Information Extraction in Finance

WITPRESS

WIT Press publishes leading books in Science and Technology.
Visit our website for the current list of titles.
www.witpress.com

WITeLibrary

Home of the Transactions of the Wessex Institute, the WIT electronic-library provides the
international scientific community with immediate and permanent access to individual
papers presented at WIT conferences. Visit the WIT eLibrary at
http://library.witpress.com

Advances in Management Information Series

Objectives of the Series

Information and Communications Technologies have experienced considerable advances in the last few years. The task of managing and analysing ever-increasing amounts of data requires the development of more efficient tools to keep pace with this growth.

This series presents advances in the theory and applications of Management Information. It covers an interdisciplinary field, bringing together techniques from applied mathematics, machine learning, natural language processing, data mining and data warehousing, as well as their applications to intelligence, knowledge management, marketing and social analysis. The majority of these applications are aimed at achieving a better understanding of the behaviour of people and organisations in order to enable decisions to be made in an informed manner. Each volume in the series covers a particular topic in detail.

The volumes cover the following fields:

Information
Information Retrieval
Intelligent Agents
Data Mining
Data Warehouse
Text Mining
Competitive Intelligence
Customer Relationship Management
Information Management
Knowledge Management

Series Editor

A. Zanasi
Security Research Advisor
ESRIF

Associate Editors

P.L. Aquilar
University of Extremadura
Spain

M. Costantino
Royal Bank of Scotland Financial
Markets
UK

P. Coupet
TEMIS
France

N.J. Dedios Mimbela
Universidad de Cordoba
Spain

A. De Montis
Universita di Cagliari
Italy

G. Deplano
Universita di Cagliari
Italy

P. Giudici
Universita di Pavia
Italy

D. Goulias
University of Maryland
USA

A. Gualtierotti
IDHEAP
Switzerland

J. Jaafar
UiTM
Malaysia

G. Loo
The University of Auckland
New Zealand

J. Lourenco
Universidade do Minho
Portugal

D. Malerba
Università degli Studi
UK

N. Milic-Frayling
Microsoft Research Ltd
UK

G. Nakhaeizadeh
DaimlerChrysler
Germany

P. Pan
National Kaohsiung University of
Applied Science
Taiwan

J. Rao
Case Western Reserve University
USA

D. Riaño
Universitat Rovira I Virgili
Spain

J. Roddick
Flinders University
Australia

F. Rodrigues
Poly Institute of Porto
Portugal

F. Rossi
DATAMAT
Germany

D. Sitnikov
Kharkov Academy of Culture
Ukraine

R. Turra
CINECA Interuniversity Computing
Centre
Italy

D. Van den Poel
Ghent University
Belgium

J. Yoon
Old Dominion University
USA

N. Zhong
Maebashi Institute of Technology
Japan

H.G. Zimmermann
Siemens AG
Germany

Information Extraction in Finance

Marco Costantino

Royal Bank of Scotland Financial Markets, UK

&

Paolo Coletti

Free University of Bolzano Bozen, Italy

WITPRESS Southampton, Boston

M. Costantino
Royal Bank of Scotland Financial Markets, UK

P. Coletti
Free University of Bolzano Bozen, Italy

Published by

WIT Press
Ashurst Lodge, Ashurst, Southampton, SO40 7AA, UK
Tel: 44 (0) 238 029 3223; Fax: 44 (0) 238 029 2853
E-Mail: witpress@witpress.com
http://www.witpress.com

For USA, Canada and Mexico

WIT Press
25 Bridge Street, Billerica, MA 01821, USA
Tel: 978 667 5841; Fax: 978 667 7582
E-Mail: infousa@witpress.com
http://www.witpress.com

British Library Cataloguing-in-Publication Data

A Catalogue record for this book is available
from the British Library

ISBN: 978-1-84564-146-7

Library of Congress Catalog Card Number: 2008924037

*The texts of the papers in this volume were set
individually by the authors or under their supervision.*

Contents

5 LOLITA and IE-expert systems 75

Preface

This book analyzes the state of the art of applied research in a challenging field: natural language understanding of financial news. Currently, thanks to the worldwide technological spreading, stock market traders are overwhelmed with financial information, both numerical and textual that has to be analyzed quickly in order to react before market conditions change again. While there are several well-known numerical techniques for quantitative data, textual information is usually manually examined investing a lot of precious human time. This book shows how information extraction (IE) can be successfully applied to this task, at the same time speeding up the process and freeing the trader from this workload.

The book's main focus has therefore a double identity: finance, especially intraday trading with large amounts of news arriving at a too fast pace to be examined manually, and IE, especially real-time analysis of predetermined events. Both sectors bring new problems and innovative techniques that are overviewed through many examples.

We start with an historical introduction to the first IE systems built in the 80s for the TREC competitions and then to the most promising approaches of MUC competitions, both statistical and rule-based, some of which lead to the development of the most interesting techniques in use today. Then we present recent systems, with a particular focus on their mixing of statistical and rule-based strategies. Finally, we show in deep detail the LOLITA system, together with its application IE-expert, two good examples of how IE and an expert systems can be applied to financial news analysis. Moreover, we introduce systems for other tasks, from which new ideas can be borrowed into this sector.

Biographies

Marco Costantino (marco.costantino@advanced-finance.com) achieved BSc and BA in Economics and Business Administration at the University of Trento, Italy. He then obtained a PhD in Computer Science at the University of Durham, UK. He worked in technology, analytics, and trading at JPMorgan equity derivatives in London and New York. He is currently head of equity derivatives quantitative development technology at Royal Bank of Scotland Financial Markets.

Paolo Coletti (paolo.coletti@advanced-finance.com) achieved BS and MSc in Mathematics at the University of Trento, Italy. After his PhD in Applied Mathematics in the field of computational fluid dynamics, he worked as a researcher in the field of natural language understanding. He is currently professor of Computer Science and Information Processing at the School of Economics and Management at the University of Bolzano, Italy.

List of figures

1 Financial information and investment decisions

Finance is one of the many fields which has received large benefits in the last 20 years from the availability of high technological tools and their interconnection. Markets can now be accessed very quickly even by non-professional investors and market data are continuously stored by computers which are powerful enough to handle these huge amounts of data and perform real-time analysis on them.

Therefore investors have nowadays access to a vast amount of information, provided by agency press news providers, historical archives, government agencies and private organisations which collect, organise, process and distribute different types of data. They are connected in real-time through the Internet to the news providers, drastically reducing the lag between when news happens and when it is assimilated by the operator. The cost of this information has decreased rapidly, making it accessible even by small and private investors.

This information revolution started, as in many other information-based sectors, in the late 70s with the development of the first commercial fast computer networks and continued in the 80s. The first target was to provide as much information as possible in real time. Quantity was the target at that time. Therefore, the quantity of the services and information available has been growing exponentially, leading to the current paradoxical situation, in which financial operators suffer from **data overload**. Operators have access to information, most of which is irrelevant, which they cannot profitably use because of the time they have to spend in selecting and understanding the appropriate data for their needs. Operators try to select the most important information, leaving for further and deeper analysis the less important one, for example analysis of price behaviour. In the 90s, therefore, the emphasis has shifted from the **quantity** of the provided information to the **quality**. Quality can be improved by providing analysis and automatic selection on this large amount of information. The financial operator, using this improved quality information, can drastically reduce the time he needs to select the appropriate data and even receive a structured summary of the needed information.

The very large amount of information to which financial operators have access is therefore of a varying degree of quality.

Quantitative information consists of information which can be expressed by numbers and which can therefore be automatically used, without any further elaboration, for analysis by investors or by computer programs. For example, as can be seen in Figure 1.1, from the **price** of an equity the investor can immediately also see the **percent change** with respect to the previous day, which gives him a clear overview of the market's current trend, or several other information derived from historical data compared to current data, such as the **highest and lowest prices** of the current day and of the current year or the **beta coefficient**, a measure of a stock's volatility in relation to the rest of the market. Another quantitative information often provided is the **volume**, the number of exchanged shares from the market daily opening or the total value of the exchanged shares, which together with the **market capitalisation**, the total value of the shares outstanding excluding shares which are not available for public trading gives to the investor an idea of the importance of this stock in the market. Other historical numeric information usually complete the view, such as the **earnings per share** (EPS), calculated as the yearly profit divided by the number of shares, and information on **dividends**. All this information, both real-time and historical, is aimed at letting the investor have an idea of the market trends for that stock and of the risks that he is facing when buying or selling that stock.

The information is typically provided all together in a table, sometimes with a small graph for quick qualitative glances, and very often is also automatically processed by computers to extract, using conventional forecasting tools, clear buy or sell signals. Other times the information is summarised, together with historical

Microsoft Corp MSFT.O (NASDAQ)

Sector: Technology **Industry:** Software & Programming ▸ View **MSFT.O** on other exchanges

As of 9:36 AM EST	Price Change	Percent Change
$29.64 USD	▲0.24	▲0.82%

▸ Independent Research ▸ Broker Research

Previous Close	$29.40	Volume	13.7M	
Open	$29.71	Avg Volume	75.2M	
Day High	$29.72	Mkt Cap.	$283.60B	
Day Low	$29.44	Shares Out	9.6B	
52-Week High	$31.84	EPS (TTM)	$1.42	
52-Week Low	$23.85	Div & Yield	0.40 (1.35%)	
Beta	1.07	Ex Div Date	08/14/07	

Jul Oct Dec Feb Apr Jun
2006 2007
1d 5d 3m 6m **1y** 2y 5y max

Research a stock: [Enter Symbol] [Stock Overview ▾] [Go] Symbol Lookup

Figure 1.1: Example of quantitative information available to financial operators (from Reuters).

data, in graphs as the one of Figure 1.2, which range from short-time graphs of the current day up to long-time graph of the current decade. Several graphs are overlapped on the same axes for an immediate global overview of the current market trends. This kind of analogical information is obviously only aimed at a human use and is on the border between quantitative and qualitative information.

Qualitative information is, on the other hand, information which may not be expressed in numeric terms. For example, a sentence such as "There are rumours of an increase in the European interest rate." from a news article may not be put in

Figure 1.2: Example of quantitative information available to financial operators (from Reuters).

any numeric format, neither does it say anything clearly numeric or precise. But, in any case, information such as the one represented by this sentence are taken in great consideration by financial operators and can determine strong rise and fall of the markets.

Qualitative information may come in two main forms:

- **Analysis** produced by internal analysts from historical data which includes forecasts for the main markets, indices and companies normally covering a period of one week.
- **News** from on-line news providers, such as Dow Jones, Reuters or Bloomberg, which report the latest relevant news for the specific market, region or company, such as in Figure 1.3. These news are the main source of qualitative information employed by traders to develop their view of the market.

While the first kind of information is often used for long-term investment decisions, the second one is used by investors to have an immediate view of the market while trying to take trading decision before the market situation changes.

Market news usually arrive at the financial operator as in Figure 1.3, in a sequential list, which may be ordered by date, and may be filtered by company, sector, market or country. Several pages of news may appear for large sectors or markets or even for some companies when particular events, such as an acquisition attempt, are taking place. The titles of the news scroll continuously on the screen and the operator can click on a title displaying the full article, such as in Figure 1.4. Complete articles are usually not too long, designed to be read in a short time, but since the author tries to put inside as much information as possible, they often take some minutes to be read carefully. A high number of articles per minute are displayed on the screen: the global-markets section of the screen shown in Figure 1.3, for example, tends to display an average of 30 articles per hour, while interfaces for professional operators display much more articles, averaging one every 10 s. Financial operators are unable to capture and analyse this amount of information in such a short time and, therefore, most of the qualitative information is lost. Another important limitation of current systems is that there is no link between quantitative and qualitative information, except for some simple hyperlinks which switch from quantitative to qualitative pages, and traders must therefore carry out manually this further analysis.

The distinction between quantitative and qualitative information, even though it can be applied to the vast majority of cases, presents some borderline situations which require particular attention. Many old numeric historical data are affected by human transcription errors, while more recent data show other errors due to not predicted situations, such as for example a stock splitting or a change in an index composition. If these errors are frequent, these data are usually considered as qualitative, since they require an interpretation and elaboration before being able to be used for an automatic analysis. On the other hand there are non-numeric data, which express events or even rumours, coded and organised in such a structured way that they can be directly used as computer programs' input without any

Company News

Microsoft Corp MSFT.O (NASDAQ)

SATURDAY, JANUARY 27, 2007

DAVOS-Internet to revolutionise TV in 5 years -Gates
10:58 AM

'Is Your Family Set?' Campaign Rolls in to Southern California
3:01 AM

FRIDAY, JANUARY 26, 2007

US STOCKS-Dow, S&P dip on rate worry, tempered by Countrywide
5:05 PM

US STOCKS-Indexes end flat; M&A talk offsets rate worry
4:09 PM

DAVOS-A good news story from Africa, for a change
3:39 PM

US STOCKS-Market slips on rate worries, Amgen falls
2:43 PM

US STOCKS-Dow drops on rate concern, Nasdaq flat
12:58 PM

US STOCKS-Indexes fall as data stirs rate concern
11:58 AM

US STOCKS-Market slips on rate worries after data
11:20 AM

US STOCKS-Indexes fall after home sales report
10:15 AM

Company News Archives for MSFT.O

View headlines from | Today ⌄ | GO   Saturday, January 27, 2007
Page 1 of 15 Next

Figure 1.3: Example of qualitative information available to financial operators
(from Reuters).

human or artificial intelligent's preprocessing; these data are often considered to
be quantitative. A typical example of this latter case can be a database of takeover
events, with very well-structured fields containing coded information on the date,
the involved companies, the cost and the takeover's type.

In summary, the investor tries to gather as much information as possible to
have a clear view of the current market condition and tries to reach the highest

Dow and S&P dip on rate worry

Fri Jan 26, 2007 5:08pm ET

By Emily Chasan

NEW YORK (Reuters) - The Dow and the S&P 500 ended slightly lower on Friday on concerns that strong economic reports will hurt chances for an interest-rate cut. But those worries were tempered by a report that Bank of America Corp. (BAC.N: Quote, Profile , Research) and Countrywide Financial Corp. (CFC.N: Quote, Profile , Research) may be in early deal talks.

Stocks had been substantially lower for most of the day, but those losses were pared when Countrywide shares shot up 12 percent to a lifetime high at $45.15 in the last hour of trading after the Financial Times reported that talks between the largest U.S. mortgage lender and Bank of America could lead to a merger or joint venture. <ID:nN26424399>

A strong profit outlook from Microsoft Corp. (MSFT.O: Quote, Profile , Research) lifted technology stocks and enabled the Nasdaq to finish the day with a tiny gain.

Figure 1.4: A typical news article available to financial operators (from Reuters).

possible level of knowledge before taking investment decisions. The investment decision-making process can therefore be summarised as following (Figure 1.5):

1. The trader assesses the global position and risks of the current portfolio using the quantitative information available.
2. The trader takes a view of the market, based on the current quantitative and qualitative information available.
3. The trader decides the strategy to put in place using the quantitative and risk-management information available.

Clearly, the faster the first two steps are performed, the faster the decision may be taken before the market changes again. Therefore it is crucial to consider all the relevant information in a very short time, in particular the qualitative information which is continuously growing in quantity and which requires a lot of time to be properly analysed and to extract the investor-relevant information from it.

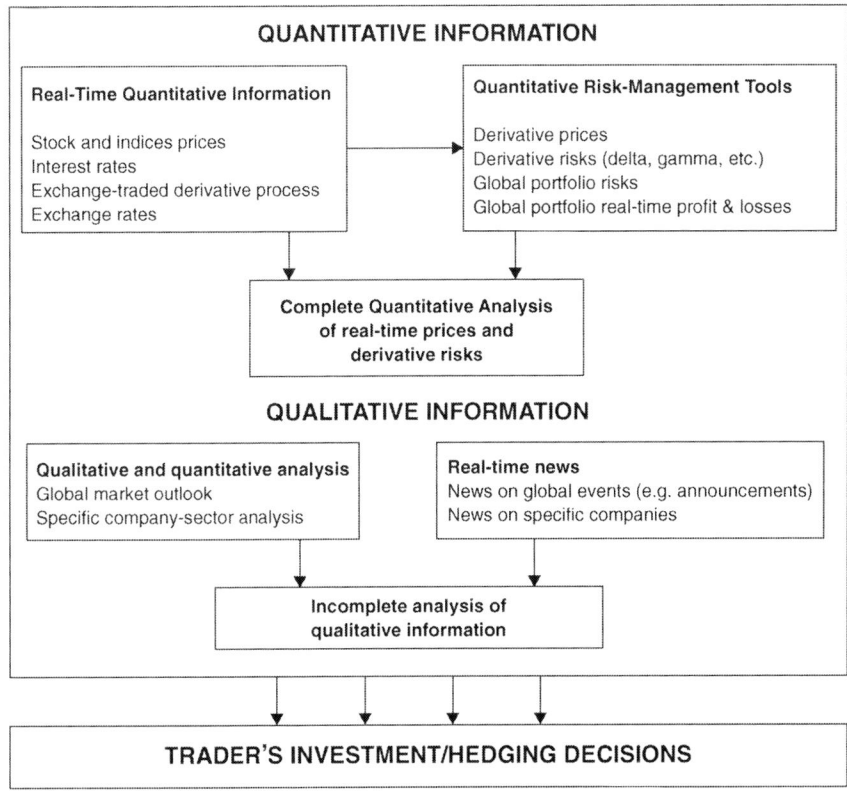

Figure 1.5: The decision-making process of a financial operator.

Financial tools are instruments used to perform this selection and to produce new inferred data. We can define them as tools that are used to support the decision-making process of the investors, by summarising, selecting or producing some analysis of the original source data or suggest some operative decisions. They are, therefore, instruments used to perform economical analysis of the stock market. Many different kinds of financial tools have been developed. In this book, we present examples of tools used in decision-making processes dealing with the trading of securities issued by companies and quoted in the stock exchange, but which can be extended to other financial markets. We also present tools used in other domains, but which can be adapted to this one or which can bring good contribution to further development of systems for our domain. We do, however, not consider tools regarding forecast analysis of other kinds of prices, profit predictions and economic forecasts. Financial tools can be classified according to three different criteria:

- The technique on which the tool is based (conventional or innovative).
- The input/output of the system (quantitative or qualitative).

- The task that the tool performs for the financial operator (explanatory, forecasting or general support).

Depending on the technique on which it is based, financial tools can be grouped into **conventional tools** and **innovative tools** [16]. Conventional tools are based on mathematical, statistical and probabilistic algorithms. These techniques are deeply studied, highly optimised and effective on particular sets of data and have been experimented for a long time. Conventional tools can be further classified in systems based on **statistics**, which perform analysis and calculations on data consisting of historical time series of share prices, on **econometrics**, which try to identify the mathematical and economical relations and models which are able to interpret and explain the evolution of the economical phenomena (called **fundamental analysis**), and on **heuristics**, which try to explain the financial events without an underlying economical or mathematical relation, but basing on experimentation, trial-and-error algorithms and knowledge available within the financial community. Innovative tools have instead been introduced in the last 20 years and are mainly based on techniques borrowed from **Artificial Intelligence** (AI), such as **neural networks**, a computational model for information processing based on a connectionist approach (described in Section 2.2.2) and **expert systems**, computer programs which possess some specific knowledge which usually belongs to human experts (described in Section 2.3.1).

According to the input and output of the system, financial tools can be also classified as **quantitative** or **qualitative** tools [16]. Quantitative tools are tools used to produce quantitative or qualitative information from quantitative data. Differently, qualitative tools are tools which process qualitative data and produce qualitative or quantitative information.

Finally, we can distinguish financial tools between **explanatory tools** (e.g. historical price analysis), **forecasting tools** (e.g. linear prediction, which also falls in the category of the tools based on conventional techniques, and neural networks for prediction of prices, which also falls into the AI category) and **general support tools**. Explanatory tools can be defined as financial tools which are used for explaining the movements of markets and which cannot normally be used for the prediction of future prices. Forecasting tools, on the contrary, are tools used to predict future prices. General support tools are used as support for the analysis of the financial operator or to preprocess the information, but cannot be used for explaining movements of share prices or for predictions.

In this book we outline how natural language processing (NLP) information extraction (IE) and expert systems can be used to process the qualitative information available to the traders, suggesting possible investment decisions and providing a link between quantitative and qualitative information which is missing in today's financial tools. We start with a general overview of traditional financial tools, which typically provide only historical and real-time information to the investor, often accompanied by a simple qualitative general support tool. Then we switch to financial tools which use NLP techniques to convert qualitative information contained in financial news' text to structured summarised information. Research in this topic started to be successful in the 90s with TREC [17–20] and Message Understanding Competition (MUC) competitions [21–25], when news information was available and computers started to have enough computational power for real-time applications. We analyse in deep detail one of the best natural language-processing system, LOLITA [26–28], that, together with its infrastructure IE-Expert [29, 30], is an innovative support tool. In Appendix A we present other system which contributes to the MUC competitions, in Appendix B we show evolutions of financial tools and the future research directions, while in Appendix C we give an overview of other general support tools whose aim is not direct IE from news, but which may be of help to the investor and to current researches in this topic.

2   Financial tools

This chapter discusses in deeper details the types of financial tools that are available to the financial operators. The main tools are traditional quantitative tools, such as technical analysis or linear prediction, and artificial intelligence techniques, such as neural networks or genetic algorithms. Then, it switches to more modern qualitative financial tools, which are the main topics of this book, namely NLP and expert systems.

2.1   Conventional quantitative tools

We define **quantitative tools** as the tools that are used to produce quantitative or qualitative information from quantitative data (Figure 2.1). For example, a quantitative tool can process the price-history of a particular share, taking into account any selected variable that is relevant and show the main periodical cycles and trends, and return a qualitative indication of the current market's trend. Other tools can be used to predict the future prices of the same shares or to suggest when is the best time to sell or buy a particular share. Many quantitative tools have been historically based on conventional techniques. More recently, tools based on innovative techniques have been introduced. For example, neural networks are mostly used in finance as quantitative tools for prediction of shares. Expert systems, instead,

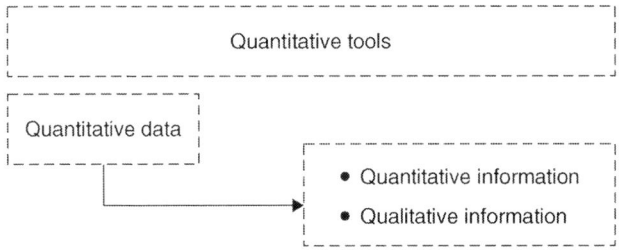

Figure 2.1: The kind of input and output of a quantitative tool.

	Technical analysis	Forecasting
Conventional	Moving average Moving average convergence divergence (MACD) indicator Stochastic index Trading bands	Linear and non-linear prediction Logistic regression
Innovative	Expert systems	Neural networks

Figure 2.2: Different kinds of quantitative tools.

have been applied to both quantitative and qualitative problems. Figure 2.2 presents a brief summary of quantitative tools based on different techniques.

Conventional technical analysis tools and forecasting tools are based on mathematics, statistics and probabilistic techniques, adapted and enhanced for the use in finance, which have been studied for centuries and therefore the current state-of-the-art of these technique is well mature and they always form a basis for the choice of every financial operators. We do not go in further details on these systems, which are described in a very wide literature, as for example in Refs. [31–35].

However these techniques present two major drawbacks. Their produced information consists only of numbers and has to be interpreted by the financial operators thus slowing-down their investment decision-making process. For example, the input and output of neural networks is strictly numeric [36], often difficult or impossible to understand for humans. Another main disadvantage of most traditional quantitative techniques is that they rely only on statistical analysis of past data, failing whenever new unpredictable events happens. This latter problem is presently a study topic for "complexity economics", an application of the complexity science theory to economics whose key feature is that agents' behaviour is modelled individually and not collectively, using inductive rules of thumb for decisions from incomplete information and using mechanism to adapt over time, thus being able to react to unpredictable events. Further information can be found in Refs. [37, 38].

2.2 Artificial intelligence techniques

The decision-making environment for business is becoming more and more complex on a daily basis. This is partly caused by the exponential increase of the global marketplace, which leads to a even greater increase of information to be processed by the financial operators [36]. Financial companies like Fidelity, Bloomberg, Dow Jones and Dreyfus are offering all kinds of data and services, such as stock quotes, electronic trading, research reports and analysis of companies, prices etc. These data are available on cheap and efficient networks such as, for example the Internet. Financial operators must therefore process a larger amount of information in a shorter period of time. Decision making in this complex and global environment requires therefore a high-quality and appropriate knowledge.

As we have already seen in the previous sections, statistical and probabilistic techniques are relatively simple and efficient methods to analyse and forecast quantitative data. However, they are unable to work in a highly complex and irregular market where decisions are taken not on the basis of previously observed patterns or cycles, but are mainly guided by emotive and psychological factors.

Towards the end of the 70s, the first financial tools based on new techniques borrowed from AI were introduced. These techniques offered the possibility to explain and predict data, which did not necessarily follow a certain pattern or cycle. Nowadays, most of actual AI financial tools are based on neural networks, which are **example-based** tools, and expert systems, appeared in the early 80s, which are instead **rule-based** tools [36].

John McCarthy coined the term AI in 1956 defining it as "the science and engineering of making intelligent machines" [39, 40]. The term itself is one of the properties of machines or programs: the intelligence that the system demonstrates, which means that the machine should exhibit reasoning, knowledge, planning, learning, communication and perception.

Early AI researchers developed algorithms that imitated the process of conscious, step-by-step reasoning that human beings use when they solve puzzles, play board games or make logical deductions. These early methods were unable to handle incomplete or imprecise information but by the late 80s and 90s, AI research developed highly successful methods for dealing with uncertainty, employing concepts from probability and economics [41]. During the 90s the "intelligent agent" paradigm became widely accepted, borrowing concepts from decision theory and economics into the study of AI. An intelligent agent is a system that perceives its environment and takes actions which maximises its chances of success. The simplest intelligent agents are programs that solve specific problems. The most complicated intelligent agents would be rational, thinking human beings. Also in the 90s, stochastic and probabilistic methods were used in AI, such as Bayesian networks applied to uncertain reasoning, learning and planning (using decision networks), and hidden Markov models, Kalman filters and dynamic Bayesian networks applied to processes that occur over time.

When the first companies specialising in AI systems appeared on the market, they were directly related to university labs and they were working for and within that environment. The second generation of AI companies understood that the biggest potential sectors is constituted by the financial community and they started studying specific applications and techniques. Nowadays, the financial industry is the primary commercial adapter of AI techniques worldwide [42]. The financial companies are the first to try to use the new AI techniques in real situations and the quickest to substitute conventional techniques with the new ones. Several reasons can be thought but the two most obvious are: access to cash and direct and immediate impact of the new technologies on the results [42]. Financial institutions, in fact, are extremely keen on investing and testing new AI techniques that can potentially result in an exponential and immediate increase in the profits. Using AI techniques, financial operators can get better information from data which they already own and improvements can be measured in terms of monetary returns. Given the fact that a financial tool is normally used to support the decision-making process for buying/ selling decisions, the performance of these decisions can be measured within a short period of time, if not in real-time. In comparison, an industrial company is not able to obtain such a clear overview of the impact of the new technology. This is because the introduction of the new technique and the results are not directly related but have to be linked to the impact in the production, quality-control or diagnoses, faster customer services, predictive maintenance and, in general, the stage at which the new technology is introduced. The financial community is, therefore, one of the biggest real-user of AI techniques, compared to other sectors, which are likely to make use of more known and conventional technologies.

One of the most addressed research problems of AI is **knowledge representation**, since a very important part of AI is to store knowledge so that programs can process it and achieve the verisimilitude of human intelligence. Representing knowledge in some ways makes certain problems easier to solve, and therefore AI scientists have borrowed representation forms from cognitive science, such as frames, rules and semantic networks.

2.2.1 Semantic networks

A semantic network is very often used as a form of knowledge representation, starting from basic assumption that the meaning of a word can be represented by the set of its verbal associations. It is a directed graph consisting of vertices and arrows. Each vertex represents a concept while each arrow represents the semantic relation between the two concepts.

The most typical semantic relations between A and B are:

- Meronymy: A is part of B or B has A as a part of itself.
- Holonymy: B is part of A or A has B as a part of itself.
- Hyponymy or troponymy: A is subordinate of B or A is kind of B.
- Hypernymy: A is superordinate of B.
- Synonymy: A denotes the same as B.
- Antonymy: A denotes the opposite of B.

Semantic networks were first developed for computers in the early 60s by Richard H. Richens, Robert F. Simmons and M. Ross Quillian. John F. Sowa suggests [43–45] six most common kinds of semantic networks:

Definitional networks represent categories and sub-categories, where the relation is a *is a.*

Assertional networks represent propositions, whose connection can therefore be true or false. For example, Figure 2.3 shows a semantic graph of an assertional network.

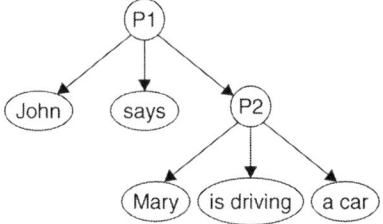

Figure 2.3: Semantic graph for the sentence "John says Mary is driving a car".

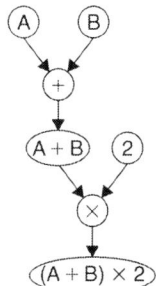

Figure 2.4: Semantic graph for the mathematical expression $(A + B) \times 2$.

Implicational networks represent casuality or inference. Their relation usually is *causes* and can be further distinguished between logical implicational networks, where the consequence is certain, and probabilistic ones, where to each arrow a probability is associated.

Executable networks are dynamic networks, which include mechanism to change the structure of the network or the content of the nodes. A common example is the graph in Figure 2.4 where the value of each node changes according to the value of nodes A and B.

Learning networks are able to change to better adapt to exogenous conditions, from simple value changes to arrows' weights changes and up to complete network's structure change. The typical representatives of this category are neural networks which are further analysed in Section 2.2.2.

Hybrid networks are combinations of different network types, which may be kept separated but able to interact or joined together in a single network.

Semantic networks are often used as of machine-readable dictionary, the most famous example being **WordNet** [46], a large lexical database of English, publicly available for download from Princeton University wordnet.princeton.edu, where words are grouped into **synsets**, sets of cognitive synonyms, each expressing a distinct concept. They are interlinked by means of conceptual-semantic and lexical relations building a semantic network which can be navigated by a browser or used in computer applications.

2.2.2 Neural networks

Neural networks are the most common innovative system for the prediction of share prices. Although few expert systems are still in use, neural networks have proven to be effective tools for supporting financial operator's trading decision, once they have been correctly trained. Neural networks are therefore forecasting tools, rather than explanatory tools. Neural networks in finance are mostly used to produce quantitative information (e.g. expected prices of shares). However, with a suitable output interface, they can produce qualitative results.

Neural networks have been created with the purpose of modelling and simulating the components and functionalities of the brain. The main component of a neural network is an element modelled after a neuron and called **neuron**, **node** or just **element**. Neurons are connected each other with a network of paths which carry the output of a neuron to the next one (Figure 2.5). The fact that the communication on a single path is uni-directional does not prevent the creation of a two-way connection, since it is possible to create an additional link from the destination to the source neuron. Each neuron, although connected to many other neurons, produces a single-output impulse each time, which is sent to other neurons.

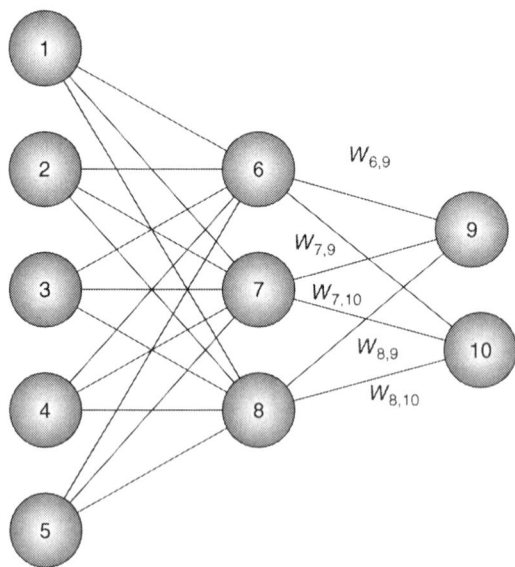

Figure 2.5: A three-layers neural network with 10 nodes.

The most important parameter of the neural network is the **strength** or **weight** with which the neurons are linked. If two neurons, i and j are connected with two uni-directional links, the links will both have two separated weights w_{ij} and w_{ji}. The weights are extremely important, since they are the elements where the knowledge is stored and represent the way in which the neural network is able to learn new knowledge, through the **training of the network**. Associated to each neuron is also a **state**, which is usually implemented as an extra weight and must therefore also be estimated [47].

The neurons are connected using two different types of connection [48]:

Excitatory: In which the output of a neuron increases the potential action of the neuron connected.

Inhibitory: In which the connected node will reduce its activity by receiving the output of the source neuron.

In most neural networks, however, all connections are excitatory. The neurons are then grouped into **layers** or **slabs** that are inter-connected. Each layer performs a specific operation – i.e. a input layer consists of neurons which receive input from the external environment. We do not further discuss the analytic representation and structure of a neural network, since it is not relevant in the context of this work: additional information can be found in many sources, for example [48–50].

The important aspect to notice here is that the neural network, to be of any use, must learn from the external world and this process is called **training**. The knowledge, as we already observed, is stored as weights given to the links between the neurons. The learning method is the most relevant distinguishing factor among neural networks and, in case of financial neural networks, represents the most important aspect. The learning method can be **supervised**, if the output of the net is compared with results which are already known during the training of the net, or **unsupervised**. More important, it can be **off-line** or **on-line**. In the former case, the neural network is trained as a separate process and cannot be updated during its use. Viceversa, an on-line neural network can learn while it is being used and, in the case of financial tools, this possibility is extremely important. Training can be a long and expensive process and is a time-consuming operation. In case of financial forecasting, the operator is usually required to input a relevant number of items (usually consisting of price of stocks) in the system and to periodically update the network, before this can be used in real-time prediction.

Two different sets of information are needed to perform the training process of the network. First, the designers need to acquire knowledge regarding the aspects of the domain (e.g. the share price of a particular company) that can influence the outcome of the decision-making process [36]. Then, the designer must collect a huge amount of data that is used to train the network according to the criteria identified in the first set of information. These data typically consist of historical price databases regarding price shares connected to the specific criteria identified. An important point to notice is that the data to be collected must be free of noise or errors, which would otherwise cause the production of non-accurate forecasts. The training process can last from hours to weeks, depending on the amount of data that is used for the training. The training of neural networks is becoming a very important issue in the financial community and various techniques to improve the process are being studied. The most common ones are the selection of a set of weights that minimises a cost criterion, using common gradient descent numerical methods or more complex methods such as simulated annealing [51], to avoid the local minimum problem of gradient descent, or expectation-maximisation algorithms [52], which find the maximum-likelihood estimates of the weights.

There are many types of neural networks according to their structure and to how does it changes during the process:

Feed-forward network is a neural network where connections between the units do not form a directed cycle. It was the first and simplest type of artificial neural network devised. In this network, the information moves in only one direction, forward, from the input nodes, through the hidden nodes and to the output nodes. Therefore, there are no cycles nor loops in the network. The earliest kind of neural network is a **single-layer perceptron network**, which consists of a single layer of output nodes: the inputs are fed directly to the outputs via a series of weights. In this way, it can be considered the simplest kind of feed-forward network. The sum of the products of the weights and the inputs is calculated in each node, and if the value is above some threshold the neuron takes the activated value; otherwise it takes the de-activated value. An extension of this is the **multi-layer perceptron**, which consists of multiple layers of computational units, usually interconnected in a feed-forward way. Each neuron in one layer has directed connections to the neurons of the subsequent layer.

Radial basis function RBF network is a neural network, which uses radial basis functions as activation functions. Typically it has three layers: an input layer, a hidden layer with a non-linear RBF activation function, usually a Gaussian and a linear output layer. A RBF network with enough hidden neurons can approximate any continuous function with arbitrary precision and they do not suffer the local minimum problem of other functions.

Kohonen self-organising map network is a neural network where the training of the weight, through vector quantisation, tries to produce a low-dimensional (typically two dimensional), discredited representation of the input space. The representation, called map, seeks to preserve the topological properties of the input space.

Recurrent neural network has bi-directional data flow, being therefore also to propagate data from later processing stages to earlier stages. They may be further divided into simple recurrent network, with a standard three-layers network and a alternation of feed-forward and back-propagation steps where the hidden layer influences the input layer, and fully recurrent network, where every neuron receives input from all the other neurons without any layers arrangement.

Stochastic neural network is a network with random variations, which can be viewed as Monte Carlo sampling applied to neural networks. The most famous is the **Boltzman machine** [53], a simulated annealing stochastic recurrent symmetric neural network.

Modular neural network is composed of small neural networks, which collaborate to solve problems. They can be differentiated through random initial variation and cooperate through a voting system.

Trading systems based on neural networks are nowadays extremely wide-spread. Neural networks are commonly used for the prediction of shares prices. They have also been applied to currency price forecasts, derivative forecasts, etc. [54]. The performance of the system in terms of predictions compares well with those provided by conventional methods, for example regression [55].

Neural networks and expert systems can be integrated to overcome the limitations of each technique. Although most of the best systems developed by big financial operators are not publicly available, an enormous quantity of neural networks systems are available even to the small investor. Many small AI firms specialise in neural network systems, which are sold to end-users (some products are [56, 57], while a brief list of AI companies specialising in neural networks products can be found in Ref. [54]). Neural networks have been used for other purposes in finance including forecasting foreign exchange rates [58, 59], bonds prices forecasting [60] and for the prediction of corporate mergers [61]. Further information on neural networks applied to finance can be found in Ref. [62].

2.2.3 Genetic algorithms

Genetic algorithms are search techniques used in computing to find approximate solutions to optimisation problems. Genetic algorithms are inspired by evolutionary biology and in fact it tries to imitate its features: inheritance, mutation, selection and crossover (also called recombination).

Genetic algorithms in economics are implemented as a computer simulation in which a population of abstract representations (called **chromosomes** or the **genotype** or the **genome**) of candidate solutions (called **individuals**) to an optimisation problem evolves towards better solutions. Traditionally, solutions are represented as binary strings, but other encodings are also possible. The evolution usually starts from a population of randomly generated individuals and happens in generations. In each generation, the fitness of every individual in the population is evaluated, multiple individuals are stochastically selected from the current population (based on their fitness), and modified (recombined and possibly mutated) to form a new population. The new population is then used in the next iteration of the algorithm.

The genetic algorithm generally consists of a population of n agents with m strings, initially randomly generated. Each string is assigned a fitness value through a defined method which is used as a measure of performance. The strings are updated through a series of operations: **reproduction**, which attempts to imitate successful agents, **crossover** and **mutation**, which are implemented to bring diversity into the system.

Reproduction, works by attempting to imitate: it selects another agent to observe its fitness value and if its fitness value is greater than its own, then it elects to adopt the other agent's string, otherwise it preserves its own. These strings are then placed into a pool to undergo crossover and mutation. Most functions are stochastic and designed so that a small proportion of less fit solutions are selected. This helps to keep the diversity of the population large, preventing premature convergence on poor solutions.

Crossover is a genetic operation to vary the programming of a chromosome or chromosomes from one generation to the next. It is an analogy to reproduction and biological crossover, upon which genetic algorithms are based.

Mutation is a genetic operator used to maintain genetic diversity from one generation of a population of chromosomes to the next. It is analogous to biological mutation. The classic example of a mutation operator involves a probability that an arbitrary bit in a genetic sequence will be changed from its original state. A common method to implement mutation involves generating a random variable for each bit in a sequence. This random variable tells whether or not a particular bit will be modified. The purpose of mutation is to prevent the population of chromosomes from becoming too similar to each other, thus slowing or even stopping evolution.

These processes ultimately result in the pool of strings that is different from the initial parent pool. The selection operator then works by comparing the fitness of the parent strings to the potential fitness of the offspring pool. If the offspring string has a higher fitness value, it will replace the parent string in the population. Otherwise, the parent string will stay. Generally the average fitness of the population is increased after this procedure, since only the best strings are selected.

Further information on genetic algorithms can be found in Refs. [63, 64] and on genetic algorithms in finance can be found in Refs. [65, 66].

2.3 Qualitative tools

We define a qualitative tool a tool that process qualitative data and produce qualitative or quantitative information (Figure 2.6) [67].

While quantitative data are identifiable in prices of stocks, historical time-series of share, bonds, inflation, interest rate and all sort of relevant numerical data,

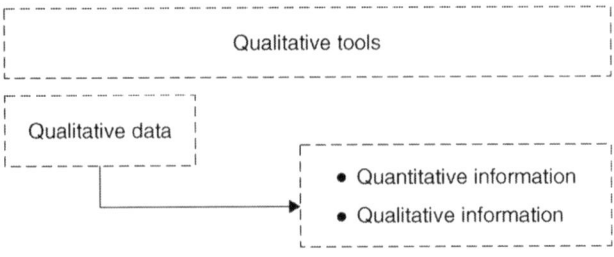

Figure 2.6: The kind of input and output of a qualitative tool.

qualitative data are more difficult to define. In fact, quantitative data can be used in mathematical or statistical equations, which does not normally apply to qualitative data. Qualitative data are difficult to express in a numeric format, or, when in a numeric format, they contain so many errors and omissions that classical mathematical tools cannot be applied successfully. For example, data regarding rumours, fears, broker's recommendations, takeovers etc. are all qualitative data. A sentence such as: *"There are rumours of a possible takeover of Apple, the i-Pod computer manufacturer"* represents an information that is extremely relevant to the financial operators, since it will probably very soon cause a marked movement in the quotation of Apple's shares as well as those of the possible buyers. However, taking it into account in a mathematical/statistical equation would be extremely difficult. These kinds of news are extremely important because they affect the expectations of the operators regarding a particular share. The way in which the operators are influenced depends on how an operator perceives the information. Even if, in theory, it could be possible to conceive a complete econometric model that takes into account all possible variables and expected behaviours of the players, the complexity of the financial world makes it impossible to practically produce such a model which would anyway be extremely expensive in terms of the necessary computing power. A similar situation is found in macro-economics. The advanced econometric macro-economics models employed by the central banks often fail to predict the development of the economical cycles, crisis and expansions. Only very few macroeconomic relations (e.g. interest rates) are actually widely used and effects of a change in one of the variable is easily predictable.

Qualitative data are much more difficult to process than quantitative. Therefore, while all sorts of quantitative financial tools are nowadays available on the market, very little progress has been done in the processing of qualitative information, which is usually left to the financial operators.

In the financial community, news, rumours and facts are among the most important factors that determine the operators behaviour. Operators, in fact, are much more influenced by news than by analysts forecasts or historical price analysis of shares. When a news such as *"The inflation rate is expected to increase next month."* arrives, the consequences are immediately visible and operators base their decisions on their personal experience and on other's people behaviour, rather than on expensive and complex forecasts produced by complicated neural networks financial forecasting systems. Quantitative methods work fine and help the operators' decision-making process by suggesting a possible path of the prices but then it may be drastically changed by the reaction to news events.

The financial operators and information providers understood the importance of qualitative data as the key-point in the trading decision-making process a long time ago. Therefore, the emphasis has been on providing as much as relevant qualitative information as possible. Financial operators receive in real-time news regarding companies (announcements, rumours, profit forecasts), macro-economics (movements of inflation rate, unemployment), politics (changes in general macro-economic policy of the government, tax policies). They also have access to huge quantities of past information. The ideal situation would be a system that is able to process the qualitative information, take into account any possible factor and produce a response such as "buy/sell". Unfortunately, excluding conventional mathematical and statistical techniques, current AI techniques are not sophisticated enough to produce such an output and, therefore, the decisions are still mainly taken by the operators.

Current development of qualitative tools is therefore concerned with, selecting, reducing, summarising or partitioning the news according to specific criteria, rather than inferring decisions from them. This is equivalent to performing simple analysis on quantitative data (e.g. the MA index), rather than producing a clear operative decision. Explanatory or forecasting qualitative tools have yet to be developed.

Expert systems have already been analysed as quantitative tools in Section 2.3.1 However, they can be successfully used for using qualitative input and qualitative output, such as suggesting buy/sell decisions. One technique that can be considered strictly qualitative is NLP, which is discussed in detail in Chapter 4.

2.3.1 Expert systems

An expert system can be defined as a "knowledge-based system that emulates expert thought to solve significant problems in a particular domain of expertise" [68].

The main characteristics of expert systems compared to neural networks is that they are **rule-based**. This means that the expert system contains a pre-defined set of knowledge, which is used for all decisions. The system uses the pre-defined rules to produce results by using inference rules which are coded into the system. Depending on the kind of input and the rules used, expert systems can either be used as quantitative or qualitative tool.

A generic expert system (Figure 2.7) will consists of two main modules: the knowledge base and the inference engine. The **knowledge base** contains knowledge of the system regarding the specific domain or area for which it is designed to solve problems or make recommendations. For example, if the system works in the financial domain, the knowledge base includes specific rules such as decisions concerning shares. The knowledge base is coded into the system according to a specific notation, which is usually found in the form of rules, predicates, semantic nets, frames and objects.

The **inference engine** processes and combines the facts related to the particular problem, case and question, using the part of the knowledge base that is relevant. The selection of the appropriate data in the knowledge base is performed according to searching criteria. The way in which inference rules are written and applied to the information in the knowledge base varies greatly from system to system and can follow different paths. Among the others, two methods of reasoning are often employed **forward chaining** and **backward chaining** [69].

The most important step for the development of financial tools based on expert systems is the acquisition of the domain specific knowledge, consisting of the methods that would be used by a domain expert for making appropriate decisions [36]. This knowledge normally consists of heuristics which, unfortunately, are extremely

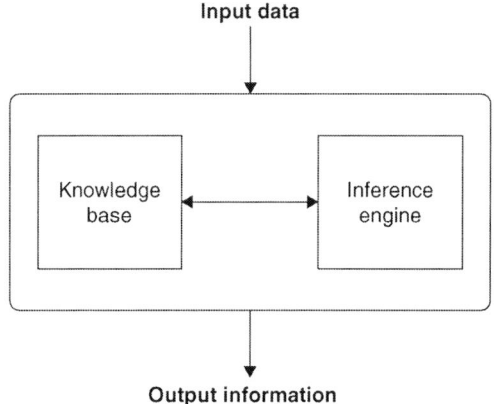

Figure 2.7: The main components of an expert system.

difficult to verbalise and the interview process to identify and the collection of these heuristics can last for a long time.

We do not describe in further detail the architecture of expert systems, but we concentrate here on their applications in finance; additional information on expert systems can be found in Refs. [48, 70, 71]. Unfortunately, information about such systems is generally limited, since disclosure of successful approaches by the financial operators can lead to the loss of competitive advantage and large sums of money. As a general point, financial operators today tend to prefer neural networks for real-time forecasting, while expert systems now tend to be used more in other financial fields, where the outcome of the system must be a clear decision – i.e. validating user's credit-card accesses. Expert systems, for example, are used in accounting [72], auditing [73], decisions in insurance companies [74]. In general, present expert systems in finance are normally used to support the operator's decision, rather than as decision makers [75].

2.3.2 Natural language processing and information extraction

The goal of IE, which belongs to the field of NLP, is to extract specific kinds of information from a source article [76]. In other words, the input of an IE system is a collection of documents (e.g. a set of newspaper articles), while the output is a representation of the relevant information from the source documents, according to specific extraction criteria. Using a IE system a structured summary, called **template**, of the original article is automatically created. The templates contain the most important relevant information from the source article, while the non-relevant information or non-relevant articles are not be extracted. Figure 2.8 shows a news-article processed by an IE system and the template generated by the system.

Quarto Group, the USM-traded publishing and printing services company, announced that it is buying Front Line Art Publishing, the California-based publisher of art prints and posters, for up to Dollars 9m (Pounds 6m). An initial payment of Dollars 7m will be satisfied by Dollars 5.3m cash and a Dollars 1.7m loan note. There is a further performance-related payment of up to Dollars 2m. For the 2003 year Front Line made profits of Dollars 1.4m, excluding owner remuneration, on turnover of Dollars 5m. Net assets at December 31 were Dollars 1.6m.

Template extracted by the system:

```
Template: TAKEOVER
      COMPANY_TARGET:    Front Line Art Publishing
      COMPANY_PREDATOR:  Quarto Group
      TYPE_TAKEOVER:     FRIENDLY
      VALUE:             9 million dollars
      ATTRIBUTION:       Quarto Group
```

Figure 2.8: A template extracted from a financial news article.

Merger	Takeover	Flotation	New Issue
Company 1: Company 2: New name: Date of announce: Date of merger: Comments: Attribution: Denial:	Company target: Company predator: Type of takeover: Value: Bank adviser predator: Bank adviser target: Expiry date: Attribution: Current stake predator: Denial:	Company name: Price: Value: Announce date: Listing date: Financial adviser flotation: Attribution: Denial: Industry sector:	Company: Company financial adviser: Issue currency: Issue value: Announce date: Launch date: Listed: Attribution: Purpose: Denial:
Privatisation	**Market Movement**	**Bankruptcy**	**Broker's recommendation**
Company name: Stake to be privatized: Price of shares: Value of shares: Announce date: Privatisation date: Bank adviser company: Attribution: Denial:	Company name: Type of securities: Movement percentage: Movement amount: Reason:	Company name: Receivers: Date of announce: Denial:	Recommendation source: Company name: Racommendation:
Overseas listing	**Dividend announcement**	**Profit/sales results**	**Director's dealings**
Company name: Overseas exchange: Type of securities: Announce date: Date of listing: Attribution: Denial:	Company name: Dividend per share: Type of dividend: Change:	Company name: Category: Value: Comment: Change:	Company name: Director name: Type of security: Type of dealing (buy/sell): Value:

Figure 2.9: The most important templates definitions in LOLITA system.

```
Template-name:          T=TAKEOVER Variables:
                        V=COMPANY1 is an organisation
                        V=COMPANY2 is an organisation
                        V=VALUE is money.

Template main-event:    V=COMPANY acquired V=COMPANY2
                        V=COMPANY1 acquired V=COMPANY2 with V=VALUE
                        The acquisition of V=COMPANY2 by V=COMPANY1
                        The V=VALUE  acquisition of V=COMPANY2 by
                        V=COMPANY1
                        V=COMPANY1 paid V=VALUE for V=COMPANY2.
                        V=COMPANY1 acquired a majority stake in
                        V=COMPANY2.
                        V=COMPANY1 took full control of V=COMPANY2.
Definition of slots:

S=COMPANY-PREDATOR:     V=COMPANY1
S=COMPANY-TARGET:       V=COMPANY2
S=TYPE_OF_TAKEOVER
HOSTILE:                T=TAKEOVER is hostile
FRIENDLY:               T=TAKEOVER is not hostile.
S=VALUE-TAKEOVER:       The cost of T=TAKEOVER
                        V=VALUE
S=ATTRIBUTION:          The person or organisation who announced
                        T=TAKEOVER.
```

Figure 2.10: The definition of a user-definable template.

IE is different from **information retrieval**. Information retrieval engines are able to locate the relevant documents within a collection, but they are unable to extract information from the relevant documents according to specific criteria. The power of an IE system compared to an information retrieval system is therefore in the ability to extract the relevant information in the articles according to specific extraction criteria and represent them in structured templates. A number of NLP and information extraction systems have been developed. However, most of these systems have been designed and tested within government agencies and the scientific community, and very few real applications have been commercially successful. A particularly interesting group of systems are those which participated in the MUC competitions [23–25], a scientific competition for the evaluation of IE systems using standard evaluation measures within a specific domain. Among the best performing systems in the competitions are: the Hasten system [3], the Shogun system [77], the PLUM and SIFT System [78, 79], the NYU system [1, 80], the TASC System [81] and the LOLITA system [26].

Very few IE systems have been specifically designed for the financial domain. One of them is the Durham financial IE system [28, 67] which is used in IE-Expert expert system as an IE engine. The system, which uses the LOLITA system as its NLP core [26, 82–84], provides a set of pre-defined financial templates designed to capture the main financial events which can influence the securities prices. Figure 2.9 shows the full list of pre-defined templates available in the system, while Figure 2.9 shows the definition of some of the templates. In addition, the system allows the user to define additional templates using a user-friendly natural language user-definable template interface. For example, the takeover template shown in Figure 2.10 can be defined by the user using natural language sentences.

Further information on information retrieval, IE and NLP can be found in Chapter 4 and Appendix B, while on LOLITA and IE-Expert in Chapter 5.

3 Traditional approaches on qualitative information

In this chapter, we describe the main systems which use a traditional approach to provide quantitative (e.g. stock and indices prices, exchanges rates, etc.) and qualitative (e.g. news) data to the professional players in the financial market. We call these systems traditional because the functionality and analysis of the qualitative data is performed using traditional techniques (e.g. keyword or pre-defined categories searching), rather than being based on more advanced techniques such as IE.

Although a very high number of somewhat similar systems are available in the marketplace, we decide to focus on two main ones: the Reuters Xtra system and the Bloomberg workstation. They are extremely widespread among the professional market operators, specifically within the trading rooms of investment banks, hedge funds, fund managements and even smaller banking institutions. These two systems are extremely reliable and, most importantly, they are able to provide real-time data from all stock exchanges as well as providing worldwide news and information edited by their own journalists. In this chapter, we briefly describe the two systems analysing in detail the qualitative information they provide and their limitations.

3.1 Reuters 3000 Xtra

Reuters 3000 Xtra, together with its interface **Reuters Kobra 5**, is Reuters' premium desktop application product. It integrates and combines in one consistent environment all types of data from multiple sources such as Reuters or third-party real-time market data, historical data, database content, web contents and calculated data. It also integrates multiple applications, for example Reuters applications, operator's own applications or ActiveX components.

Reuters 3000 Xtra brings fast, comprehensive news from more than 500 company and stock market reporters and distributes more than 5000 real-time company announcements every day. Moreover it provides real-time prices from 166 exchanges worldwide and official market fixings for over 50 currencies.

Figure 3.1: Reuters 3000 Xtra menu.

The financial operator, through the **company profile**, can get a detailed picture of a security: fundamental data, ratios, earnings estimates, including detailed and consensus estimates, and the latest corporate actions, and retrieve deep ownership information for listed companies globally, including the top holders, their holdings and how these have changed over time. The **polling unit** module gives notice of the news on bond yields, short-term interest rates, currencies and economic indicators. Real-time pricing is complemented by real-time analytical support that gives an instant view of yields, price sensitivities, spreads and reference data.

Using pre-defined models the user can get a snapshot of a stock's price events including current price quote, price charts and news, or ascertain a stock's track record by examining stock price and volume history against a selected index. Displays can be created linking prices, quotes and news. Moreover, the user can set up watch-lists with summary prices on up to 40 user-defined stock groupings. In parallel he can monitor related fixed income issuance, credit default swaps, convertibles, warrants and options. Through the same graphical interface the user can access the market directly for a fast buy/sell order.

News are grouped by category, geographical region and asset class so that it is easy to find the required news headlines [85]. In addition, it is possible to search for news by keyword, subject or language or, within certain constraints, specify a specific search criteria. News are typically displayed in Reuters 3000 Xtra in a headline format such as the one displayed in Figure 3.1, or they can be accessed clicking on the security, such as in Figures 3.2 and 3.3.

Quantitative quotes (e.g. stock quotes or bond information) can also be displayed at any time by double clicking on the corresponding ticker. An example quote can be seen in Figure 3.4.

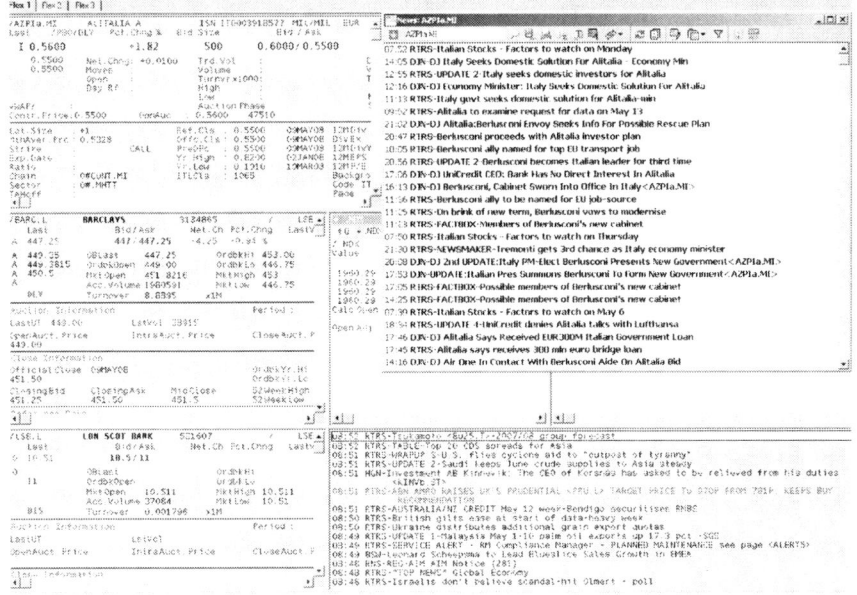

Figure 3.2: Reuters 3000 Xtra news menu.

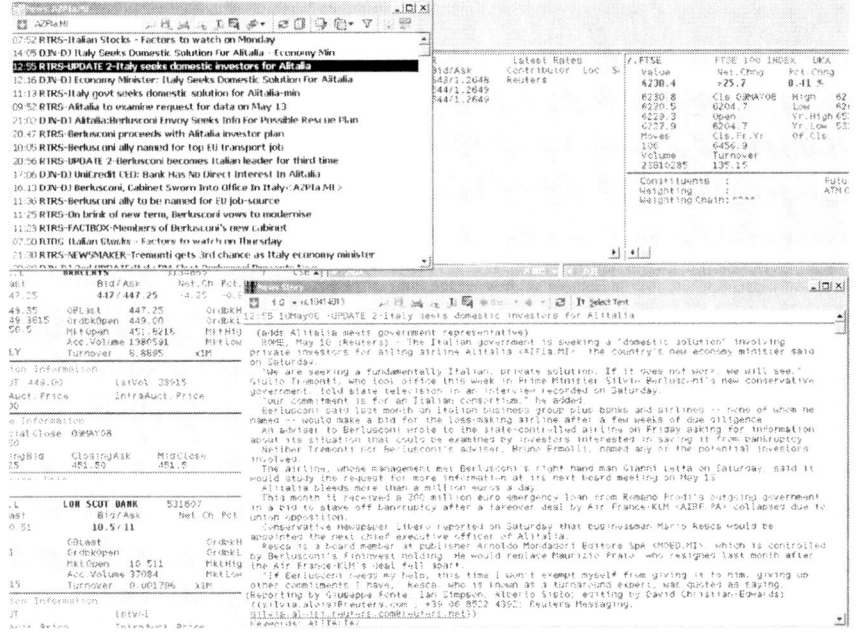

Figure 3.3: Reuters 3000 Xtra news.

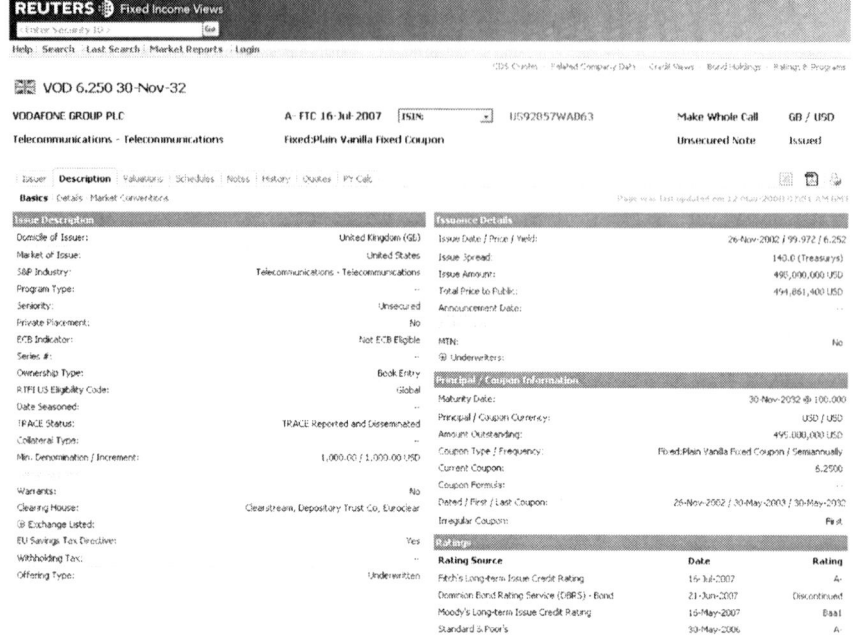

Figure 3.4: Reuters 3000 Xtra bond information.

Searching for information or specific news in Reuters 3000 Xtra is constrained to keyword and category searches. A first way to search for specific information is to type the stock ticker or the company name in the headline object. This shows historical and real-time news for the specific company. The wild card asterisk operator may be used in this case. Another way is to type a keyword, such as "petroleum", in the same window to retrieve headlines containing the word petroleum. Headlines can also be filtered, showing for example only news after or before a certain date, only news regarding a specific topic, such as for example interest rates, or a specific country. Finally, search expressions can be combined in different category codes, such as dates, keywords and filters in order to create news searches on specific topics. This can be done entering *OR*, *AND* or *NOT* within the search criteria. For example *(GB-POL) NOT ("BSE" or "MAD COW")* will search for British politics not containing the words *BSE* nor *mad cow*.

We consider the Reuters 3000 Xtra an excellent product. It is highly rated by all financial professionals who make use of it for taking trading decisions. The main limitation of the product are its news analysis capabilities. Similarly to most other financial qualitative information systems, searching is mainly limited to keyword searching or pre-defined categories. No AI techniques are used and, therefore, it is impossible to extract real-time templates.

In December 2006, Reuters started a project [86] to tag with keywords, with the help of its financial journalists, its news archive from 2003 until today. The aim of this project is not machine's comprehension of the news nor information extraction, but a statistical analysis of the relation between tags and large markets' movements. Reuters plans to have by 2011 a sophisticated set of algorithmic trading system based on news information as well as market data.

3.2 Bloomberg

Bloomberg, which started its network activities 15 years ago approximately in the same period as Reuters, took a completely different approach. Its services strongly rely on the World Wide Web technologies, having thus developed an extensive financial news website (see Figure 3.5). On their website the user finds news about financial markets, politics and economics, and all the markets' quantitative data, from stocks and bond prices (see Figure 3.6) and indices, up to currencies, funds and mortgage rates. Its strength is its usability: today every financial operator has access to a web browser with a broadband connection and can therefore take benefit from the user-friendly interface and also from the other web-services offered, such as online portfolio management, news podcast, audio and video reports, and interactive calculators for financial operations.

Figure 3.5: Bloomberg website's homepage.

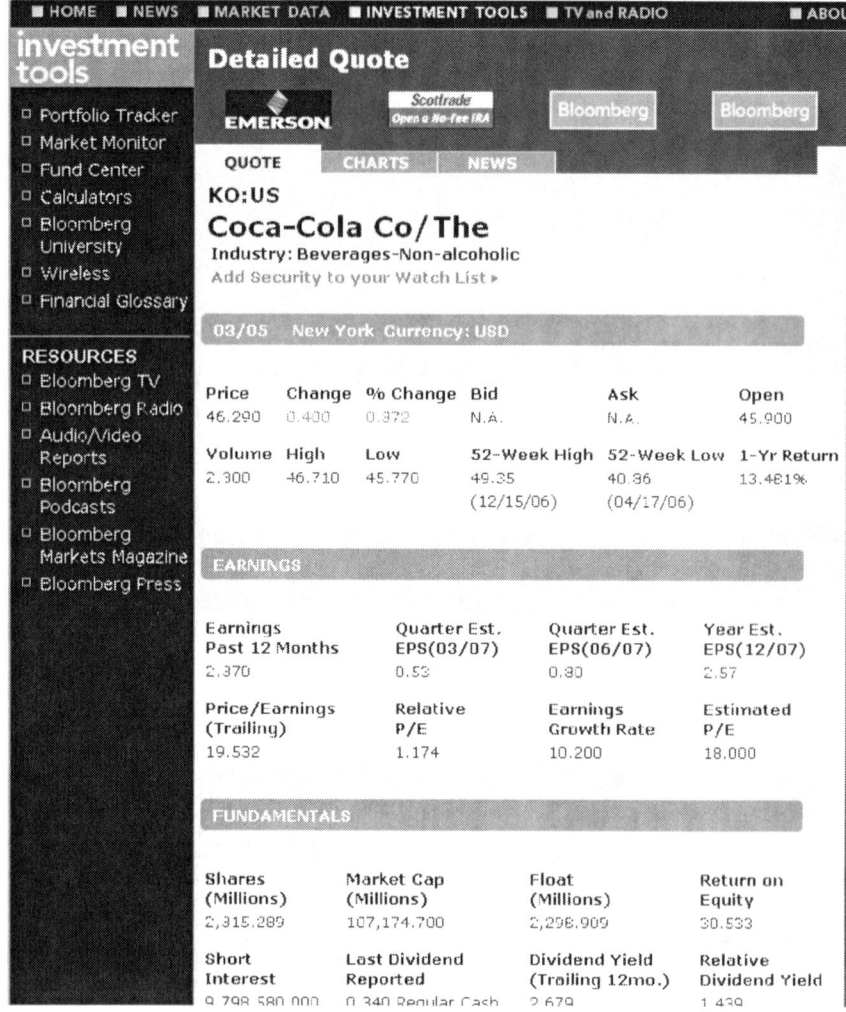

Figure 3.6: Bloomberg bond information.

Even though Bloomberg does sell the double-monitor **Bloomberg terminal**, a computer system that enables financial professionals to access the information service, its main entrances are not, as for Reuters, the selling of the platform and data, but extra services. For example, with a subscription to **BloombergAnyWhere**, users may access the website via mobile telephone. Advertisement is also a strong entrance for Bloomberg, which, as for many websites, presents very well-targeted announces and sponsored links. Even though Bloomberg now apparently looks like one of the many financial news websites, with some services dedicated to non-professional users such as the financial tutorials and glossaries, its huge database

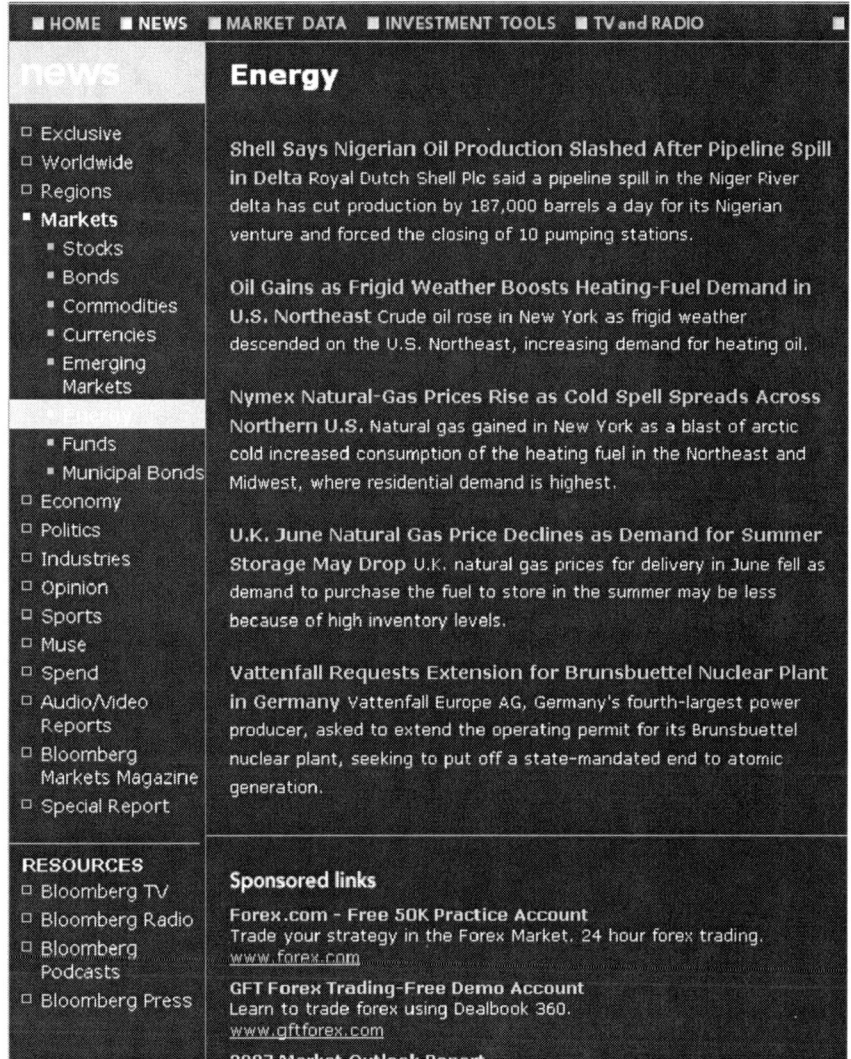

Figure 3.7: Bloomberg news menus.

of financial data and the long-time experience of its analysts make it one of the favourite websites for professional users.

The way information is presented and categorised is also quite different from Reuters. News tend to be more structured, with menus and submenus that drive the user to the right section (see Figure 3.7), or with a drop-down menu that gives direct access to the wanted section. Headlines are obviously provided to select the more interesting news among those provided. Every time a news is selected,

Figure 3.8: Bloomberg news.

similar news are suggested on the right pane. A search engine is present, however its use is very limited without any advanced search options. Moreover, there is no interaction between a single news (see Figure 3.8) and quantitative market data, thus preventing the user reading qualitative information to quickly switch to see the impact on numeric data.

Although the examples of Bloomberg screenshots shown above represent a very limited subset of the information that can be retrieved through it, it gives a clear indication of the strengths and the limitations of the platform. The main strength is the structured approach to the information which, therefore, is clearly and easily available to the user. This strength, however, also translates into the main weakness of the platform, which is the limited availability of tools and criteria for retrieving specific news.

3.3 Other information systems

Other companies provide information systems, such as **Thompson Financial News** service. This service behaves in the same way as Reuters, limiting the information extraction to the link between news and the corresponding company's market data.

FactSet provides the usual news and market information together with a lot of static information, such as phone number, password, type of conference call and important company investor relations contact information. However, it concentrates mostly on corporate events, such as conference call, for which it provides dates and transcripts. This system also provides analysis and expert's estimates, trying to give to the professional user access to as many different sources as possible.

Dow Jones MarketWatch tries to integrate, via a website, the newspaper format with hyperlinks to other news or to quantitative data (Figure 3.9).

Figure 3.9: Dow Jones MarketWatch.

3.4 Weaknesses of traditional approaches

We briefly discussed two of the most important and widespread traditional real-time systems the Reuters and Bloomberg applications. These systems represent the state of the art in traditional techniques and provide the users with outstanding real-time capabilities and news.

From the brief examples discussed in the above sections, however, clear limitations of the systems arise: almost no analysis is carried out on the news itself and the searching capabilities are extremely basic. The tools make use of simple keyword searching techniques, completely skipping any use of more intelligent techniques such as information extraction. Any additional analysis of the news, such as information extraction of the main events or automatic investment suggestions or possible impact on the stock prices from the news is not available.

These limitations are technological limitation of the current state of the art of commercial programs. These programs must be reliable, real-time and especially validated through many years of use as non-crucial subsidiary tools. Information extraction techniques are still undergoing major changes and for this reason they still have not been adopted by major financial software producers. However, we believe that coupling the great amount of information provided by current commercial systems together with more intelligent tools based on AI techniques such as information extraction would greatly improve the quality of the service without forcing end-user to radical changes.

4 Natural language processing and information extraction

In this chapter, we introduce the research field of IE and its most relevant techniques, approaches and systems. Since many of the statistical and probabilistic techniques used in IE are borrowed from information retrieval, we briefly analyse information retrieval focusing on the most important techniques which can be applied to IE. We later focus on the basic IE systems that have been developed, specifically those developed for the MUC competitions.

4.1 Information retrieval

Information retrieval is the extraction of relevant texts from a large collection of documents. Typically, information retrieval techniques are used to flag relevant documents from a large collection (newspaper articles, legal documents, etc.). They can be identified according to specific criteria supplied by the user. These criteria are generally called a **query**, which represents the user's requirements for the selection of the relevant documents. This first kind of information retrieval is sometimes called **ad hoc information retrieval** (e.g. in the TREC conferences [87]). Another aspect of information retrieval is the **routing** of a stream of incoming documents, which are discriminated between **relevant** and **non-relevant** documents given specific criteria. Some authors [88] consider information retrieval as a global term covering any sort of extraction or identification of data in source article and document retrieval as the identification of relevant documents in a collection. We here prefer to consider information retrieval as the process used for the identification of relevant documents among a collection of documents, rather than as a global term.

An important aspect of the information retrieval area is **efficiency** and **effectiveness**. Efficiency is usually quantified in terms of computer resources needed by the program, such as memory and CPU time and it is therefore very difficult to measure as a machine-independent value. Moreover, it should be measured taking into consideration the effectiveness of obtaining the information requested. Effectiveness is usually measured in terms of **precision** (accuracy) and **recall** (completeness).

Precision is mathematical defined as the ratio of the number of retrieved relevant documents to the total number of retrieved documents:

$$\text{precision} = \frac{\text{number of retrieved relevant items}}{\text{total number of retrieved items}}.$$

Recall is the ratio between the number of retrieved relevant documents and the total number of relevant documents (both retrieved and not retrieved) [89]:

$$\text{recall} = \frac{\text{number of retrieved relevant items}}{\text{total number of relevant items in the collection}}.$$

These two measures are often combined to obtain the **F-measure**:

$$\text{F-measure} = \frac{2 \times \text{precision} \times \text{recall}}{\text{precision} + \text{recall}},$$

or, more generally using the parameter α,

$$\text{F-measure} = \frac{(1 + \alpha) \times \text{precision} \times \text{recall}}{\alpha \times (\text{precision} + \text{recall})}.$$

The F-measure gives also an idea of how different precision and recall are, strongly penalising systems with a high precision and a low recall or viceversa. For example, with the same value of precision and recall, the system will have an F-measure equal to the precision, while with α equal to 1 and a recall 2 times smaller than the precision, the system will have a F-measure equal to two thirds of the precision.

Another measure, sometimes used, is **fallout**, which is defined as the ratio between the number of retrieved non-relevant items and the total number of non-relevant items in the collection:

$$\text{fallout} = \frac{\text{number of retrieved non-relevant items}}{\text{total number of non-relevant items in the collection}}.$$

The techniques that are available for extracting relevant information from a text are numerous. It is useful to classify them into statistical probabilistic approaches, linguistic approaches and a combination of the two approaches.

While the statistical probabilistic approach makes wide use of these techniques to find the relevant information in the text, the linguistic approach's goal is to perform a deeper analysis of the source text involving the analysis of the meaning of the sentences in order to select the information that is needed. The third approach combines the two approaches, the techniques based on statistics and linguistics.

4.1.1 Statistical and probabilistic approaches

The first approaches to information retrieval use keyword searches and statistical techniques in order to retrieve the relevant documents. These approaches achieve good results in terms of speed, but have many disadvantages mainly related to the fact that the meaning of the text is not understood by the information retrieval application.

The boolean retrieval

A very simple retrieval method, which also is the basis of many commercial retrieval services, is the boolean retrieval. This method, unfortunately, provides low performance in terms of precision and recall. The term "boolean" is used to emphasise the fact that query specifications are expressed as words or phrases combined using operators coming from boolean logic. The boolean method retrieves documents, which are able to match exactly the terms that form the query and thus there is no distinction among the retrieved documents. The main problem of this method is that it does not allow any ranking of the documents of the collection. In fact, it is quite unlikely that every document is relevant in the same way as everyone else. Moreover, boolean retrieval is an **exact-matching retrieval** method, thus it only allows retrieval of documents that match exactly the query; excluding documents from the retrieved set because they do not exactly match the query, maybe due to an orthographic mistake or a plural noun or a conjugated verb, is very reductive. This is different from **best-matching** methods, that retrieve documents matching the query in the best way.

Web search engines

Web search engines started developing in the mid-90s using boolean retrieval techniques. Very soon, however, it became obvious that returning a disordered list of websites did not help the user, especially when only a single keyword was entered as a search criteria. Many search engines tried to rank the results, but it was Google in the early 2000s that managed to order the search result in the best way. Its scoring system uses, as every information retrieval system should do, extra information derived from the World Wide Web structure. The whole WWW is harvested and the webpages' links produce a huge scoring matrix which is used to find out the websites, which are considered the most important by their peer community [90]. This scoring system has a great success, pointing out that all available information should be inserted in the search process.

The vector space model

Another approach is based on the frequency of a word in a document and, thus, on the identification of key terms in the document which can be matched with the queries supplied by the user, through a process is known as **indexing**. In fact, a term appearing often in the text may be more important for the identification of relevant information than a term appearing rarely. In contrast, if the same term occurs in many documents, it will probably be irrelevant for finding the relevant information. Therefore, the specificity of a given term as applied to a given document can be measured by a combination of its frequency of occurrence inside that particular document (the term frequency (tf)) and an inverse function of the number of documents in the collection to which it is assigned (the inverse document frequency (idf), be computed as 1 divided by the document frequency). A possible weighting function for a generic term i appearing in the document j can be [91]

$$w_{ij} = \text{tf}_{ij} \times \text{idf}_i,$$

where the second factor shown in the formula above, the inverse document frequency of a term, can be obtained in advance from a collection analysis, while the term frequencies can be computed from the individual documents, as needed.

Using the weighting formula, the documents of the collection can be ranked in connection with the query of the user. The first documents will be those where the specific terms occur frequently in the document, and very rarely in the rest of the collection. Such terms will in fact distinguish the relevant documents from the non-relevant ones.

The main disadvantage of the simple word-based approach considered above is that single words are rarely specific enough to accurately discriminate documents, and their grouping is often accidental [92]. A better method is to identify groups of words that create meaningful phrases, thus stop looking at words and search for phrases. A good example [92] is the phrase *Joint Venture* that can be much more important in a financial article than either *Joint* or *Venture* alone. In large databases comprising hundreds of thousands of documents, the use of phrasal terms is not just desirable, but it becomes necessary. The terms that used to extract information from a text are usually preprocessed through four main techniques: **removal of high-frequency words, suffix stripping, detection of equivalent stems** and **addition of synonyms**.

High-frequency words are eliminated because they are supposed to be too common and, thus, not significant for the identification of relevant information in a document. This phase is normally implemented by comparing the input text with a **stop list** of words that are supposed to be common, such as, for example, *about, into, cannot, our*. The advantages of the process are not only that non-significant words are removed and will not interfere with the searching process, but also that the size of the original text will be reduced consistently [89].

The second process, suffix stripping, is more complicated. The words involved in the searching process are checked and common suffix are removed from the word, obtaining the stem. For example, verbs are reduced to their stem (e.g. *started* is reduced to *start*). A standard approach to do this is to have a complete list of suffixes and to remove the longest possible one. Unfortunately, suffix stripping can lead to errors in the searching process, and the suffix must be removed taking into account the context. In addition, many words, even if they look equivalent are not, and special algorithms must be used as well as lists of irregular words. Moreover, the suffix stripping algorithms are often different from one language to another. The most important advantage of the suffix stripping algorithms consists in the fact that words sharing the same stems should represent the same concept and, thus, the number of words to be used in the search process can be reduced.

Another process that can be useful to improve the recall performance of information retrieval applications is to add to the query synonyms of the original terms or broader terms. The last step that can be useful in order to reach a better performance in the searching process is normalisation. This process is normally lexicon based and, thus, a dictionary is needed in order to construct the proper word. For example, the word *move* is reduced to *mov* by the word stripping algorithm and reconducted to *move* by the normalisation algorithm.

Techniques such as suffix removal, addition of synonyms, addition of related or broader terms leads to an improvement in recall – enhancing strategies but, unfortunately the use of these techniques leads to a loss of precision. In fact, it is often possible to notice a trade-off between recall and precision and every operation that causes a broadening of the terms to search will generally lead to an increase of recall, while a narrowing of the terms will lead to an improvement of the precision. In fact it usually happens that the harder a system tries to extract all the relevant information (i.e. the more aggressively configured it is), the more likely it is to extract erroneous information [93].

The probabilistic approach

Another approach to information retrieval is based on the use of statistics and, thus, the model is called the probabilistic retrieval model. Probabilistic information retrieval models are based on the **probability ranking principle** [94]. This states that a way to discriminate among the documents in a collection is to rank the documents according to the order of probability to match a certain query. Clearly, the ranking process takes into consideration the limited information available at the time it is made. The probability ranking principle, thus, assumes that it is possible to calculate the probability of relevance of a document and, also, to estimate it accurately. The problem that arises trying to calculate the probability above is that the percentage of the relevant documents among all the others is unknown and, therefore, must be estimated. Following the probabilistic retrieval model, the most valuable documents for retrieval purposes are those whose probability of relevance to a query is largest [95] and, in this, the approach differs quite a lot from the simple word-matching search. The relevance property of a document is estimated by taking into consideration the relevance of the individual terms in the document. Various different probabilistic formulations have been proposed and they differ mainly in the way in which they estimate the probability of relevance of a document. A possible relevance weighting function can be:

$$\text{tr}_i = \log\left(\frac{N - n_i}{n_i}\right) + \text{constants}$$

where N is the collection size and n_i represents the number of documents in the collection with term i [95].

The term-discrimination approach

A different approach to information retrieval is the term-discrimination model. This model assumes that the most useful terms for finding relevant information in the collection of documents are those which can distinguish the documents of a collection from each other. Thus, "the value of a term should be measured by calculating the decrease in the density of the document collection that results when a given term is assigned to the collection" [95]. The density of the documents is high when they are indexed by many of the same terms. With the term-discrimination approach the terms that occur often in all the documents of the collection become the less useful to search for relevant information, while the terms that make it possible to distinguish between the documents are preferred. In other words, the best words to be used should be those which appear neither too often in the documents, nor too rarely. The term-discrimination model, thus, is based on the assumption that terms that are able to distinguish a document among the others document of the collection are those which are enough specific but not too much to be rare.

Other non-linguistic approaches
In recent years, researchers moved towards new directions in information retrieval. The common thought is that better performance in information retrieval tasks can be obtained if the algorithms are able to understand in some way the meaning of the text in order to extract the relevant embedded information. In this view [96], information retrieval is an inference or **evidential reasoning** process in which the goal is to estimate the probability that the information needed by the user is available given a document as evidence. The retrieval method based on **inference networks** follows this approach [96] and it is based on **Bayesian inference networks** [94] which are directed, acyclic dependency graphs in which nodes represent prepositional variables or constants and edges represent dependence relations between propositions. The basic document retrieval inference network consists of two component networks: a document network and a query network. The document network represents the collection of the documents through a variety of representation schemes. The document network is built at the beginning for a particular document collection, and it does not change while the search process takes place. While the document network consists of many nodes, the query network consists of a single node, which represents the query supplied by the user. Moreover, while the document network is built when a particular collection of documents is given, the query network is built each time the user supplies a query and is modified during the search processing as existing queries are redefined or new queries are added to perform better search. A complete description of the algorithms can be found in Refs. [91, 96]. However, at the moment the inference networks method does not seem to be largely used in information retrieval applications.

4.1.2 Linguistic approaches

The linguistic approach to information retrieval is based on the assumption that the statistical and probabilistic techniques are limited in the sense that they are not able to understand the meaning of the text. Other authors [97] refer to the linguistic approach as a **meaning-oriented approach**. The linguistic approach is based on the idea that a technique that can deeply understand the text performs much better than statistical and probabilistic techniques. Once the meaning of the text is understood, the user can retrieve information by simply providing queries in natural language to the system, obtaining the information needed in the desired form. In other words [98], an information retrieval application based on the linguistic approach is able to process the collection of documents by a natural language understanding system, and to extract the meaning of the documents. The user's requests are processed by the same natural language understanding system and the information can be identified since the system has already understood the meaning of the text.

Unfortunately, the systems that have been built until now are still not able to cope with the free text of a general domain and, usually, work only in limited domains. In addition, linguistic approaches tend to be slower than systems based on statistics and probability and require very large computing power. Current research in information retrieval is therefore oriented towards the improvement of techniques based on statistics and probability through the use of linguistics methodologies and these approaches are usually called **knowledge-based approaches**.

4.2 The TREC competitions

The Text Retrieval Conference (TREC), co-sponsored by the National Institute of Standards and Technology (NIST) and U.S. Department of Defense, started in 1992 as part of the TIPSTER Text program. Its purpose was to support research within the information retrieval community by providing the infrastructure necessary for large-scale evaluation of text retrieval methodologies. In particular, TREC workshops have the following goals:

- to encourage research in information retrieval based on large test collections;
- to increase communication among industry, academia and government by creating an open forum for the exchange of research ideas;
- to speed the transfer of technology from research labs into commercial products by demonstrating substantial improvements in retrieval methodologies on real-world problems;
- to increase the availability of appropriate evaluation techniques for use by industry and academia, including development of new evaluation techniques more applicable to current systems.

For each TREC workshop, NIST provides a testset of documents and questions to participants, which run their own retrieval systems on the data, and return to NIST a list of the retrieved top-ranked documents. NIST judges the retrieved documents for correctness, and evaluates the results. The TREC ends with a workshop where participants share their experiences.

This evaluation effort has grown in both the number of participating systems and the number of tasks each year. 117 participating from 23 different countries participated in TREC-2005 [99]. The TREC test collections and evaluation software are available to the retrieval research community at large, so organisations can evaluate their own retrieval systems at any time.

TREC has also sponsored the first large-scale evaluations of the retrieval of non-English (Spanish and Chinese) documents, retrieval of recordings of speech, and retrieval across multiple languages. TREC has also introduced evaluations for open-domain question answering and content-based retrieval of digital video. The TREC test collections are large enough so that they realistically model operational settings. Most of today's commercial search engines include technology first developed in TREC.

4.2.1 Tasks

TREC-2005 [100] contains seven areas of focus called **tracks**. Two tracks focuses on improving basic retrieval effectiveness by either providing more context or by trying to reduce the number of queries that fail. Other tracks explore tasks in question answering, detecting spam in an e-mail stream, enterprise search, search on terabyte-scale document sets, and information access within the genomics domain.

Information retrieval track is concerned with locating information that will satisfy a user's information need. Originally, the emphasis has been on text retrieval: providing access to natural language texts where the set of documents to be searched is large and topically diverse. In the last years, however, document was interpreted as any unit of information such as a database record, a web page, or an e-mail message. The prototypical retrieval task is a literature search in a library. In this environment, the retrieval system knows the set of documents to be searched, but cannot anticipate the particular topic that will be investigated. This is called an **ad hoc retrieval task**, reflecting the arbitrary subject of the search within its short duration. Other examples of ad hoc searches are Internet search engines, lawyers looking for precedences in case law, and financial analysts searching news for particular political or economical events. A retrieval system's response to an ad hoc search is generally a list of documents ranked by decreasing similarity to the query. Most of the TREC-2005 tracks include some sort of an ad hoc search task.

A **known-item search** is similar to an ad hoc search but the target of the search is a particular document that the searcher knows to exist in the collection and wants to find again. Once again, the retrieval system's response is usually a ranked list of documents, and the system is evaluated by the rank at which the target document is retrieved. The **named-page-finding task** in the terabyte track and the known-item task within the enterprise track are examples of known-item search tasks.

In a **categorisation task**, the system is responsible for assigning a document to appropriate categories. In the **spam track**, deciding whether a given e-mail is spam is a categorisation task; the genomics track has several categorisation tasks in TREC-2005 as well.

4.2.2 Evaluation metrics

Retrieval runs on a test collection can be evaluated in a number of ways. In TREC, ad hoc tasks are evaluated using a distributed package [101]. This package reports about 85 different measures for a run, including recall and precision at various

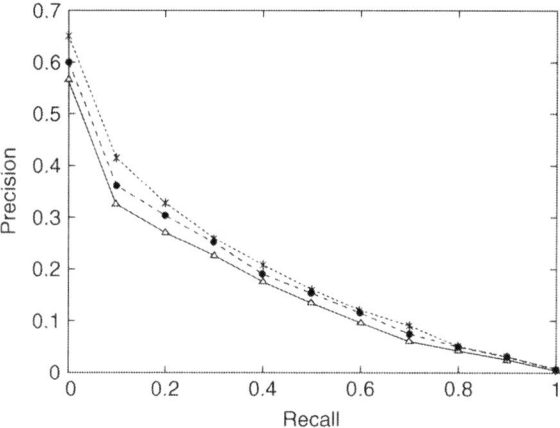

Figure 4.1: Precision recall curve for LowLands' system.

cut-off levels plus derived summary measures. A **cut-off level** is a rank that defines the retrieved set; for example, a cut-off level of 10 defines the retrieved set as the top 10 documents in the ranked list. The evaluation program reports the scores as averages over the set of topics where each topic is equally weighted. At varying cut-off levels, recall and precision tend to be inversely related since retrieving more documents will usually increase recall while degrading precision and viceversa. The interpolated recall–precision curve and mean average precision are the most commonly used measures to describe TREC results. A precision–recall curve plots precision as a function of recall (Figure 4.1).

Precision–recall graphs show the behaviour of a retrieval run over the entire recall spectrum. **Mean average precision** is the single-valued summary measure used when an entire graph is too cumbersome. The **average precision** for a single topic is the mean of the precision obtained after each relevant document is retrieved, using zero as the precision for relevant documents that are not retrieved. The mean average precision for a run consisting of multiple topics is the mean of the average precision scores of each of the individual topics in the run. The average precision measure has a recall component in that it reflects the performance of a retrieval run across all relevant documents, and a precision component in that it weights documents retrieved earlier more heavily than documents retrieved later. Geometrically, average precision is the area underneath a recall precision curve.

4.3 Information extraction

The goal of IE is to extract specific kinds of information from a document [76]. In other words, the input of the system is a stream of text while the output is some representation of the information previously contained in the texts [102]. The main difference between information retrieval and IE is that while the main objective of information retrieval is to identify relevant documents among a generic collection

Original text with relevant information

Source: Dow Vision, a service of Dow Jones.
Date: Jan 18, 2007 Time: 9:34 am
Banker Trust New York Corp. (BT) said its 2006 earnings were affected by persistently difficult market conditions, which hurt trading revenue.
The company said trading revenue was 49 dlrs million in the latest fourth quarter, down from 449 dlrs million in the year-ago quarter, while trading-related net interest revenue fell to 50 dlrs million in the latest fourth quarter from 187 dlrs million a year earlier.
Banker Trust said many of its proprietary trading businesses, principally fixed income instruments, recorder lower revenues during the latest fourth quarter as market conditions remained generally unsettled. The company said trading results also declined significantly in the emerging markets of Asia and Latin America, and said the volume of traditional risk management products slowed.
The company said revenue increased from its client-related businesses that provide financing, advisory and transaction processing services.
Bankers Trust said it reclassified 423 dlrs million of leveraged derivative contracts as receivable in the loan account and placed them on a cash basis during the last fourth quarter. Of the amount, the company said 72 dlrs million was subsequently charged off to the allowance for credit losses. About half of the remainder related to transactions with Procter and Gamble Co. (PG).
With the transfers and charge-offs, the company said it has taken action on the leveraged derivative transactions that likely will not perform according to the contract and has charged off the balances deemed to be uncollectible.
Bankers Trust said net charge-offs for the latest fourth quarter were 85 dlrs million, compared with 184 dlrs million a year ago.

Extracted fragment containing relevant information

Banker Trust New York Corp. (BT) said its 2006 earnings were effected by persistently difficult market conditions, which hurt trading revenue. The company said trading revenue was 49 dlrs million in the latest fourth quarter, down from 449 dlrs million in the year-ago quarter, while trading-related net interest revenue fell to 50 dlrs million in the latest fourth quarter from 187 dlrs million a year earlier.

Figure 4.2: Information extraction using fragments from the original document.

of documents, IE tries also to identify relevant information inside documents and to produce a representation of the information. Thus, IE systems must not only be able to judge the relevance of a particular document in the collection but also to spot where the relevant information is inside the documents.

Finally, the output of the two systems is rather different. The output of a classical information retrieval system is simply the collection of relevant documents retrieved, while the output of an IE system can be of different types. One kind of output is simply a fragment of relevant text found in the documents of the collection (see Figure 4.2).

Alternatively, the output of an IE system consists of templates (Figure 4.3). A **template** is as a structure with a predefined set of slots, one for each type of information to be extracted from the text [76].

Original text with relevant information

A car bomb exploded outside the Cabinet Office in Whitehall last night, 100 yards from 10 Downing Street. Nobody was injured in the explosion which happened just after 9 pm on the corner of Downing Street and Whitehall. Police evacuated the area.

First reports suggested that the bomb went off in a black taxi after the driver had been forced to drive to Whitehall. The taxi was later reported to be burning fiercely. (THE DAILY TELEGRAPH 31/10/92)

Extracted template

Incident: The bomb explosion outside the Cabinet Office and outside 10 Downing Street in a black taxi.

Where: Outside the Cabinet Office and outside 10 Downing Street in the black taxi that a driver drove to Whitehall.

When: Last night (30 October). When a forceful person forced a driver to drive t Whitehall a black taxi that fiercely burned.

Responsible: Unknown.

Target: Cabinet Office. 10 Downing Street.

Damage: Human: nobody. Thing: the black taxi that a driver drove to Whitehall.

Source: Telegraph.

Source date: 31 October 1992.

Certainty: facts.

Other relevant information: Police evacuated Downing Street.

Figure 4.3: Information extraction using templates.

Clearly, the way the template is presented to the end user is crucial for the effective usefulness of an IE system. In Ref. [102] three different but interacting considerations are indicated for an effective template:

- The template as representational device.
- The template as generated from input.
- The template as input to further processing, by humans or programs or both.

The design of templates has to take into consideration many different aspects, often in competition between themselves [103]:

Descriptive adequacy: The template should present all the relevant information for a particular task or application. The relevant information should include all supporting information such as measurement units, etc.

Clarity: The information included in the template should not be ambiguous, for both the human end-user of the template or for further processing of the information by computer applications.

Determinacy: There should be only one way of representing the extracted information inside a template.

Perspicuity: "The degree to which the design is conceptually clear to the human analysts who will input or edit information in the template or work with the results" [103]

Monotonicity: Adding new information to a template already filled, there should be no new objects in the template and none of the existing slots should be removed.

Reusability: Templates can be used in other domains and, therefore, must be designed to be manually converted.

4.3.1 The scripts-frames systems

The first attempts to understand the meaning of a text and to produce summaries or templates from it were mainly based on the concepts of frames or scripts. A **frame** can be defined [104] as "networks of nodes and relations the highest level of which are things which are always true about the situation, the lowest level being slots which are filled by the details of a particular instance of the situation". In a similar way, a **script** can be defined [104] as "a predetermined, stereotyped, sequence of actions that define a well-known situation". The systems based on scripts and frames were thus based on a collection of predefined stories and their task was, therefore, to identify which one was suitable for the text analysed. Various attempts have been made using the script-frame approach. The most important systems based on these approaches are here analysed. However, the analysis will not be very deep, because more advanced techniques have been introduced in recent years [105].

SAM

SAM [106] is a system based on scripts. Each script provides pre-stored expectations about what will be read, based upon what has already been seen. The main problem of SAM, as well as for other systems based on scripts or frames, is that it cannot be used for analysing texts for which it does not have a pre-stored script. SAM, in fact, does not deeply understand the meaning of the text and bases its knowledge on the scripts. Moreover, SAM, unlike other programs based on script or frames, is not prepared to deal with unknown information in a text. This means that, if a particular text does not exactly match any script, the program will fail to classify and predict its contents and, therefore, will not be able to produce any output for it. The main module in SAM is the **script applier**, whose task is to introduce the largest script for a particular story. Once the script has been applied, predictions are made for what has to be the subsequent input. If the following text does not match any more the predictions contained in the script, the script applier will look for another script. Clearly, the main problem arises when the script applier is not able to match any script to the text.

PAM

A different approach is followed by PAM [106], which identifies two main problems of the scripts-frames approach. The first is that it is not always possible to identify a single frame that classifies the entire text. The second is that the selection of an appropriate frame for a specific text can be ambiguous. Some texts, in fact, can potentially fit in more than one frame. Moreover, the authors of PAM consider the fact that it is very unlikely that one single story (text) is based on a single goal and it is more likely that in a single story different goals will appear together. PAM is thus based on the analysis of the goals that can be found in a particular story [106]:

Goal subsumption: A situation in which many recurrences of a goal are planned at the same time.

Goal conflict: A story can include goals in conflict between themselves.

Goal competition: Different goals can be in competition.

The behaviour of PAM is therefore directed to the understanding of the goals of a particular text and, thus, predict the subsequent text.

FRUMP

Another script-based system is FRUMP [107]. The program, like others, tries to match a particular sketch script to the text being analysed and tries to make predictions about the further contents of the text. The main characteristic of this program, is that it just skips the parts of the text that do not satisfy its predictions.

Scrabble

Another scripts-frames based system considered here is Scrabble [104]. One observation made by its authors is that a system should not skip over sections of text which do not follow the pre-loaded scripts. Scrabble is composed by five main modules: an **English semantic parser**, a combined stereotype management module, a stereotype application module, a **text representation summariser** and an **English generator**. The interesting modules in this context are the stereotype management module, the stereotype application module and the English summariser.

The **stereotype management module** analyses the text coming from the parser and suggests a possible stereotype suitable for the text. It is important to notice that, unlike other systems, more instances (scripts) can be activated at the same time. Thus, the stereotype management module must also be able to decide whether an instance has to be de-activated or a new instance activated. An instance that is not used in a particular situation but has not been removed yet is called suspended.

The **stereotype application module** waits for the incoming text and checks if the predictions available in the currently activated instances, supplied by the stereotype management module are satisfied.

The task of the **summary generator** is to produce the summary of the original text and supply it to the English generator for the final output of the program. The summary generator receives three kinds of input. The first is the list of all activated and suspended stereotype instances. The second is a list of all parsed sentences that were not expected by the activated instances (this second input is given because Scrabble does not skip unexpected part of a text like FRUMP). Finally, the third input that is supplied to the summary generator is a "data structure which represents the textual interrelationships of the propositions in the input text which gave rise to the elements of the other two" [104]. The first step taken by the summary generator is to attempt to choose between related instances used to analyse the text by further processing them. The summary generator attempts, in fact, to reduce the number of instances. This means that some instances may be killed or suspended for a particular text. The process in this step differs from the equivalent one made in the stereotype management module, for the fact that the assumption made in the summary generator algorithm are much stronger that in the stereotype management module, so that less instances are analysed. Once the relevant instances have been chosen, the elements that will be later included in the summary can be also identified. However, the contents of the summary is not yet known and, therefore, each stereotype-instance is processed to produce the data structure coming from the input and this is combined with the part of the text that was unexpected and, thus, impossible to process. The approach suggested seems to be better than others in the sense that it also considers the parts of the text that were unexpected and does not just skip them.

ATRANS

The first commercially successful program based on the scripts-frames approach was ATRANS, from Cognitive Systems [108]. The task that ATRANS (Automatic Funds TRANSfer Telex Reader) performs is to extract information from Telex messages [109]. More precisely, the messages that ATRANS processes are requests for money transfers that banks send to each other. ATRANS first extracts the relevant information and then uses it to produce an output that can be later used for an automatic execution of the transfer. The form of the output can be viewed as a template containing information such as the amount of money to be transferred, the date, the beneficiary and so on. The Telex messages given as input to ATRANS can vary considerably due to the fact that a money transfer can be sent from any part of the world. In fact, the English form of the messages will vary in spelling, sentence construction, standard abbreviations, amounts, date conventions and so on. ATRANS is able to extract correctly 80% of the relevant information in the Telex messages, while about 15% of relevant information is lost and 5% is identified incorrectly. The evaluation, however, was not carried out within a formal framework and was influenced by the very restricted domain.

ATRANS is based on the scripts-frames approach. This means that, as well as other systems based on this approach, it will first try to fit an appropriate script to identify the relevant information in the text. There are various script available in the system, according to the different kind of transfers that can be processed such as, multiple intermediary banks, different methods of payments, more then one beneficiary and so on.

The architecture of ATRANS is similar to that of other script-based systems. ATRANS consists of four parts: the message classifier, the text analyser, the message interpreter and the output formatter.

The **message classification** module is similar to script-applier modules found in other systems and determines the type of message currently processed, choosing the appropriate script from those available in the system. However, more than one script can be applied to the same Telex. This mainly happens in the case of multiple transfers and the message classification module identifies the common portions of the transfer (using one script) and composes several single transfer messages.

The output of the message classification module is given as input to the **text analyser** module, which is defined as the "heart of the system" by the authors. This module uses the chosen script and the dictionaries available and tries to identify the frames being referred in the text following the predictions of the script, such as, for example payment, test and cover.

The analyser does not try to verify the information extracted or check its consistency. This task is performed by the **message interpreter** module, which verifies and consolidates the extracted information items. However, the output of the message interpreter is still in an internal representation form.

The conversion from the internal representation to the final output form is made by the **output generator** module. The form varies according to the particular user of the system (e.g. the Swift and Chips banking networks).

Systems based on the scripts-frames approach were the first attempt to produce summaries and templates from a text. However, many other approaches have been developed in subsequent years and, thus, they will not analysed here in more detail.

4.4 The MUC competitions

A particular group of interesting systems are those developed for the MUC tasks [21–25]. The target of the MUC competitions was to improve the technology of IE systems performing specific tasks set for each of the MUC conferences.

The procedure was equivalent for all MUC competitions. The first step was the definition of the tasks to be performed by the participating systems. Once the tasks were defined, a set of training documents, the associated keys and an automatic scoring program were made available to the participants. The participants could use the set of training documents for developing and training the systems and carrying out an initial unofficial evaluation of the systems. After a specific amount of time allowed for the development and training of the systems, the actual evaluation was carried out. A final set of evaluation documents was released to the participants which were asked to submit the results using this set of documents. The final evaluation of the results was carried out matching the results produced by the systems against a set of predefined keys for the set of evaluation documents. In the MUC-6 competition one of the evaluation tasks was released to the participants only 1 month prior to the final evaluation to emphasise the portability of the systems.

We will briefly analyse the tasks of the MUC conferences, the main techniques employed by the systems that participated, in particular the MUC-6 and MUC-7 conferences, and the measures used for the evaluation.

The first two MUC competitions, known as MUCK-I and MUCK-II [110] represented initial experiments related to the evaluation of systems performing rather simple tasks on source texts. However, the evaluation set was extremely limited (just five texts for the MUCK-II competition) and, therefore, the results themselves are not particularly useful. The MUC-3 evaluation, instead, was significantly more relevant, both in terms of tasks and systems which entered the competitions. However, the most important MUC competitions in terms of kind of tasks, number and quality of the systems that entered the competition and results were the number 5 [23] and number 6 [24] which will be here described in more detail.

MUC competition testsets are still used after 10 years in many modern systems (see Appendix B), since they are a very large set of publicly available documents, and therefore they are considered to be one of the best text sets to compare different systems. Also the systems presented in the two last MUC competitions, MUC-6 and MUC-7, represent the basis for the development of the next generation of IE systems.

MUC-3 tasks

The MUC-3 task was to extract information about terrorist attacks from articles from newspapers, TV and radio news, speech and interview transcripts, rebel communications, etc. The systems had to extract the relevant information and represent it into a pre-defined template. Differently from MUCK-I and MUCK-II, the MUC-3 competition required the systems to discriminate between relevant and irrelevant information (information filtering). In Figure 4.4 an example MUC-3 article is shown, while in Figure 4.5 an example MUC-3 template produced from the same article is shown.

The systems that entered the competition were based on various techniques such as statistical, keyword, finite-state analysis, deep NLP, etc. The specific systems will not be analysed here, since most of them participated in the subsequent editions of the MUC competitions.

TST1-MUC3-0080
BOGOTA, 3 APR 90 (INRA VISION TELEVISION CADENA 1) [REPORT] [JORGE ALONSO SIERRA VALENCIA] [TEXT] LIBERAL SENATOR FEDERICO ESTRADA VELEZ WAS KIDNAPPED ON 3 APRIL AT THE CORNER OF 60TH AND 48TH STREETS IN WESTERN MEDELLIN, ONLY 100 METERS FROM A METROPOLITAN POLICE CAI [IMMEDIATE ATTENTION CENTER]. THE AN- TIOQUIA DEPARTMENT LIBERAL PARTY LEADER HAD LEFT HIS HOUSE WITHOUT ANY BODIGUARDS ONLY MINUTES EARLIER. AS HE WAITED FOR THE TRAFFIC LIGHT TO CHANGE, THREE HEAVILY ARMED MEN FORCED HIM TO GET OUT OF THIS CAR AND GET INTO A BLUE RENAULT.
HOURS LATER, THROUGH ANONYMOUS TELEPHONE CALLS TO THE METROPOLITAN POLICE AND TO THE MEDIA, THE EXTRADITABLES CLAIMED RESPONSIBILITY FOR THE KIDNAPPING. IN THE CALLS, THEY ANNOUNCED THAT THEY WILL RELEASE THE SENATOR WITH A NEW MESSAGE FOR THE NATIONAL GOVERNMENT.
LAST WEEK, FEDERICO ESTRADA VELEZ HAD REJECTED TALKS BETWEEN THE GOVERNMENT AND THE DRUG TRAFFICKERS.

Figure 4.4: A MUC-3 document in the terrorist domain.

Message ID: TST1-MUC3-0080
Template ID: 1
Date of incident: 03 APR 90
Type of incident: KIDNAPPING
Category of incident: TERRORIST ACT
Perpetrator: ID of indiv(s): THREE HEAVILY ARMED MEN
Perpetrator: ID of org(s): THE EXTRADITABLES / EXTRADITABLES
Perpetrator: confidence: claimed or admitted: THE EXTRADITABLES /
    EXTRADITABLES
Physical target: ID(s): *
Physical target: total num: *
Physical target: type(s): *
Human target: ID(s): FEDERICO ESTRADA VELEZ (LIBERAL SENATOR /
    ANTIOQUIA DEPARTMENT LIBERAL PARTY LEADER / SENATOR /
    LIBERAL PARTY LEADER / PARTY LEADER)
Human target: total num: 1
Human target: type(s): GOVERNMENT OFFICIAL / POLITICAL FIGURE:
    FEDERICO ESTRADA VELEZ
Target: foreign nation(s): -
Instrument: type(s): *
Location of incident: COLOMBIA MEDELLIN (CITY)
Effect on physical target(s): *
Effect on human target(s): -

Figure 4.5: A MUC-3 terrorist template.

MUC-4 tasks

The MUC-4 competition [22] was held 1 year after the MUC-3 competition. The tasks for the MUC-4 competition were rather similar to the MUC-3 ones. Few differences can be found in the templates, where some slots which included two pieces information were split into two separated slots. For example, the MUC-3 slot *Type of incident* became two MUC-4 slots *Incident: type* and *Incident: stage of execution*. Similarly, other slots were separated and few other changes were carried out on the template definition.

The main change in MUC-4 regarded the evaluation metrics [111] which, for the first time, included the F-measure (see Sections 4.1 and 4.4.1) for a combined evaluation of precision and recall.

A greater number of systems entered the MUC-4 competition. We do not describe these systems and the techniques on which they were based, since most of them entered the subsequent MUC-5 competition.

MUC-5 tasks

The MUC-5 competition comprised two domains (joint ventures and microelectronics) and two languages, English and Japanese, thus obtaining four language/domain pairs. Each pair was associated to about 1200 to 1600 articles. In the case of the joint venture domain for the English language (the only domain here considered) the articles were extracted from more than 200 sources, including *The Wall Street Journal, Jiji Press, The New York Times, The Financial Times, Kyodo Services* and a variety of other technical publications in fields such as communications, airline transportation, etc. The articles were mainly extracted using statistical and prob-abilistic information retrieval techniques. However, manual filtering techniques were also used. A number of non-relevant documents, about 5% of the total, were also included to test the system's ability to discriminate between relevant and non-relevant documents in the collection. Each of the documents of the collection was associated with a hand-made template to be used for the subsequent evaluation by the scoring program. The developers had access to numerous sources of different kinds of data, such as the English language gazetteer, provided to regularise geographic location information, lists of currency names and abbreviations, national adjectives, lists of countries and used abbreviations, the hierarchical classification of all the industry or business type in the U.S.

The joint venture domain of MUC-5 is relevant in the context of this work because it can be considered a subset of the financial domain. However, the joint venture domain was extremely limited because it considered only a very limited partition of the financial domain. The MUC-5 systems were in fact built to skip over any kind of information not regarding the joint venture domain and, even if the overall results of the competition were in absolute terms significant, the restricted domain in which they were achieved has to be taken into account. In Figure 4.6 a typical joint venture MUC-5 article is shown.

A MUC-5 template was supposed to be able to identify the joint venture, the participants, the capital of the new company and all the other relevant information related to the joint venture (Figure 4.7). The MUC-5 task was not therefore limited for the kind of template regarding the joint venture which, in fact, was enough to explain all the important information related to it, but for the extremely restricted partition of the financial domain considered: the joint venture domain.

Bridgestone sports co. said Friday it has set up a joint venture in Taiwan with a local concern and a Japanese trading house to produce golf clubs to be shipped to Japan. The joint venture, Bridgestone sports Taiwan co., capitalised at 20 million new Taiwan dollars, will start production in January 1990 with production of 20,000 iron and "metal wood" clubs a month. The monthly output will be later raised to 50,000 units, bridgestone sports official said.
The new company, based in Kaohsiung, southern Taiwan, is owned 75% by Bridge-stone sports, 15% by union precision casting co. of Taiwan and the remainder by Taga co., a company active in trading with Taiwan, the officials said.
...
With the establishment of the Taiwan unit, the Japanese sports goods maker plans to increase production of luxury clubs in Japan.

Figure 4.6: A MUC-5 document in the joint venture domain.

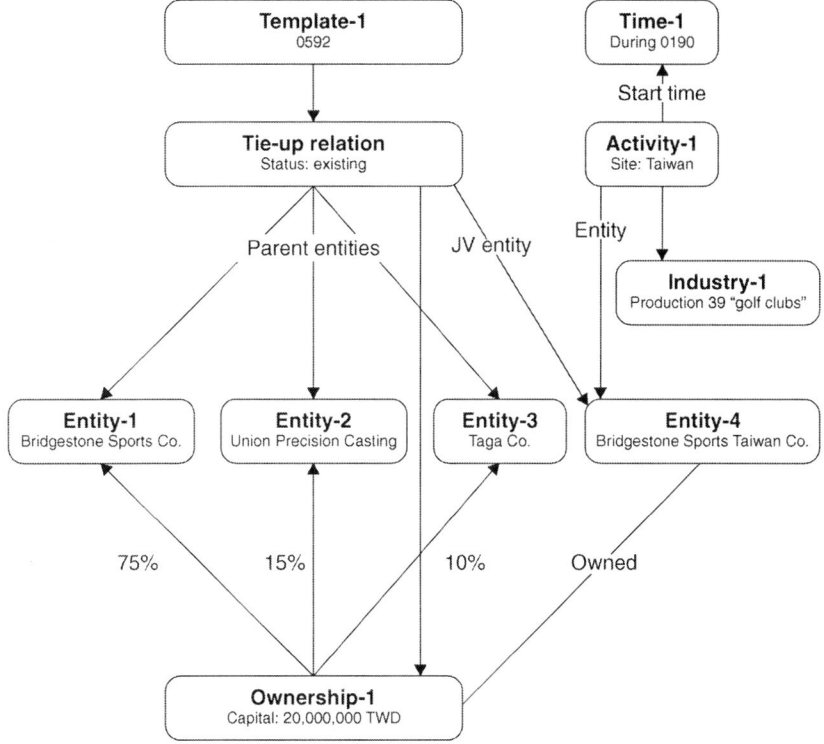

Figure 4.7: The MUC-5 joint venture template schema.

MUC-6 tasks

Differently from MUC-5, the MUC-6 competition [24] consisted of four different tasks:

Named-entity recognition: This task involved the recognition of entity names (for people and organisations), temporal expressions, place names and numeric values such as money and percentages. The task cannot be defined a proper IE task. However, it is usually a necessary step to produce a template or a summary of the original text.

Co-reference: This task involved the identification of co-reference relations. Different kind of links had to be identified. For example, pronouns like *it* had to be linked to their corresponding entity such as the name of a company.

Information extraction mini-MUC (template filling): This task involved the extraction of information about a specified class of events and the filling of a template for each instance of such an event. The IE task included the identification of people, organisations and artifacts. An example of MUC-6 organisation template can be found in Figures 4.6 (text) and 4.8 (schema).

Org-1-name: BRIDGESTONE SPORTS CO.
Org-1-alias: BRIDGESTONE SPORTS / BRIDGESTON SPORTS
Org-1-descriptor: SPORTS GOODS MAKER
Org-1-type: COMPANY
Org-1-nationality: JAPAN
Org-2-name: UNION PRECISION CASTING CO.
Org-2-alias: UNION PRECISION CASTING
Org-2-descriptor: A LOCAL CONCERN / CONCERN
Org-2-type: COMPANY
Org-2-locale: TAIWAN COUNTRY
Comment: uninformative descriptor
Org-3-name: TAGA CO.
Org-3-descriptor: TRADING HOUSE
Org-3-type: COMPANY
Org-3-nationality: JAPAN
Org-4-name: BRIDGESTONE SPORTS TAIWAN CO.
Org-4-type: COMPANY
Org-4-descriptor: A JOINT VENTURE
Org-4-locale: KAOHSIUNG CITY / KAOHSIUNG PROVINCE
Org-4-country: TAIWAN
Comment: A JOINT VENTURE is the most substantive descriptor
Art-descriptor: GOLF CLUBS
Comment: ART-TYPE not specifiable without rest of task

Figure 4.8: A MUC-6 organisation template.

Scenario templates: These templates had to be created following the guidelines contained in a scenario that was released only 1 month before the final evaluation of the systems. A sample training scenario was released together with the training data which, however, was substantially different from the final one. The late release of the scenario forced the systems to be more flexible and increase their portability towards new domains. Differently from the MUC-5 or the mini-MUC templates, the scenario templates included references to other templates. The final evaluation scenario template, called *management scenario*, regarding changes in the management of companies and is shown in Figure 4.9.

MUC-7 tasks
MUC-7 competition [25] had tasks very similar to MUC-6. Named-entities recognition was carried out in Chinese and Japanese in a side competition called MET-2 concurrently with English in MUC-7. The **template relations** task was added, consisting of marking relationships between template elements. It was limited to relationships with organisations (*employee of, product of, location of*); however, the task is expandable to all logical combinations and relations between entity types. An example of template relations from MUC-7 can be found in Figure 4.10.

The multi-lingual named-entity evaluation was run using training and test articles from comparable domains for all languages, with the domain for training being airline crashes and the domain for testing launch events. The domain change between the dry run and the formal run caused similar effects across languages.

```
<TEMPLATE>:= //
   DOC_NR:                    number
   CONTENT:                   <SUCCESSION_EVENT>

<SUCCESSION_EVENT>:=
   SUCCESSION_ORG:            <ORGANIZATION>
   POST:                      position title | no title
   IN_AND_OUT:                <IN_AND_OUT>
   VACANCY_REASON:            {Departure of workforce, Reassignment,
                              New position created, Other unknown}

<IN_AND_OUT>:=
   IO_PERSON:                 <PERSON>
   NEW_STATUS:                {In, In acting, Out, Out acting}
   ON_THE_JOB:                {Yes, No, Unclear}
   OTHER_ORG:                 <ORGANIZATION>
   REL_OTHER_ORG:             {Same org, Related org, Outside org}

<ORGANIZATION>:=
   ORG_NAME:                  name
   ORG_ALIAS:                 alias
   ORG_DESCRIPTOR:            descriptor
   ORG_TYPE:                  {Government, Company, Other}
   ORG_LOCALE:                locale string
   ORG_COUNTRY:               normalised country | normalised region

<PERSON>:=
   PER_NAME:                  name
   PER_ALIAS:                 alias
   PER_TITLE:                 title
```

Figure 4.9: The MUC-6 management scenario template.

```
Employee-of-9602040136-5:=
 Person: entity-9602040136-11
 Organisation: entity-9602040136-1
Entity-9602040136-11:=
 Ent-name: Dennis Gillespie
 Ent-type: PERSON
 ENT-descriptor: Capt./the commander of Carrier Air Wing 11
 ENT-Category: PER-MIL
Entity-9602040136-1:=
 Ent-name: NAVY
 ENT-type: ORGANISATION
 Ent-category: ORG-GOVT
```

Figure 4.10: A MUC-7 template relation.

4.4.1 Evaluation of the MUC results

The evaluation measures used in the MUC competition are very important, because they have been used for the evaluation of a relevant number of systems using a relevant amount of data.

The MUC-5 measures were based on several basic scoring categories. These data were computed matching the templates produced by the systems to hand-made templates by a scoring program and were:

Correct: If the key in the hand-made template matched exactly the response of the system.

Partial: If the key matched the response, although not exactly.

Incorrect: If no match was identified between the key and the response.

Missing: If the key had a fill and the response did not.

Spurious: If the response had a fill which was not present in the key.

The primary performance measure in MUC-5 was the **error per response fill** which was calculated as the number of wrong responses divided by the total and it was chosen because it gives an indication to the developers about the source of errors. Three secondary measures were used: **undergeneration, overgeneration** and **substitution**. These three measures represent different elements of the overall error and can be used to view particular aspects of the error. The primary measure and secondary measures were mainly designed to satisfy the developers' need. However, another different measure was used, mainly because of its independence from the system, the **richness normalised error**, which was designed for measuring errors related to the amount of information to be extracted from the texts [112]. This error was calculated by dividing the number of errors per word by the number of key fills per word. The error can be subdivided in minimum and maximum error.

MUC-5 used as unofficial secondary metrics, mainly to assure continuity with the precedent editions, the precision and recall measures, which were slightly different from the one normally used in information retrieval (see Section 4.1). Recall was defined as the percentage of possible correct answers, while precision was defined as the percentage of actual correct answers given [112]. The last measure used in MUC-5 was the F-measure that represents a way to combine the precision and recall measures into a unique value and was first introduced by van Rijsbergen [89]. The F-measure, as combination of precision and recall, gives a values that falls between them. The α positive parameter in the F-measure represents the relative importance given to recall over precision and in the case recall and precision are of equal weight, α assumes value 1.0. The F-measure presents a higher value if precision and recall are more at the centre of the recall–precision graph than if they are at the extremes of it. For example, if a system has precision and recall both of 50%, the F-measure will be higher than a system that has recall of 20% and precision of 80%. This is because the aim of the formula is to direct developers towards an improvement of both recall and precision. The measures explained above are shown in Figure 4.11.

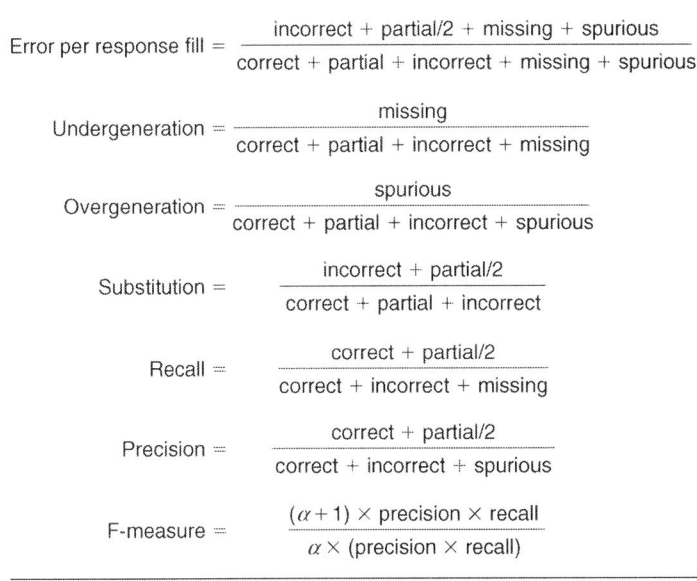

$$\text{Error per response fill} = \frac{\text{incorrect} + \text{partial/2} + \text{missing} + \text{spurious}}{\text{correct} + \text{partial} + \text{incorrect} + \text{missing} + \text{spurious}}$$

$$\text{Undergeneration} = \frac{\text{missing}}{\text{correct} + \text{partial} + \text{incorrect} + \text{missing}}$$

$$\text{Overgeneration} = \frac{\text{spurious}}{\text{correct} + \text{partial} + \text{incorrect} + \text{spurious}}$$

$$\text{Substitution} = \frac{\text{incorrect} + \text{partial/2}}{\text{correct} + \text{partial} + \text{incorrect}}$$

$$\text{Recall} = \frac{\text{correct} + \text{partial/2}}{\text{correct} + \text{incorrect} + \text{missing}}$$

$$\text{Precision} = \frac{\text{correct} + \text{partial/2}}{\text{correct} + \text{incorrect} + \text{spurious}}$$

$$\text{F-measure} = \frac{(\alpha + 1) \times \text{precision} \times \text{recall}}{\alpha \times (\text{precision} \times \text{recall})}$$

Figure 4.11: The MUC-5 evaluation measures.

Within the MUC-5 evaluation the performance of humans against machines were compared [113]. The result of the comparison is that machine performances are still far below the humans in terms of precision and recall. In fact, four human analysts were able to extract up to 79% of the information (recall) and, of all the information extracted, 82% was relevant (precision). The best three performing systems in MUC-5 were able to extract in average 53% of the relevant information and about 57% of the IE was relevant. On the other side, machines notably outperformed humans in terms of speed. In fact, while a human took an average of about 37 minutes to produce a complete template, the three best systems were able to produce the template in an average of 143 s.

The evaluation of the MUC-6 systems was based on the same measures as MUC-5. The scoring of the named-entity task was slightly different from the template-element (mini-MUC) and the similar (from a scoring point of view), scenario templates [114]. The evaluation indices were based on the results of a scoring program which was available to the participants for the training of the systems. Although the scorer, as the MUC-5 scorer, evaluated also partial fills, the assumption was that the template should have been filled with exact copies of the source text. In fact, the scoring of MUC-7 systems considered partial results as incorrect.

MUC-6 and MUC-7 competitions yield better results when compared with human annotators on the named-entity extraction task: the best MUC-6 system obtained 97% precision and 96% recall (human results were both 98%) while the best MUC-7 obtained 92 and 95% (98 and 95%). Unfortunately, on the scenario template the best human annotator obtained 97% precision and 98% recall, while no MUC-7 system managed to go further than 70% precision and 50% recall.

The MUC competitions provided a general evaluation framework for a relevant number of systems performing IE on a high number of source texts, and contributed to the improvement of the research in the field of IE. However, one main criticisms can be made. It is in fact questionable whether the MUC tasks are useful for the end-user of an IE system. Tasks such as the named-entity recognition or co-reference would probably not be directly useful for a potential user of an information extraction system, although they could be incorporated in more general systems. Callaghan [115] argues that there is some artificiality in the MUC tasks and suggests that the scoring should be weighted according to how useful the answers are.

4.5 The MUC systems

In this section, we describe briefly the main and most interesting systems that participated to the last two MUC competitions. Further details and other systems's descriptions is in Appendix A, while a very detailed description of LOLITA system is in Chapter 5.

MUC systems usually follow a very similar generic structure with a sequence of modules in cascade which progressively convert each part of text, usually a sentence, into a structured object, using knowledge taken from various dictionaries, hard-coded sentences prototypes, or, in some cases, statistical training. Most of these steps are performed through pattern-matching techniques.

Hobbs described the architecture of a generic MUC-5 IE system in order to better compare and analyse the systems that entered the competition. The structure of such generic system is composed of 10 modules performing different tasks, depicted in Figure 4.12, which handle sequentially the sentence obtaining their input from the preceding module's output. Given the large importance of the generic structure of MUC systems, the following description up to the end of this Section 4.5 is taken entirely from Hobbs' article [116].

Text zoner

This module parses the text into text segments. At a minimum it would separate the formatted from the unformatted regions. Some systems may go farther and segment the unformatted text into topic areas, either by looking for discourse particles like *meanwhile*, or by statistical means.

Pre-processor

This module takes the text as a character sequence, locates the sentence boundaries, and produces for each sentence a sequence of lexical items. The lexical items are generally the words together with the lexical attributes for them that are contained in the lexicon. This module minimally determines the possible parts of speech for each word, and may choose a single part of speech. It makes the lexical attributes in the

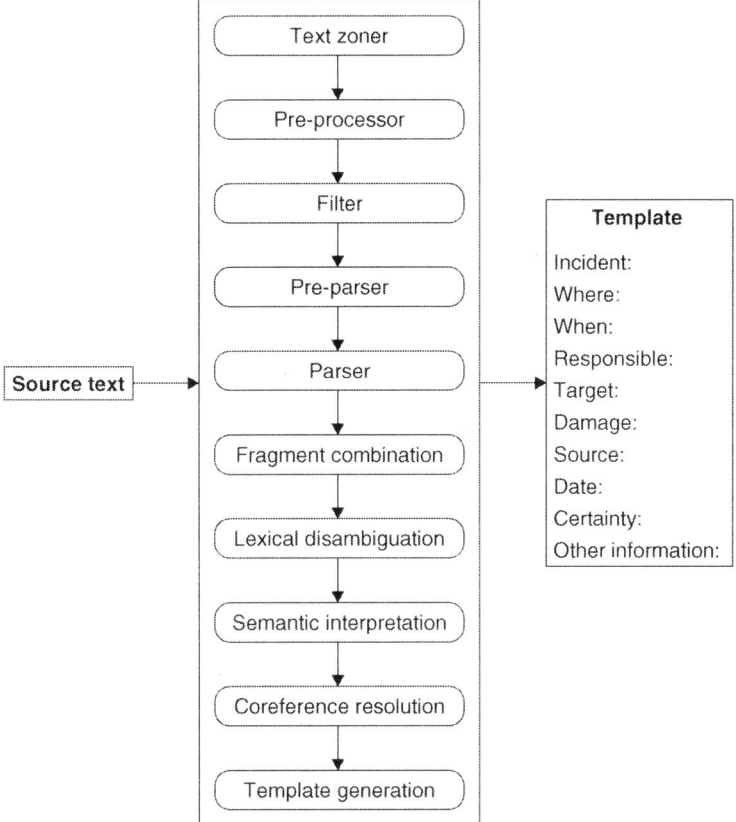

Figure 4.12: The generic information extraction system.

lexicon available to subsequent processing. It recognises multi-words. It recognises and normalises certain basic types that occur in the genre, such as dates, times, personal and company names, locations, currency amounts and so on. It handles unknown words, minimally by ignoring them, or more generally by trying to guess from their morphology or their immediate context as much information about them as possible. Spelling correction is done in this module as well.

The methods used here are lexical lookup, perhaps in conjunction with morphological analysis; perhaps statistical part-of-speech tagging; finite-state pattern-matching for recognising and normalising basic entities; standard spelling correction techniques; and a variety of heuristics for handling unknown words.

The lexicon might have been developed manually or borrowed from another site, but more and more they are adapted from already existing machine-readable dictionaries and augmented automatically by statistical techniques operating on the key templates and/or the corpus.

Filter

This module uses superficial techniques to filter out the sentences that are likely to be irrelevant, thus turning the text into a shorter text that can be processed faster. There are two principal methods used in this module. In any particular application, subsequent modules will be looking for patterns of words that signal relevant events. If a sentence has none of these words, then there is no reason to process it further. This module may scan the sentence looking for these keywords. The set of keywords may be developed manually, or more rarely if ever, generated automatically from the patterns.

Alternatively, a statistical profile may be generated automatically of the words or N-grams that characterise relevant sentences. The current sentence is evaluated by this measure and processed only if it exceeds some threshold.

Pre-parser

Certain small-scale structures are very common and can be recognised with high reliability. The Pre-parsing module recognises these structures, thereby simplifying the task of the Sentence Parser. Some systems recognise noun groups, that is, noun phrases up through the head noun, at this level, as well as verb groups, or verbs together with their auxiliaries. Appositives, words placed on the side in order to clarify or modify another (e.g. in the phrase "my father John", words "my father" are appositive to word "John"), can be attached to their head nouns with high reliability, as can genitives, *of* prepositional phrases, and perhaps some other prepositional phrases. *That* complements are often recognised here.

Parser

This module takes a sequence of lexical items and perhaps phrases and normally tries to produce a parse tree for the entire sentence. Systems that do full-sentence parsing usually represent their rules either as a phrase structure grammar augmented with constraints on the application of the rules, or as unification grammars in which the constraints are represented declaratively. The most frequent parsing algorithm is chart parsing. Sentence are parsed bottom-up, with top-down constraints being applied. As fragmentary parsing becomes more prevalent, the top-down constraints cannot be used as much. Similar structures that span the same string of words are merged in order to bring the processing down from exponential time to polynomial time.

Recently more and more systems are abandoning full-sentence parsing in IE applications. Some of these systems recognise only fragments because although they are using the standard methods for full-sentence parsing, their grammar has very limited coverage. In other systems the parser applies domain-dependent, finite-state pattern-matching techniques rather than more complex processing, trying only to locate within the sentence various patterns that are of interest in the application.

Grammars for the parsing module are either developed manually over a long period of time or borrowed from another site. There has been some work on the statistical inference of grammar rules in some areas of the grammar.

Fragment combination

For complex, real-world sentences of the sort that are found in newspapers, no parser in existence can find full parses for more than 75% or so of the sentences. Therefore, these systems need ways of combining the parse tree fragments that they obtain. This module may be applied to the parse tree fragments themselves. Alternatively, each fragment is translated into a logical form fragment, and this module tries to combine the logical form fragments. One method of combination is simply to take the logical form of the whole sentence to be the conjunction of the logical form fragments. A more informative technique is to attempt to fit some of the fragments into unfilled roles in other fragments.

The methods that have been employed so far for this operation are ad hoc. There is no real theory of it. The methods are developed manually.

Semantic interpretation

This module translates the parse tree or parse tree fragments into a semantic structure or logical form or event frame. All of these are basically explicit representations of predicate-argument and modification relations that are implicit in the sentence. Often lexical disambiguation takes place at this level as well. Some systems have two levels of logical form, one a general, task-independent logical form intended to encode all the information that is in the sentence, and the other a more specifically task-dependent representation that often omits any information that is not relevant to the application. A process of logical-form simplification translates from one to the other.

The method for semantic interpretation is function application or an equivalent process that matches predicates with their arguments. The rules are acquired manually.

There are a number of variations in how the processing is spread across the last four modules. It may be as I have outlined here. The system may group words into phrases, and then phrases into parsed sentences, and then translate the parsed sentences into a logical form. The more traditional approach is to skip the first of these steps and go directly from the words to the parsed sentences and then to logical forms. Recently, many systems do not attempt full-sentence parsing. They group words into phrases and translate the phrases into logical forms, and from then on it is all discourse processing. In a categorical grammar framework, one goes directly from words to logical forms.

Lexical disambiguation

This module, if it is such, translates a semantic structure with general or ambiguous predicates into a semantic structure with specific, unambiguous predicates. In fact, lexical disambiguation often occurs at other levels, and sometimes entirely so. For example, the ambiguity of *types* in "He types". and "The types ..." may be resolved during syntactic processing or during part-of-speech tagging. The ambiguity of "... rob a bank ..." or "... form a joint venture with a bank ..." may be resolved when a domain-dependent pattern is found. The fact that such a pattern occurs resolves the ambiguity.

More generally, lexical disambiguation generally happens by constraining the interpretation by the context in which the ambiguous word occurs, perhaps together with the a *priori* probabilities of each of the word senses.

These rules are in many cases developed manually, although this is the area where statistical methods have perhaps contributed the most to computational linguistics, especially in part-of-speech tagging.

Coreference resolution or discourse processing

This module turns a tree-like semantic structure, in which there may be separate nodes for a single entity, into a network-like structure in which these nodes are merged. This module resolves coreference for basic entities such as pronouns, definite noun phrases and *one* anaphora. It also resolves the reference for more complex entities like events. That is, an event that is partially described in the text may be identified with an event that was found previously; or it may be a consequence of a previously found event, as a death is of an attack; or it may fill a role in a previous event, as an activity in a joint venture.

Three principal criteria are used in determining whether two entities can be merged. First, semantic consistency, usually as specified by a sort hierarchy. Thus, "the Japanese automaker" can be merged with "Toyota Motor Corp.". For pronouns, semantic consistency consists of agreement on number and gender, and perhaps on whatever properties can be determined from the pronoun's context; for example in "its sales", *it* probably refers to a company.

Secondly, and more generally, there are various measures of compatibility between entities; for example, the merging of two events may be conditioned on the extent of overlap between their sets of known arguments, as well as on the compatibility of their types.

The third criterion is nearness, as determined by some metric. For example we may want to merge two events only if they occur within N sentences of each other (unless they are in *The Financial Times*). The metric of nearness may be something other than simply the number of words between the items in the text. For example in resolving pronouns, we are probably better off favouring the subject over the object in the previous sentence; this is simply measuring nearness along a different path.

The term *discourse processing* as used by MUC sites almost always means simply coreference resolution of application-relevant entities and events. There have been no serious attempts to recognise or use the structure of the text, beyond simple segmenting on the basis of superficial discourse particles for use in nearness metrics in coreference resolution.

Template generation

This module takes the semantic structures generated by the NLP modules and produces the templates in the official form required by the rules of the evaluation. Events that do not pass the threshold of interest defined in the rules are tossed out. Labels are printed, commas are removed from company names, percentages are rounded off, product-service codes are pulled out of a hat, and so on. And on and on.

4.5.1 New York University: Proteus

NYU system for MUC-6 can be found in Section A.6. In MUC-7 NYU presented a slightly changed system, with a core extraction engine called **Proteus** with its graphical interface **PET**.

In detail, as can be seen in Figure 4.13, the first module is the **lexical analysis** which, using online dictionaries and domain-specific words, assigns syntactic categories and tries to disambiguate, using also statistical techniques, when several meanings are possible (like "he types" and "the types").

The next three phases (in grey in Figure 4.13) are parsing programs that progressively try to match known part of sentences, starting from the smallest and easily identifiable token, such as proper names, temporal expressions, expressions for numeric entities and currencies, in the **name recognition**, going to detection of nouns and verbs in the **partial syntax** and up to high-level syntactic constructions in the **scenario patterns**, which is the domain-dependent part of the parsing action. The text is therefore split into these constructions called logical forms, which correspond to events, relationships and entities, and to each one is associated a corresponding class.

The **reference resolution** deals with all the coreferences and pronouns which are referred to other entities. The **discourse analysis** is in charge of solving the problem when the template information is spread among several logical forms, joining them together and handling temporal references. Finally, the **output generation** fills the output of the MUC structure.

The patterns used in Proteus are organised in a bottom-up way: at first the most general patterns are applied, and these are hard-coded in the program. Then very generic domain-specific patterns are used, which are taken from libraries called

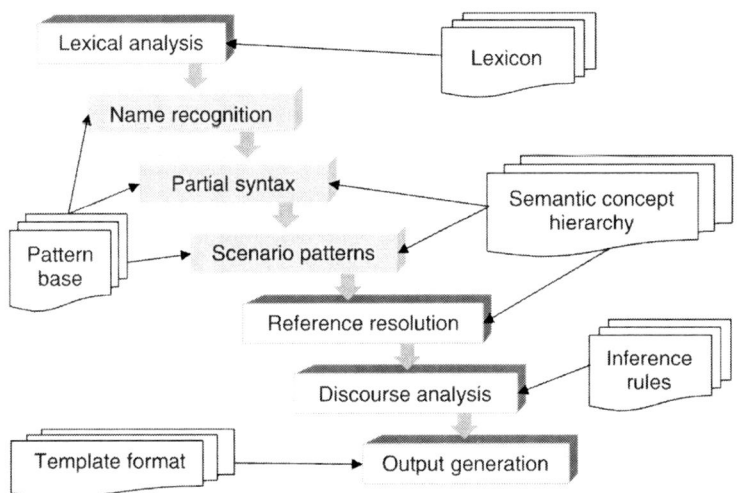

Figure 4.13: MUC-7 NYU Proteus system architecture (from Ref. [1]).

pattern base and finally through the graphical interface PET the system gets the most domain-specific directly from the user. The user is in charge therefore to input the domain patterns in a high-level format, such as *company verb company*, while PET tries to broaden them to other cases; then the user specifies how pattern elements are used to fill slots in the corresponding event template.

Proteus system is therefore customisable by non-expert users but only at high-level patterns and templates, while to update middle-level patterns or low-level on-line dictionaries program or database modifications must be made.

Pattern-matching techniques

Pattern builders are algorithms that are able to automatically build new pattern-matching rules, examining several relevant documents without any human tagging, to adapt IE systems to new domains. Traditional pattern builders are called **subject–verb–object** (SVO), since they try to detect typical sentences using grammar rules and a verb database. They unfortunately are not able to get some entities when the sentence construction is not the typical one. Especially,

Free word order is one of the most significant problems in analysing bad structured sentences or syntax-free languages (such as Japanese or Italian). To capture all the possible patterns given a verb and its arguments, a permutation of the arguments is needed, producing therefor an extremely large number of different patterns.

Relationship between a verb and a modifier of one of its arguments is another thing which is not captured by standard SVO patterns. This is the case when relevant entities appear not only as an argument of the verb that describes the event but also in other places within the sentence, such as in the MUC-3 terrorism scenario where word *bomb* appears in the same sentence without being the argument of the verb (i.e. "One person was killed as the result of a bomb explosion").

Clausal boundaries can prevent the system from detecting relations. For example in the sentence "A Palestinian suicide terrorist triggered a massive explosion in the heart of downtown Jerusalem today, killing himself and three other people" a SVO model would extract only *Palestinian suicide terrorist* as subject and *himself and three other people* as victim, missing the location, since it is a modifier of noun *heart*, and not being sure whether the subject and the victim are related to the same event, since they belong to two different sentences.

NYU system [117] overcomes these problems developing a **tree-based representation of patterns** (TBP). It starts from building a directed tree, called **dependency tree**, whose nodes are phrasal units and whose arcs represent the dependency between two phrasal units: A → B means that B depends on A (e.g. A is the subject and B is the verb). However, dependency relationships are not only those between a case-marked element and a verb, but also include those between a modifier and its head element, and this covers most of the relationships within sentences. Each TBP is defined as a path in the dependency tree passing through nodes within the tree. For matching with TBP, the target sentence is parsed into a dependency tree. Then all the verbs are detected and the sub-trees which have a verb node as a root are considered to find a match with a pattern.

The first step of the system is the **morphological analysis**, performed on the training data by **JUMAN** [118], and then a **named-entity tagging**, performed by a NE-system [119], which is based on a decision tree algorithm. Then the system retrieves the 300 documents that describe the events of the scenario of interest, called the **relevant document set**, using **CRL's stochastic-model-based information retrieval system** [120].

The system then calculates an affinity score of relevance to the scenario for each sentence in the relevant document set and retrieves the 300 most relevant sentences as the source of the patterns. The retrieved sentences will be the source for pattern extraction in the next section. The score is, when w is a noun, verb or named-entity:

$$\text{score}(w) = \text{tf}(w)\frac{\log{(N + 0.5)}}{\text{df}(w) \times \log{(N + 1)}},$$

and zero otherwise. N is the number of documents in the collection, $\text{tf}(w)$ the frequency of w in the relevant document set and $\text{df}(w)$ the document frequency of w in the collection. Then, the system calculates the score of each sentence s based on the score of its words, penalising unusually short or long sentences:

$$\text{score}(s) = \frac{\sum_{\forall w \in s} \text{score}(w)}{\text{length}(s) + |\text{length}(s) - av|},$$

where $\text{length}(s)$ is the number of words in s and av the average number of words over all the sentences.

Based on the dependency tree of the sentences, patterns are extracted from the relevant sentences. First, the retrieved sentence is parsed into a dependency tree, also finding the verbs in the tree. Then, the system takes all the verbs in the tree and uses them as the roots of their own sub-trees. Then each path from the root to a node is extracted, and these paths are collected and counted across all the relevant sentences. Finally, the system takes those paths with frequency higher than some threshold as extracted patterns. Figure 4.14 shows an example of extracted TBPs.

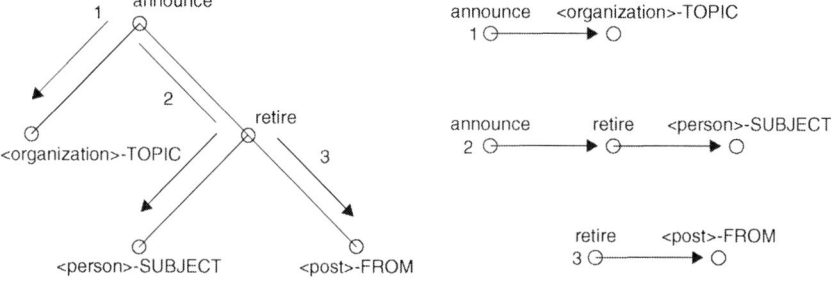

Figure 4.14: NYU system's example of dependency tree and tree-based patterns.

Experiments were performed without a complete IE system with an appropriate template generation module. Therefore simply the match of the patterns with sentences was tested. One false match was scored for every matched pattern that did not contain any named-entity and the number of missing named-entities was scored for every not matched pattern that did contain named-entities.

The system was tested on robbery arrest sentences and on 79 sentences from executive management succession sentences taken from MUC-6, events in which corporate managers left their positions or assumed new ones with the following data to extract: date, person, organisation and title. We concentrate our attention on the second testset, where results were confronted with a baseline performed by a standard SVO system. The highest recall for TBP was 0.34 while the baseline got 0.29 at the same precision level. In contrast, at the same level of recall, TBP got higher precision (0.75) than the baseline (0.70). Strangely, both TBP system and baseline got at lower recall (below 0.20) an unusual low precision between 0.50 and 0.60.

NYU built another extraction pattern model with improved TBPs. It starts from the consideration that the TBP model, also called **chain model**, has its own weakness in terms of accuracy due to the lack of context. For example, from the sentence *"A Palestinian suicide terrorist triggered a massive explosion in the heart of downtown Jerusalem today"* to extract the date entity the TBP model needs the pattern *triggered <date>*, but which also extracts a wrong date from *"The inflation rose by 1 point and triggered a marked reaction last week"*. The new model, called **sub-tree model** [121], is a generalisation of the previous model, such that any subtree of a dependency tree in the source sentence is regarded as an extraction pattern candidate. Its obvious advantage is the flexibility in creating suitable patterns, spanning multiple levels and multiple branches. Pattern coverage is further improved by relaxing the constraint that the root of the pattern tree be a verb node. However, this flexibility can also be a disadvantage, since often a very large number of pattern candidates must be considered. An efficient procedure is required to select the appropriate patterns from the candidates pool, using a ranking function for pattern candidates which assigns a larger score to patterns with a more relevant context.

The architecture of this system is very similar to the previous one, with the main difference being in the choice of patterns. The algorithm finds which sub-trees appear more frequently than a given threshold by constructing the sub-trees level by level, while keeping track of their occurrence in the corpus. Thus, it efficiently avoids the construction of duplicate patterns and runs with a computational complexity almost linear in the total size of the maximal tree patterns contained in the corpus. The following ranking function is used to rank each pattern candidate i:

$$\text{score}(i) = \text{tf}(i) \times \left(\log \frac{N}{\text{df}(i)} \right)^{\beta}$$

where N is the total number of documents in the collection, $\text{tf}(i)$ the number of times that sub-tree i appears in the documents of the relevant document set and $\text{df}(i)$ the number of documents in the collection containing sub-tree i. β is used to control the weight of the right factor of the scoring function, to focus on how specific a pattern is to a given scenario. For high β values a more specific pattern like *triggered explosion-OBJECT* <*date*> is ranked higher than *triggered* <*date*>. In testing this system an optimal value of 8 was chosen for β, however the system has also an automatic tuning algorithm for β. Then patterns with less than three occurrences or with more than eight nodes are filtered out, being respectively too rare or too complex to be useful.

Experiments on MUC-6 executive management succession sentences comparing this system with standard TBPs showed the same precision at recall levels below 0.35 and a precision from 0.01 to 0.10 larger for recall levels above 0.35.

4.5.2 University of Sheffield: LaSIE

Large Scale Information Extraction, LaSIE [122, 123], developed by University of Sheffield, was the only system to take part in all of the MUC-7 tasks. Its basic approach philosophy is pragmatic way between the shallow analysis, since IE tasks may not require full text understanding, and the deep analysis to avoid preclusion of the application of arbitrarily sophisticated linguistic analysis techniques where these may prove useful. The result is a mixture of techniques including finite-state recognition of domain-specific lexical patterns, partial parsing with a context-free grammar, simplified semantic representation of each sentence in the text and a formal representation of the whole discourse.

LaSIE is pipeline of nine modules each of which processes the entire text before the next is invoked, called via the graphical interface. A **tokeniser** and a **sentence splitter** identify token and sentence boundaries, the **pattern matcher** looks for domain specific full names and keywords, a **tagger** assigns part-of-speech tags to each token, then a **morphological analyser** and the **buchart parser** follow. The parser is one of the two key modules of the system, for which 17 sub-grammars were developed independently and grouped into two sets of 10 specialist named entity grammars and 7 general phrasal grammars. The first set is composed of 400 hand-coded rules that use part of speech tags, semantic tags added in the tokeniser stage and lexical items, while grammars for the second set were manually written adopting a high precision but low recall strategy to avoid false positives. If grammatical relations are missed, they can be added during discourse interpretation, where lexical-semantic information is available to the system.

After a **name pattern matching**, the **discourse interpreter** adds the best parse to a semantic net and resolves co-references. Inside the interpreter is stored all domain specific knowledge which is not retrieved by the parser. This knowledge is expressed using a semantic network (see Section 2.2.1) whose nodes represent concepts, with an associated structure of attribute and value with properties and relations of the concept, and whose arcs model a concept hierarchy and property inheritance. This semantic network is built starting from the template definition which defines the properties of the nodes. To each instance of the text and additional property, called consequence property, is added to trigger other hypothesis; for example the presence of the verb "to buy" triggers automatically the nodes of *company name* and *money value*. Excluding the insertion of some specific world knowledge, the semantic network is built entirely automatically using only the template definition. Semantic information is also added to the network, especially to deal with synonyms and even to extend the use of the system to other similar languages, which may be inserted as synonyms. One of the key features of the semantic network is inheritance: nodes inherits properties of their parents; for example the *company name* inherits from its parent *name* the property *number*=1.

The coreference resolution algorithm takes the set of instances and compares each one with the set of instances already in the semantic network, looking for coreferences first at intra-sentential level and then at inter-sentential level. Each pair of compatible instances a similarity score is calculated based on the distance between the instances' parent classes in the concept hierarchy and on the number of shared properties. The highest scoring pair is merged in the semantic network combining the properties of both instances. Finally, the **template writer** puts the result in a template format.

LaSIE systems evolved later into **GATE framework**, which is described in Section B.3.

4.5.3 BBN technologies: PLUM

PLUM are systems, developed by BBN Technologies for MUC-6, uses a completely different approach, relying on statistical techniques and off-line or interactive training from preprocessed corpora. This technique has two major advantages: it increases its performances while more and more corpora become available, without any extra development effort, and it is extremely flexible when used with other domains and tasks.

BBN's PLUM, **Probabilistic Language Understanding Model** system [2] was the second best system in MUC-6. The main original features that can be found in PLUM are statistical language modelling, learning algorithms and partial understanding. The first feature is the use of **statistical modelling** to guide processing. The authors underline that the use of statistical methodologies allows the achievement of good results in terms of portability, robustness and trainability. The second feature is the use of **learning algorithms**. These kinds of algorithms were used in PLUM to obtain the knowledge bases used by processing modules and to train the probabilistic models. The authors stress that the use of learning algorithms can improve the portability of the system towards other domains. The third feature is **partial understanding**: PLUM, as well as other systems, does not fully understand the meaning of the text but it is designed to take advantage of the information that is partly understood without failing when complete information is missing. Thus, full grammatical analysis and full semantic interpretation are not performed by the system.

PLUM's architecture is based on seven different modules: the message reader, the morphological analyser, the pattern matcher, the parser, the semantic interpreter, the discourse and the template generator, as shown in Figure 4.15. The first module, the **message reader**, reads the input given to the system (a file containing one or more messages) and determines the message boundaries, identifies the message

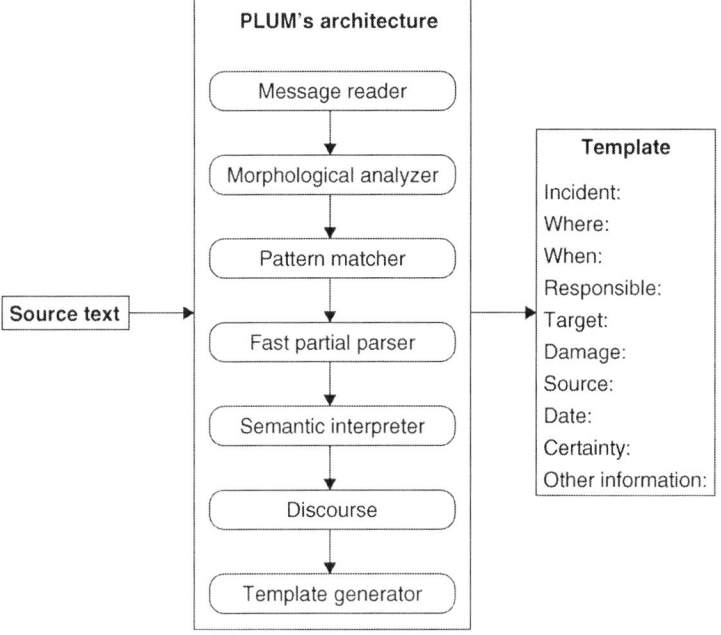

Figure 4.15: PLUM system architecture (from Ref. [2]).

header information and determines paragraph and sentence boundaries. The next step taken by BBN is **morphological analysis**: each word is classified and its parts-of-speech (e.g. proper noun, verb, adjective, etc.) identified. The assignment of part-of-speech to known words is done using a bi-gram probability model and frequency models, while probabilities based on word endings are used to assign part-of-speech to highly ambiguous or unknown words. The output of the morphological analyser is supplied as input to the next module: the **pattern matcher**. The task performed by this module is to apply patterns to the input to identify relevant groups of words such as company names, organisation names and person names. The fourth module is the **parser**. The parser produces one or more non-overlapping parse fragments. However, the parser will sometimes not be able to fully process a sentence and, therefore, will defer any decision regarding ambiguities. In case permanent ambiguities arise, the parser will leave the sentence starting to process a new one.

The output of the parser, a set of parse-fragments, is further processed by the **semantic interpreter** which consists of two sub-components: a **fragment interpreter** and a pattern-based sentence interpreter. The former applies semantic rules to each of the parse fragments produced by the parser. The semantic forms identified are entities, events, and states of affairs. Each of these forms can be classified into *known*, *unknown* or *referential*. Entities correspond to people, things, places and time intervals. The fragment interpreter is able to prevent the generation of errors, improving robustness. Moreover, the fragment interpreter is not often able to process all the parse fragments, however the system is designed to deal with partial understanding. The second sub-module of the semantic interpreter is the **sentence interpreter**. The task of this sub-module is to add extra long-distance relations between semantic entities in different fragments of the same sentence.

The sixth module is the **discourse processing**. The task performed by the module is to create a meaning for the whole message based on the meaning of the single sentences. However, the semantic information given as input may be insufficient to obtain a complete understanding. Thus, the discourse component must be able to infer long-distance relations that were not previously identified by the semantic interpreter and resolve any reference in the text. The output of the discourse processing module is a list of **discourse domain objects**. To create them, the discourse processing module fills the empty slots with the information supplied by the semantic interpreter and with those inferred. Moreover, the module tries to merge different discourse domain objects to check whether a new one is only an update of an old one. The output of the discourse processing is adjusted according to the required application-specific layout by the **template generator**. The generation of the output is based on specific requirements of the application, instead of on linguistic processing.

4.6 User-definable template interfaces

Most IE systems developed in the past have been designed and tested within government agencies and the scientific community and very few real applications have been commercially successful. The emphasis has been on the improvement of the performance of the systems in terms of precision and recall or other metrics. However, little progress has been done in making the systems user-friendly.

One of the main criticism that can be made to many of the presented IE systems is that the users can hardly configure the systems to produce other kinds of results (templates) which differ from those already available in the system. In other words, the templates are often hard-coded within the system and the user cannot modify the existing templates or add new ones without having to intervene directly on the system's code. If this can be acceptable for scientific competitions such as the MUC conferences, for real applications such as a financial IE system this problem is extremely relevant.

The lack of flexibility of IE systems has already been identified some years ago in the TIPSTER phase II project document [124], in which specific standard objects and classes for the development of standardised components within a customisable IE system were defined. The TIPSTER phase II document defines three different classes of objects for a customisable IE system.

ExtractionNeed: This class should contain the input definition of the user, consisting of a formal specification (e.g. the template and slot names) and a narrative description describing the slot fill rules (e.g. the MUC-5 slot fill rules). This should be then translated by the system obtaining the CustomisedExtraction-System.

CustomizedExtractionSystem: This class should contain the system-specific procedures for extracting the user-defined templates from the source texts. These procedures should be created employing specific operations available in CustomisedExtractionSystem.

TemplateObjectLibrary: This class should contain the system-specific rules for general concepts which might be used in the user's definitions of the templates such as person, company, etc.

The architecture proposed in the TIPSTER phase II document is particularly interesting, but has two main limitation:

- The document defines the class of objects ExtractionNeed, but does not exactly determine which kind of definitions should be entered by the user. The authors propose the MUC-5 slot fill-rules, but it is not clear how the ambiguities of such definitions would be resolved or how the user should refer to information already defined in other slots. Processing a simple MUC-6 fill rule such as *"The proper name of the organisation, including any corporate designators"* for the *ORG_NAME* slot would present several ambiguities, which require deep understanding of the source text.
- It is unclear how the system would be able to translate the input definitions into specific templates in the class CustomisedExtractionSystem. It is proposed that this class should contain the operation *Customise (ExtractionNeed): CustomisedExtractionSystem* which should be an interactive process with the user, but it is unclear how this could be implemented.
- It is unclear how the user could refer in the fill-rule definitions to the class TemplateObjectLibrary, which should contain objects commonly used.

However, the architecture proposed in the TIPSTER phase II project is a first step towards the development of customisable IE systems.

Tabula Rasa [125] is an early prototype for supporting the analyst's process in defining new templates. The user is assisted in the definition of new templates using a menu-based approach. The Hasten system which successfully participated in the MUC-6 competition [3], is an example of partially customisable IE system. The user-definable interface is based on example-patterns corresponding to relevant fragments of source texts which can be entered by the user and will be used for producing the templates. Although the interface presents the advantage of allowing the user's definition of the slots, few problems arise in the definition of a totally new template:

- The template definition is still coded in the system. The user is allowed to enter slot definitions for the templates already coded in the system, but the definition of new templates must be done by modifying the system's code.

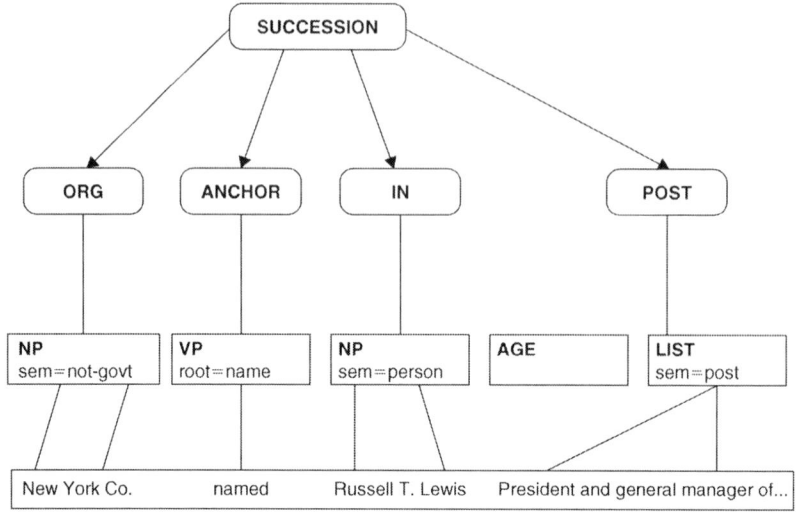

Figure 4.16: A Hasten e-graph (from Ref. [3]).

- The user is required to enter a considerable amount of example patterns for the definition of a specific slot. The problem is mainly caused by the fact that the system is based on finite-state analysis which intrinsically require a considerable amount of patterns. In Figure 4.16 an example of Hasten pattern (egraph) for the MUC-6 management succession template is shown. The pattern is however unable to capture any other configuration of the same event and, in fact, the total number of egraphs which have been used for the MUC-6 management succession template is 132 [3].

Differently from IE, in the field of information retrieval the issue of making the system as user-friendly as possible has already been tackled. For example the systems that participated in the TREC competitions were able to automatically construct a user query from paragraphs in natural language.

4.7 Conclusions

In this chapter, we introduced the field of information retrieval and IE and the most relevant techniques, approaches and systems. We particularly focused on the Message Understanding Conferences which provided a common evaluation framework for IE which allows to compare different systems performing the same tasks. Such evaluations have shown that the best MUC systems are based on finite-state analysis techniques or statistical and probabilistic techniques, with the latter increasing their performances as more corpora become available.

5   LOLITA and IE-expert systems

5.1 Introduction and scope

Large-scale, Object-based, Linguistic Interactor, Translator and Analyser
(LOLITA) system, has been under development since 1986 at the University of
Durham. Various kinds of applications have been built around the original system's
core and they include dialogue, query, translation, database front-end, IE, telephone
enquiry system, Chinese tutoring. LOLITA took part to the last two editions of the
MUC (MUC-6 and MUC-7) and was one of only six group world-wide to under-
take all of the MUC-6 tasks (named-entity, co-reference, template elements and
scenarios [26, 27]).

The system has been designed with a general-purpose core, trying to satisfy the
following principles:

- be easy to scale, working efficiently from few templates and data up to large
  databases;
- allow integration of its core into another system;
- allow extension to other domains;
- be real-time fast with present-day computers;
- be robust;
- be usable, in the sense that users should prefer it to manual news analysis.

These features are highly relevant for the implementation of a financial IE extraction
tool. The second feature means that different kind of applications can be built around
the original core which provides two main facilities: analysis, which converts text to
a logical representation of its meaning, and generation, which expresses information
represented in this logical form as text [26]. One of the advantages of using a
common general-purpose natural language core is that any improvements in the
core are reflected in the applications.

The main difference between LOLITA and the other NLP systems lies in the
semantic network, a knowledge repository for LOLITA, which is at the same
time used to improve performance of the information analysis and is updated with
incoming structured information.

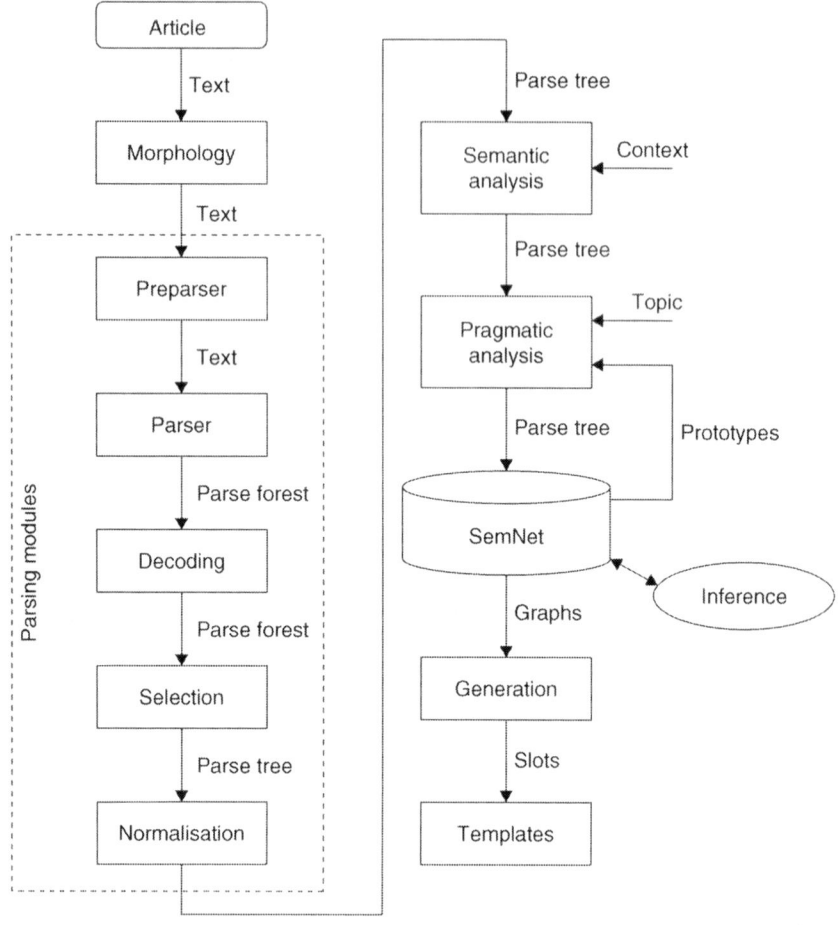

Figure 5.1: The LOLITA architecture.

5.2 Architecture of the system

A brief sketch of LOLITA's architecture with its important components is shown in Figure 5.1. The input is processed through a sequence of hierarchical modules and the analysis is stored in the **semantic network SemNet** which represents the knowledge base of the system. Natural language documents are morphologically, syntactically and then semantically analysed by LOLITA. **Semantic analysis** assigns a part of a graph to each construction. This is then passed to the **pragmatic analysis**, which before adding the new information to the network, checks whether it is consistent with the rest of the SemNet. LOLITA is built around SemNet, a dynamic semantic network which holds knowledge that can be accessed, modified or expanded using the information extracted from the input.

A fundamental point of LOLITA is that it moves away as soon as possible from the superficial linguistic structures and reaches deep structures independent of each specific natural language and close to more generic cognitive forms. The core of LOLITA has a pipeline structure. As the semantic network contains both lexical and semantic information, all its components are linked to it. A group of modules of the core are used to transform natural language text into semantic network and the **natural language generator** module that converts information represented in the semantic network back into text.

5.2.1 The semantic network SemNet

SemNet represents the core of the system, as it affects all other parts of the system and application and comprises around 150,000 nodes including WordNet (see Section 2.2.1). It is a definitional semantic network (see Section 2.2.1) where the relation "is a", here called arc, also has an attribute.

Inside this semantic network, knowledge is represented independently from the superficial linguistic structures such as grammar and lexical rules. Concepts are represented in the network by two types of nodes: **entity nodes** and **event nodes**. Simple relationships between concepts correspond to arcs in the SemNet. More complex relationships between concepts are implemented using event nodes, which have a frame-like structure. Each node has a set of **controls** or control variables and a set of **arcs**. The most important controls for IE applications are:

Rank gives quantification information: *universal* for general sets; *bounded existential* for instances of a concept where the instance depends on the particular instance of some other universal concept; *individual* for anonymous instances of a concept; *named individual* for named instances of a concept.

Type concepts are sorted into a type of lattice. The main values for this control are *entity, relation, event*.

Family control is used to classify nodes into the semantic and pragmatic group to which they belong. Examples of values for family are *living, human, inanimate, man-made*.

These mechanisms allow the network to contain an elaborate knowledge base (i.e. encyclopedic world knowledge, linguistic knowledge) which can be expanded by using most of the LOLITA applications which have been built so far and, in particular, the query application. In Figure 5.2 an example of a takeover event corresponding to the sentence "FIAT announced it acquired RENAULT with 10 billion dollars" is shown, while Figure 5.3 shows the representation of the two events corresponding to the fragment "10 billion dollars".

There are approximately 60 different arcs in LOLITA. The arcs *subject_, action_* and *object_* represent the basic roles of an event, as can be seen for example in Figure 5.2. Events can have other arcs, such as those indicating temporal

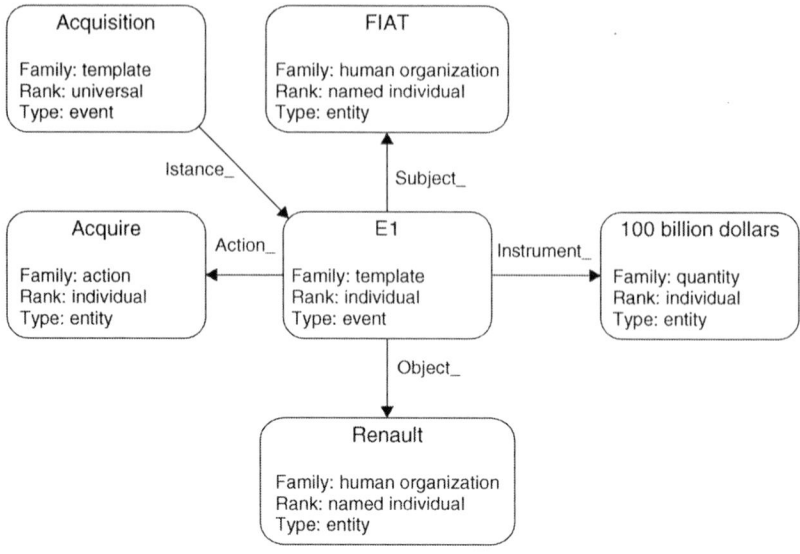

Figure 5.2: Representation of a typical financial event in the SemNet.

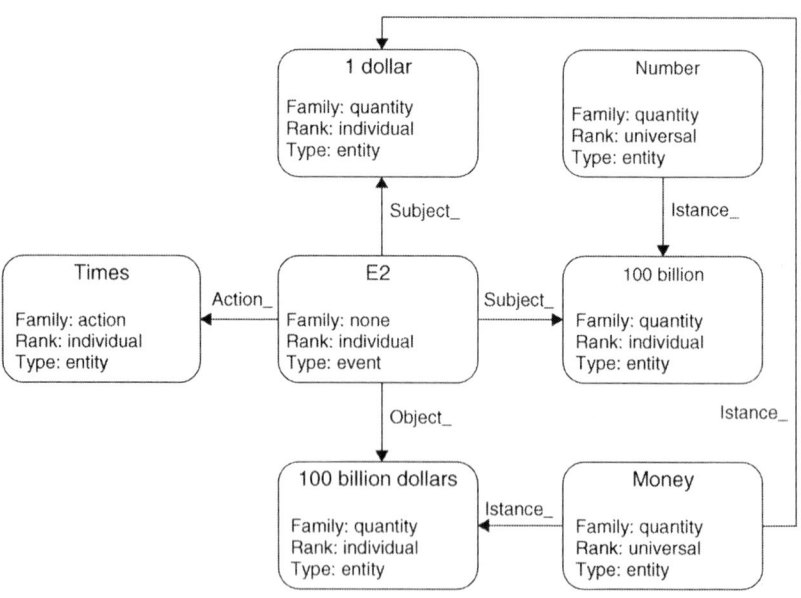

Figure 5.3: The SemNet representation for "100 billion dollars".

information, the status of the information (whether the information is certain or a hypothesis), or the indication of the source of the information. Many arcs also have their inverses, which allow the determination of the event starting from the subject. Concepts are connected with arcs such as *specialisation_* and its inverse, *generalisation_*, or *instance_* and its inverse *universal_*. Specialisation links a set to one possible subset, and through it hierarchies of concepts can be specified. The instance arc connects a concept to an instance of that concept, for example number to 100 billion such as in Figure 5.3. Other links between concepts include *synonym_* and *antonym_*.

Prototypical events

LOLITA also makes use of prototypical events, which define restrictions on events by providing template for them, for example, imposing the criterion that in an *ownership* event only human or organisations can take the subject role. For example, the *ownership* prototype which can be defined with the sentence *human owners own things*. This prototype restricts the subject of the verb to own to humans (which will belong to the set of humans who are also owners) and the object to non-humans. This information will be used by the pragmatic analysis to accept or reject new events and for the disambiguation of meanings. In a sentence such as "he owns a car", the pragmatic analysis will assume *he* as being human according to the *ownership* prototype.

In summary, SemNet holds several kinds of information:

- concept hierarchies, built with arcs such as *generalisation_*, which encode knowledge like "FIAT *is_a* company". They prevent duplication of information by allowing information to be inherited within the hierarchy;
- lexical information, which are words and their properties, stored directly in the network, as opposed to having a separate lexicon which is typical of many other systems. The lexical-level nodes are indexed via a simple dictionary, such as a mapping from root words to all the senses of that word. Lexical forms are distinct from concepts, to which they are linked by a *concept_* arc. Concepts are, in return, linked to lexical forms by a link which depends on the language of interest. For example, *company* has a link to *dog*, used for English, and a link to *cane*, used for Italian. In this way the structure of the semantic network may be used for several different languages at the same time;
- prototypical events, which define restrictions on events by providing templates for events, imposing selectional restrictions on the roles in an event;
- general events, which are other kinds of information. For example, the content of MUC articles would come in this class, when analysed.

5.2.2 Syntactic analysis

The syntactic analysis is the first step taken by the system for the processing of the input text and includes morphology, parsing and normalisation. At the end of this stage, the system has not performed any disambiguation or anaphora resolution.

Morphology

The first stage of the syntactic analysis is to build a surface representation of the input sentences. Words are separated according to the spaces in the input sentences and punctuation is used to separate the sentences into grammatical units. Contractions are expanded (e.g. *I'll* expanded to *I will*) as well as monetary and numeric expressions (e.g. *10 $ million* to *10 million dollars*). Specific idiomatic phrases are transformed (e.g. *in charge of*). Misspelt words are recovered where possible and unknown ones are guessed [126].

The morphological process extracts the roots of the input words which are linked to appropriate lexical and semantic nodes, which will be used during the rest of the analysis. A **feature system**, which assigns to every word its set of features, is used to preserve information such as number, case, word class and some semantic-based features. Words are finally labelled with all possible categories for that word.

Parsing

The task of the parser is to group the words of a sentence into a symbolic structure representing their grammatical relationships. The parser produces a forest of parse trees normalised and ordered according to penalties. There are four stages in parsing:

- the **pre-parser** which identifies and processes monetary expressions (e.g. *10 million dollars*), which is implemented using a low-ambiguity simple grammar and a parser which attempts to find the largest non-overlapping sequences which match the grammar. This grammar is a very basic grammar which is used to identify and convert into single units non-ambiguous phrases, matching only sentence parts which can only be interpreted in a specific way. Treating them with specific rules rather than allowing the LOLITA parser to fully process them, reduces the number of possibilities which are considered by the parser and the possibility that they are wrongly interpreted. For example, *100 million Canadian dollars* does not present any ambiguity and, therefore, it is possible to convert it using the simple grammar. This simple grammar includes all the possible currencies (dollars, euros, pounds), quantifications (thousands, millions), and places (Canadian, American, etc.) which can be recognised. It then uses these information to mark each word with the appropriate labels;
- the **parser** which is based on the **Tomita algorithm** [127] and uses a large and highly ambiguous grammar written in a context-free style. This algorithm takes advantage of the structure of natural language, which is not so strict as those of a programming language but neither so free as context-free languages. It is basically an extension of standard parsers typically used when parsing programming languages (which use left-recursive grammars), which is able to handle even grammatical structures typical of natural languages, with a reduced loss of efficiency. It is able to produce all possible parses out of an ambiguous sentence and to handle reference words, such as *that*, and unknown words. The result of the parser is a **parse forest**. It is a directed acyclic graph consisting of all possible

parses for the input sentence which, given the complexity of the grammar, can be extremely large;

- the **decoding of the parse forest**. The forest is selectively explored from the topmost node, using heuristics such as feature consistency and hand-assigned likelihoods of certain grammatical constructions. Feature errors and unlikely pieces of grammar involve a cost: the aim of the search is to extract the set of lowest-cost tree;
- the **selection of best parse tree**. The lowest-cost tree is ordered according to heuristics based on the tree form. Subsequent analysis (e.g. semantics) is performed on this parse tree;
- the **normalisation**. This stage applies several transformations to the parse tree with the goal of reducing the number of cases required in the semantic analysis. These transformations are performed preserving the meanings of the sentences. For example *Renault was bought by FIAT* to *FIAT bought Renault*.

5.2.3 Analysis of meaning

Once the input sentences have been transformed into an ordered parse tree forest, the best path must be interpreted and the semantic network updated with the new information by creating or updating SemNet nodes. Two modules are employed for analysing the meaning of the parse tree: semantic and pragmatic analysis.

Semantic analysis
The semantic analysis module maps the information available in the parse tree onto nodes in the semantic network. Existing nodes in the network are checked and eventually updated or linked to newly created ones. Each object or event in the parse tree must be mapped onto an appropriate existing or new node.

The first step taken by the semantic analysis is to make references absolute. For example, the reference *I* must be referred to the person, company etc. who is the source of the information, while *you* to LOLITA. Temporal references must be made absolute. For example, in the sentence "The takeover offer will expire on Monday", *Monday* must be referred to the date corresponding to the Monday after the date in which the sentence was processed. The step taken by the semantic analysis module is the disambiguation of the parse tree choosing among the possible interpretations. In the sentence "Renault rejected the price offered by FIAT because it was too low", the attribute *low* is attached to *price* rather than to *FIAT* because of the fact that *low* cannot be an attribute of a company (*human_organisation*) but it is legal for a price. The semantic analysis module makes use of the **context**, which consists of the latest sentences analysed.

Pragmatic analysis
The task of the pragmatic analysis module is to check whether the new semantic information (consisting of new and updated nodes) produced by the semantic analysis module is consistent with the one already available in the semantic network. The pragmatic analysis will therefore check and adjust the new information to

better fit into the existing network. Prototypical information are used at this stage. For example, the sentence "FIAT acquired Roberto" is rejected by the pragmatic analysis module because of the fact that the object of an acquisition cannot be a human (*Roberto*), as defined by the acquisition prototype (see Section 5.6.1), and will therefore be marked with a low level of belief. The level of belief is determined using **source controls** which implies looking at the source of the information, rather than at the information itself [128].

Another task of the pragmatic analysis is to disambiguate among possible meanings of objects. This is done using a set of heuristics which are firstly applied to disambiguate the action of the event. Once the action is known, they are applied to the other unknown nodes of the event. The pragmatic analysis module takes into consideration the current context together with the **topic** of the text (the latter is supplied to the system in advance) if available. For example, the meaning of the verb *to buy* in a financial article will normally be:

to buy: to acquire, to purchase

rather than, for example:

to buy: to accept, to believe, to trust, to gather

Using the prototypical information, the topic and heuristical rules, the pragmatic analysis module chooses the first meaning which is appropriate for the event.

5.2.4 Inference

The inference engine is used to infer information which is not directly available in the semantic network. Various kinds of inference are available within the LOLITA system such as **analogy** [129], **deduction** and **induction**.

One of the main tasks carried out by the inference engine is to retrieve specific information from the semantic network. The inference functions available in the LOLITA system are, in fact, able to answer questions by returning events from the semantic network which match the question. For example, the question *What does Roberto control?* returns the event *Roberto owns a motorbike*, since *control* is a generalisation of *own*.

The inference functions search in the semantic network for events with subject *Roberto*, action a specialisation of *control* and object a concept which shares the same properties as *thing*.

5.2.5 Generation

The LOLITA generator is used to rebuild surface language expressions from SemNet [84, 130]. The generator is widely used by most of LOLITA applications when an output in natural language is required, for example query, dialogue, translation and IE. The generator is able to produce natural language sentences from any fragment or concept of the semantic network according to various kinds of controls, such as rhythm, length and colour which will affect the way in which the final sentences are produced.

5.3 Information extraction

The LOLITA IE application is based on templates. The IE application provides an application programmer interface (API) which allows the programmer of the LOLITA system to define new templates within the IE framework.

Each template is organised as a structure of four main elements (Figure 5.4). The first element is the **template name** which identifies the specific template among the templates available in the system. The second element is the **template rule**, which defines under which condition the template must be filled by the system. The template rule is called the **main-event condition** because the template is built by the application if the condition is true. The condition can be built by checking the control variables of the new or updated nodes produced by the analysis of the source text and verify that they satisfy certain conditions. The main-event condition can also check generalisations or specialisations of nodes and, in general, follow any link of the node.

For example, the main-condition of the *incident* concept-based template (see Section 5.4.1) is built by checking if an event produced by the analysis of the source text has generalisation *incident_events* which includes *attack, explode, kill, intimidate, retaliate, wound, shoot* and *bomb*. When the main-event condition is true, the node corresponding to the successful event or entity is stored in the **TemNodes data structure**, which will include all the nodes for which the main-event condition is *true*.

The third element of the template is the **template post-condition**, which is used by the template application to decide whether to build or discard the

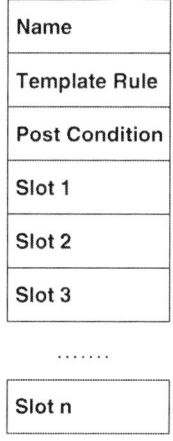

Figure 5.4: The structure of a LOLITA template.

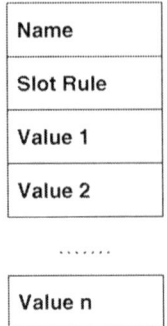

Figure 5.5: The structure of the template slots.

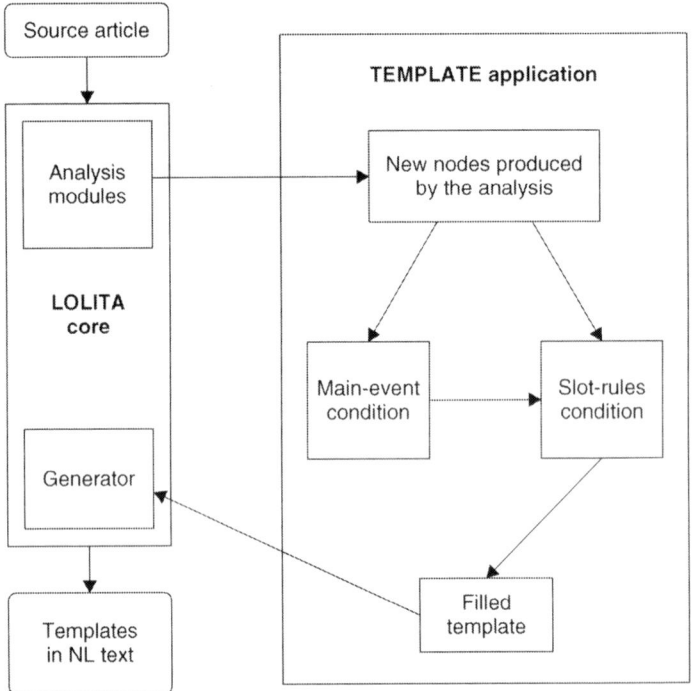

Figure 5.6: Information extraction within the LOLITA system.

template according to additional conditions and the information identified in the template.

The fourth element of the template structure are the **slots**, which are filled by the application once the template main-events have been identified. Each of the slots has a name, a rule for filling the slot with the appropriate information and a set of values which are used for filling the slot (Figure 5.5). In Figure 5.6 the way in which the template application fills a template is shown. Slot rules define a relationship that must hold. The relationship is represented in different ways depending on the type of slots involved.

5.3.1 Types of slots

Four kinds of slots can be used in a template depending on the kind of rule used: concept slot, string slot, text reference slot and template reference [131]. The slots differ in the way they are filled by the template application. The slot rule associated to each slot defines how the slot is filled by the application. Apart from the main event, the slot rule condition cannot generally be a *true/false* condition, but must produce a result in the appropriate form which will represent the final contents of the slot. Similar to the main-event condition, the slot rules can be built by checking the control variables, such as *rank, family*, etc. and the links of the nodes, such as generalisation, specialisation, etc. or using inference functions.

Concept slot
The concept slot represents the generic LOLITA template slot. The rule associated to the slot is used to identify the relevant concepts in the semantic network which are passed to the generator obtaining the corresponding English natural language text. This rule is extensively used in numerous LOLITA templates. For example, the rule for the *responsible* slot in the *incident* concept-based template (see Section 5.4.1) returns the subject of the main-event under the condition that it belongs to *family_human* and returns its *noderef.*

String slot
This slot is used to produce the output directly from a given list of strings and not by using the English generator. It is mainly useful to produce a slot with a predefined number of alternatives which may not be present in the original text. The rules associated to the slot will produce a boolean *true/false* value which will be used to choose among the various strings available.

Text reference slot
Text reference slots are used to produce output referring directly to fragments of the original text where possible and the generator if a semantic network's concept does not correspond to any fragments of the original text. The slot is used when the exact copy of the original text is needed and is used extensively in the MUC-6 templates [26]. The text reference mechanism, introduced in the system specifically for the MUC-6 competition, provides a way of referring back to the original text without using the generator. The generator, in fact, relies heavily on the core analysis, and although it performs well given a correct analysis, errors in the analysis of the source text can lead to intelligible output. Text reference slots, instead, are more robust in this sense, since their output consists of direct fragments of the original text. On the other side, the text reference mechanism does not allow information which is not

directly available in the original text to be represented, e.g. information produced by the inference system. In this case, the generator will provide the correct output.

The use of text reference slots in the MUC-6 templates was also due to the fact that the scorer required an exact copy of the source text and, therefore, the use of the generator would have reduced the number of correct fills.

Template reference slot

This slot is used to create a link to another template and, potentially, to other sources of information. The output of the slot consists of a pointer to the new template. The template reference slot provide the basic mechanism for handling hyper-templates in LOLITA which are widely used in the MUC-6 scenario templates (see Section 5.4.3). The MUC-6 scenario templates are actually an **acyclic graph**. The LOLITA hyper-templates mechanism allows the use of acyclic and cyclic templates similar to the links available in hypertext documents.

The template reference slot refers to another template by stating the destination template and the rule from which the reference depends. In addition, the definition of the slot can force the system to produce one or more than one child templates.

The LOLITA hyper-templates can be produced in HyperText Markup Language (HTML) format, which allows to follow the different templates using a standard web browser.

5.4 Templates available in the system

Three different kinds of templates can be built by the system depending on the kind of template main-event and the slots used.

5.4.1 Concept-based templates

Concept-based templates are structures where it is possible to identify a clear underlying top-level event to which all the information of the template's slots can be referred [82]. Any kind of condition can be used for the definition of the main-event.

For example, the takeover of a company by another company can be considered a suitable event for building a concept-based *takeover* template [132]. In fact, all the information regarding the takeover: amount, type of takeover, company target, company predator, etc. can be associated to the parent takeover event (see Figure 5.7).

More than one concept-based template can be identified in a source document, according to the number of relevant top-level events that are generated by the semantic analysis of the article.

Once the template main-event has been identified, each slot is filled by searching the semantic network for the relevant information according to the slot rules, starting the search from the main event.

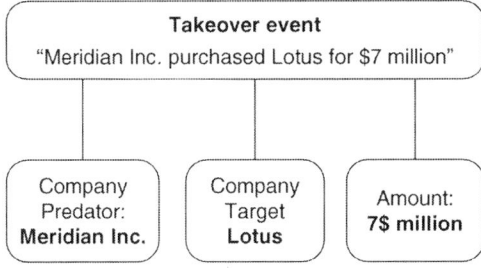

Figure 5.7: Slots in a concept-based template.

Incident template
The incident template has been the first template built in the LOLITA system and is composed of six slots as follows:

incident: the slot is filled with the main event of the template. All other slots are related to the contents of this slot;

where: the slot should contain the position or the location of the incident. Positions are defined as **coordinates in space** which do not necessarily have any concrete entity occupying that space, but are specified relatively to some of those entities. Locations are positions which are occupied by some concrete entity. A location is therefore a position, but not viceversa;

when: the slot should contain the date or time of the incident event.

responsible: the slot should be filled with the responsible of the incident. The responsible can either be the subject of the incident, in case the incident implies a human subject or the maker of the inanimate manmade that caused the incident;

target: the target of the incident is the object of the incident event. In case the object does not exist, the target is plausibly inferred from the position of the incident;

damage: the slot is filled with the objects that have been damaged because of the incident event which are identified in four different ways:

- the object of damage events with the original incident event as subject of the damage event;
- the location of the incident events that are subject of a damage event;
- the event itself in case it is a damage event.

5.4.2 Summary templates

Summary templates represent structures for which it is not possible to identify an underlying main-event. A summary template is basically a collection of objects stored in different slots which may not directly refer to the same concept or relate to each other (see Figure 5.8). For example, a summary template can be composed of personal names, organisations, locations, temporal, acronyms, monetary values, descriptions, animates, inanimates, etc.

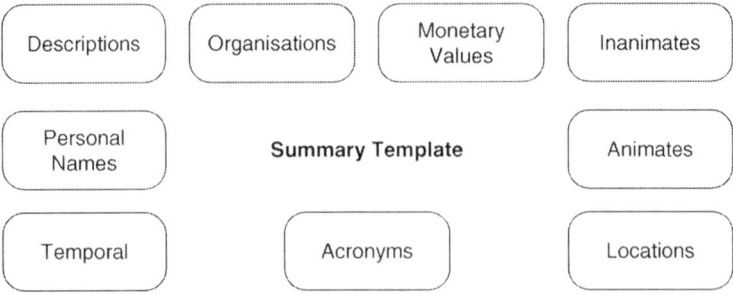

Figure 5.8: Slots of a summary template.

Summary templates are built differently from the concept-based templates. In fact, the main-event is *true* for all the new nodes generated by the semantic analysis of the source text. Consequently, the slot fill-in rules will be applied on all nodes, since the main-event is *true* for all nodes.

Although the information is stored in a template, summary templates are more similar to a named-entity task, than to a proper template. A summary template, in fact, is unable to provide any relation between the various information which have been extracted from the source text.

5.4.3 Hyper-templates

Hyper-templates are structures whose slots can refer to other templates. This mechanism is extensively used in the MUC-6 management scenario templates. The hyper-templates are implemented using template reference slots to point to the templates (see Section 5.3.1). The hyper-templates mechanism is potentially usable for linking different kinds of information to the template, not necessarily extracted from the source text, such as company databases or historical share prices.

5.4.4 The information to be extracted

As far as the type of input for the system is concerned, the target source documents that have been chosen for the LOLITA financial IE system are articles from financial newspapers and, in particular, from The Financial Times on CD-ROM. Articles from newspapers or magazines tend to include, as opposed to articles from on-line news services, analysis, interpretation and comments regarding the facts. Therefore, the financial operator has often to spend a considerable amount of time scanning through the articles trying to identify the most relevant information. In case he makes use of information retrieval packages, he needs only to identify the most relevant articles, but he still needs to identify the most relevant information within the selected articles. The IE system is instead able to select the relevant information in each of the relevant articles leading to a marked reduction of the time usually spent by the financial operator in reading and analysing the articles. Moreover, if we consider the number of articles on specific topics stored on a single CD-ROM (some thousands), the time of accessing to the relevant information by the operator is extremely high.

Articles from real-time on-line services tend instead to be rather summarised and, most of the times, a simple report of facts, excluding any sort of interpretation. Further processing of the news, although it is possible, is therefore often unnecessary. Information providers tend usually to categorise and classify the news articles and, therefore, further classification is often not needed. A financial IE system processing these kind of data would, in addition, need to extract information in real-time.

The LOLITA IE system has been designed with articles from newspapers in mind. However, the system is also able to process articles from on-line news services.

The definition of the templates of the LOLITA financial IE system has been carried out in close contact with experts of the financial sector. The potential target customers of the LOLITA financial application are any financial operator that needs to have access to qualitative information to support his decision-making process.

The design of the information to be extracted by the application started by identifying the qualitative information which is normally needed by the financial operators to support their decision-making process. Operators in the financial markets are normally interested in reading and analysing any news which is likely to influence the price of shares in the stock exchange, while they will normally skip any other news which is unlikely to influence such price. This observation has lead us to the definition of the concept of financial activity: a **financial activity** is an event which is likely to influence the price of shares and, therefore, influence the decision-making process of the players of the market regarding these securities [16].

The financial activities represent the information that the operators normally interested in reading and analyse and extract from a source article. A sentence such as: *"The European central bank has reduced the interest rate of 1 per cent"* can be considered a financial activity (interest rate movement), since the event is likely to influence people's behaviour and their investment decisions. The financial operator will therefore be extremely interested to know the relevant information about the event, such as the amount of the increase, when it has been decided, etc. since the event is likely to produce a marked positive impact on the quotations of shares in the stock exchange.

A relevant number of financial activities has been identified, with the help of financial experts and include: merger, takeover, flotation, new issue, privatisation, bankruptcy, etc. The activities chosen are those which are more likely to have a direct impact on the share price of the stock. However, since direct relations between the share-price and the various events cannot be directly measured, the choice of the activities was based mainly on the knowledge and experience of experts of the financial sector.

The LOLITA financial IE system is based on the **financial activities approach**, which consists in associating each of the financial activities with a corresponding template [16]. For example, the takeover financial activity is associated with the *takeover* template, which includes all the information which refers to the takeover in appropriate slots. The solution of having more than one template, one for each financial activity, provides a complete representation of the relevant contents of the source articles. If a particular article comprises two different financial activities (e.g. a takeover and a merger), two different templates are created for the same article (corresponding to each of the two financial activities).

5.4.5 Financial templates

Following the usability criteria of the natural language extraction approach, the user can finally define his own templates using the specific user-definable template interface provided by the system (see Section 5.5). In this way, the user can define specific templates which do not necessarily follow the financial activities approach but are needed for specific reasons.

The following financial activities have been identified: *takeover, merger, flotation, new issue (of shares), privatisation, bankruptcy, new stake, dividend announcement, overseas listing.*

Once the financial activities which can influence the financial operator's behaviour have been defined, a specific template has been associated to each of the activities. The templates have been designed identifying the **objects** which are relevant for each activity (e.g. a takeover). These objects correspond to **slots** of the templates. The objects identified for the templates represent the information needed by the financial operator to gain complete knowledge regarding the specific event. The financial operator should be able to take an appropriate investment decision based on the contents of the template without having to refer to any additional information related to the specific event. The identification of the relevant objects for each financial activity has been carried out in close contact with the experts of the financial sector.

The financial templates have been defined as follows:

- *takeover* **template:**
  the template has to be instantiated when a company is, will be or is expected to be acquired by another company, an institution or an operator.

```
company target:    the name of the company target company
predator:          the name of the person or company
                   performing the takeover
type of            {FRIENDLY, HOSTILE}
takeover:
value:             Total value of the takeover
bank adviser       the name of the bank advising the predator
predator:
bank adviser       the name of the bank advising the target
target:
```

```
expiry date:        the date in which the offer expires
attribution:        the name of the company or person source of
                    the news
current stake       the amount or value of shares already
predator:           owned by the predator in the company target
                    at the time of the takeover.
denial:             the name of the person or company who
                    denies any of the information in the
                    template.
```

- **merger template:**
  the template has to be instantiated when a company is, will be or is expected to be merged with another company.

```
company 1:          the name of the first company involved
company 2:          the name of the second company involved
new name:           the name of the new company
date of             the date in which the merger is announced
announce:
date of             the date in which the merger takes place
merger:
comments:           comments of the company's chairman or
                    directors
attribution:        the name of the company or person source
                    of the news source of the news
denial:             the name of the person or company who
                    denies any of the information in the
                    template
```

- **floatation template:**
  the template has to be instantiated whenever a company is, will be or is expected to be floated on the market.

```
company name:       the name of the company floated
price:              the price of the shares offered
value:              the nominal value of the shares offered
announce date:      the date in which the flotation is
                    announced
listing date:       the date in which the flotation takes
                    place
financial           the bank advising the flotation or the
adviser flot.:      company which is floated
attribution:        the name of the company or person source
                    of the news source of the news
denial:             the name of the person or company who
                    denies any of the information in the
                    template
industry sector:    the stock market industry sector in which
                    the company will be listed
```

- *new issue* **template:**
  the template has to be instantiated whenever a company has, will be or is expected
  to issue new shares on the market.

  ```
  company:              the name of the company issuing new shares
  comp. financial       the bank advising the new issue
  advisor:
  issue currency:       the currency in which the bonds are issued
  issue value:          the price of the bonds offered
  announce date:        the date of the announce
  launch date:          the date when the issue will take place
  listed:               the name of the stock exchange where the
                        shares
                        will be listed
  attribution:          the name of the company or person source
                        of the news source of the news
  purpose:              the purpose of the new issue of the
                        company
  denial:               the name of the person or company who
                        denies any of the information in the
                        template
  ```

- *privatisation* **template:**
  the template has to be instantiated whenever a company is, will be or is expected
  to be privatised.

  ```
  company name:         the name of the company privatised
  stake to be           the percentage of the total shares to be
  privatised:           privatised
  price of the          the price of the shares offered on the
  shares:               market
  value of the          the nominal value of the shares offered
  shares:
  announce date:        the date of the announce
  privatisation         the date in which the privatisation
  date:                 takes place
  bank adviser          the bank advising the privatisation or
  company:              the company privatised
  attribution:          the name of the company or person source
                        of the news
  denial:               the name of the person or company who
                        denies any of the information in the
                        template
  industry sector:      the sector of the stock exchange in
                        which the company will be listed
  ```

- *bankruptcy* **template:**
  the template has to be instantiated whenever a company is, will be or is expected
  to be declare bankrupt.

  ```
  company name:         the name of the company declared bankrupt
  ```

```
receivers:          the name of the receivers of the company
date of             the date of announce of the bankruptcy
announce:
denial:             the name of the person or company who
                    denies any of the information in the
                    template
```

- *new stake* **template:**
  the template has to be instantiated whenever a company or a person has, will or
  is expected to acquire a new stake in another company or an institution.

```
company target:     the name of the target company or
                    institution
company taking      the name of the person or the company
the stake:          acquiring the stake
Value:              the amount of the stake to be bought
attribution:        the name of the company or person
                    source of the news
denial:             the name of the person or company who
                    denies any of the information in the
                    template
```

- *dividend announcement* **template:**
  the template has to be instantiated whenever a company has, will or is expected
  to announce dividends.

```
company name:       the name of the company announcing the
                    dividends.
dividend per        the value of the dividend per share of
share:              the company
type of dividend:   Type of dividend to be distributed
```

- *overseas listing* **template:**
  the template has to be instantiated whenever a company is, will or is expected to
  be listed in a foreign Stock Exchange.

```
company name:
COMPANY_NAME
overseas            the name of the overseas Stock Exchange
exchange:
type of             the type of securities of the company
securities:         that will be listed at the Stock Exchange
announce date:      the date of the announce
date of listing:    the date when the listing takes place
attribution:        the name of the company or person source
                    of the news
denial:             the name of the person or company who
                    denies any of the information in the
                    template
```

5.5 Implementation of the financial templates

After defining the kind of output that the financial information system has to produce, the second important step is the definition of the rules that the system will use to fill the template's slots. The first main step is identifying the rule for the main-event. Since the financial templates are classifiable as concept-based templates (see Section 5.4.1), the identification of the correct main-event is of crucial importance. If, for example, we are trying to fill a *takeover* template (see Section 5.4.5), first of all, we need to define **when** and **under which conditions** the template has to be created. The system will then scan through all the new nodes created by the semantic analysis of the financial article, looking for specific events/nodes satisfying the main-event condition.

The identification of the appropriate rule is a difficult and complex process since, if it is done improperly, it leads to large losses of recall and precision. Therefore, the identification must be done on a significant quantity of relevant and non-relevant articles.

The identification of the appropriate rule for the main-event and, in general, for all the slots, has to be carried out designing the relevant **semantic structures** able to identify the relevant information in the source text. These semantic-structures differ from one another for the different **meaning**, rather than for differences in the structure or form of the sentence. The LOLITA semantic structures are therefore rather different from the **patterns** of IE systems based on finite-state techniques. For example, the following two sentences share the same semantic structure, although the form of the sentences is different:

```
FIAT acquired Renault.
```

and:

```
the acquisition of Renault by FIAT.
```

The semantic structure of the two sentences is:

```
action:  acquire
object:  RENAULT
subject: FIAT
```

The above notation is used in this chapter to represent semantic structures.

Once the semantic structures have been identified, it is important to verify whether they are correctly recognised by the general-purpose LOLITA semantic, pragmatics and inference rules and categorised according to the user's need or they need to be supported by domain-specific knowledge to be added to the system. Some of the rules, in fact, might present semantic output which differs from what we would expect in the analysis of a generic text. For example, the system would normally be unable to infer that the sentence *"FIAT took full control of Renault"* corresponds to a company takeover. Therefore, the domain-specific knowledge has to be added to the system. The rule therefore looks for any of the semantic structures identified and, in case of the main-event, it returns *true* and produces the template or, in case of slot rules, fills the slot with the appropriate information retrieved from the semantic network.

5.5.1 Prototypes

Prototypical information (see Section 5.2.1) is used within the LOLITA system to restrict the kind of entities that can be used within a particular event according to the appropriate action. Prototypical information is particularly useful in filling concept-based templates. This is because it ensures that the events produced from the analysis of the source text include the correct kind of entities.

5.5.2 Domain-specific knowledge

The performance of the IE system can be improved with the addition of domain-specific knowledge which may differ from the LOLITA system world knowledge. The domain-specific knowledge is used to capture specific meaning of the source text for the particular domain, for example the financial domain.

This knowledge can be placed at two different levels in the system. A first choice is to store the specific knowledge directly in the semantic network of the LOLITA system using existing facilities. The LOLITA core system would use the knowledge during the analysis of the source text. The introduction of this knowledge in the semantic network, however, can be difficult and can cause logical problems within the network. This leads to the second possibility, which is to incorporate the domain-specific knowledge directly in the IE system, rather than in the core system.

The domain-specific knowledge for the LOLITA IE system is stored directly within the application, rather than stored in the semantic network. The knowledge consists of **semantic rules** which are used to capture specific events and objects from the analysis of the source articles performed by the core system. The domain-specific knowledge of the financial application consists of semantic rules which are used to locate specific events and objects from the analysis of the source article which are relevant for the financial domain.

5.5.3 Unification

One of the most relevant issues for the success of the financial templates is the correct unification of events referring to the same concept by the LOLITA core system. This applies to the main-event and any other slot. The concept of unification is that if two events are referring to the same semantic concept, but they are reported in two different places in the same text, the LOLITA core should unify them and create a unique event, as composition of the relevant information extracted from both source events. For example, the two following sentences should be unified by the LOLITA system:

Airtours, the UK's second largest holiday tour operator after Thompson, has acquired one of the UK's leading long-haul brand names.
Tradewinds has been acquired from International Travel Connections, a privately-owned company based in Chester, for Pounds 450,000 cash.

The system should unify the two events creating one single event, as composition of the relevant pieces of information of the two sentences. A correct unified event for the two sentences should be, ideally:

Airtours, the UK's second largest holiday tour operator after Thompson, has acquired Tradewinds, one of the UK's leading long-haul brand names, for Pounds 450,000 cash.

The unification would allow the financial template application to retrieve all relevant information attached to the acquisition event, otherwise impossible to identify.

The unification is extremely important for the main-event of the template as well as any other slots (i.e. takeover value, company target, etc.). The system should also be able to identify that two different nodes refer to the same object. In the two sentences shown above, the system should be able to identify that *the leading long-haul brand names* and *Tradewinds* refer to the same object and, therefore, should share the same node.

Unification is carried out at different stages of the processing of the source text by the LOLITA core system. A first identification of possible events to be unified is carried out during the semantic analysis (Section 5.2.3) before the new knowledge is stored in the semantic network. A later stage of the analysis examines the recently built pieces of the network and attempts to unify information which meet specific criteria.

5.6 The takeover financial template

This section describes the rules that have been chosen for the *takeover* template. The analysis has been carried out on a total of 80 relevant takeover articles, identifying all the possible different semantic structures associated to the source text. The semantic structures for both the main-event and each of the slot rules have been coded directly into the financial application and they locate relevant information within the new nodes produced by the analysis of the source text.

5.6.1 The takeover main-event

The identification of the semantic structures for the main-event of the *takeover* template has been carried out analysing a total of 80 relevant takeover articles. Four different relevant semantic structures have been found for the main-event of the takeover template with different statistical relevance. Some of the semantic structures correspond to domain-specific knowledge.

Semantic structure 1

```
Event 1:
 action:  acquire | purchase | buy | take-over
 subject: company | person
 object:  company
```

This semantic structure covers situations in which the information that makes it possible to recognise a takeover is carried by the action of the sentence, thus, the verb. This semantic structure captures different kind of sentences in the financial source texts. The following sentences from The Financial Times belong to this semantic structure:

Shield Group, the holding company that owns Stickley Kent, the auctioneer and property insolvency specialist, has acquired Kamco Computer Systems.

BF Goodrich, the Ohio-based specialty chemical and aerospace company, is to acquire Rosemount Aerospace from the Emerson Electric Company for 300 million dollars in cash, pending regulatory approval.

Westcoast is set to become Canada's biggest gas utility with its proposed acquisition of Union Energy.

Archer Holdings yesterday announced that it would continue its expansion by acquiring Kellet Holdings.

Cementos Mexicanos is expected to launch a 1.7 billion dollars takeover for Spain's biggest producer, Valenciana de Cementos.

Bank of Scotland is poised to complete its takeover of the Countrywide Banking Corporation.

Alexandra Towing has conditionally agreed to a 52 million dollars takeover by Howard Smith.

The takeover of the east German oil company Minol by a consortium including the German steelmaker Thyssen and the French oil company ELF-Aquitaine has been approved.

Semantic structure 2

```
Event 1:
  action:  acquire | purchase | buy | take-over
  subject: company | person
  object:  majority stake
Event 2:
  action:  is_part_of
  subject: majority stake
  object:  company
```

This structure covers cases in which there is no mention of an acquisition or a takeover. However, it is possible to infer a takeover or acquisition from the fact that acquiring a majority stake in a company implies a takeover. This structure is an example of domain-specific knowledge stored at the application level. Example sentences from articles from The Financial Times which belong to this semantic structure are:

Brau und Brunner, the German brewery, is paying 2.112 million euros (2.42 million dollars) for a majority stake in Kamenitzka.

Arjo Wiggins Appleton, the Franco-British paper group, has taken a majority stake in Nitech, a Polish paper merchant.

Semantic structure 3

```
Event 1:
  action:  acquire | purchase | buy | take | take-over
  subject: company | person
  object:  control
Event 2:
  action:  relate_
  subject: control
  object:  company
```

This semantic structures covers cases in which there is no mention of an acquisition or takeover which can however be inferred from the fact that taking control of a company implies a takeover domain-specific knowledge. The following sentences, from The Financial times, belong to this semantic structure:

Unilever, the Anglo-Dutch food and consumer products group, is set to become France's largest ice cream producer by taking control of Ortiz-Miko.

Galeries Lafayette, one of France's leading stores groups, is taking control of Monoprix, the retail chain.

Semantic structure 4

```
Event 1:
  action:  pay
  subject: company | person
  object:  monetary value
  goal:    company
```

This semantic structure is another example of domain-specific knowledge. In fact, there is no mention of an acquisition or a takeover in the rule. However, it is possible to infer a possible takeover from the fact that a company paid an amount of money for the other company. The following sentences, from The Financial Times, belong to this semantic structure:

Conrad, the Manchester-based sports, leisure and consultancy group, has agreed to pay 1 million pounds in cash and shares for Inter Research.
Calderburn, the office furniture group, has paid an initial 6.25 million pounds for SBFI.

The 80 articles in the sample population have been divided and classified according to the semantic structure they belong to and the statistical frequency distribution of the semantic structures are:

- semantic structure 1: 75%
- semantic structure 2: 3%
- semantic structure 3: 3%
- semantic structure 4: 19%.

As the percentages suggest, the semantic structures 1 and 4 are the most relevant, while the semantic structures 2 and 3 are less frequent.

Prototypes for the takeover main-event
The *acquisition* prototype has been added to the LOLITA system for correctly processing acquisition and takeover events. The concept of acquisition, in fact, is the generalisation of takeover.
The prototype defines an acquisition as following:

Some humans acquire things

Any event in which the above occurs is recognised an acquisition event. The action chosen for the prototype is *to acquire* which is synonym of *purchase, take over* and *buy*. The subject of the acquisition is a set of humans who perform an acquisition. This also includes human-organisations and, therefore, companies, which are stored below the concept of human in the semantic network. The node *some* has been introduced to avoid saying that *all humans acquire things* which would be represented in case the restriction was not included. The object of the acquisition can be anything. The rules of the takeover template, however, restrict the object of the acquisition only to companies.

Domain-specific knowledge for the takeover main-event
Various domain-specific rules have been identified for the takeover main-event:

X buys a majority stake in Y, this implies a takeover. This rule is similar to the previous one. Basically, LOLITA would not normally assume that buying a majority stake in a company (although it knows the meaning of stake) means a takeover. It would only assume that X owns a stake of Y, but nothing else. This rule, instead, implies that a takeover is in place and it is actually equivalent to buying a majority stake. This rule corresponds to the semantic structure number 2.

X takes control of Y, this implies a takeover. This rules covers the situation in which a company takes full control of another company, without mentioning if this is a takeover. Normally, the system would not classify it as being a takeover, since the concepts of *take control* and *takeover* are not connected. However, in the specific financial context, taking control of a company, usually means taking it over or buying a majority stake, which is equivalent. This rule corresponds to the semantic structure number 3.

X pays M for Y and Y is a company, this implies the takeover of Y by X. This case covers cases in which, for example, "IBM pays 10 million dollars for Lotus Inc.". LOLITA would not normally understand that IBM bought LOTUS nor that this is a takeover. With this rule, the sentence (and all other sentences with same meaning) is understood to be an acquisition (takeover) by the financial application. This rule corresponds to the semantic structure number 4.

Rule for the takeover main-event

Once the different semantic structures have been identified, the corresponding rules for the takeover main-event can be written. These rules will locate the relevant information within the new knowledge produced by the semantic analysis of the source text.

The *takeover* template post-condition

The additional rule that must be satisfied for the template to be created (template post-condition) is that at least one of the two companies (or person for the company predator) involved in the takeover must be correctly recognized by the system. If no companies are recognized, the possible takeover main-event candidate is discarded by the template code.

5.6.2 The *takeover* template slots

This section describes the rules for the various slots associated with the *takeover* template. The identification of the relevant rules has been done in the same way as the main-event. The semantic structures for each slots have been identified from the same 80 relevant articles. The rules have been defined taking into account any relevant prototypical information and domain-specific knowledge.

Company predator

The company predator slot should be filled with the name of the company or the person which performs the takeover. The rule for the company predator slot is therefore rather straightforward. The slot is filled with the subject of the acquisition event, provided that it is either a company or a person. This rule should catch all possible semantic structures, which are the same identified for the main-event,

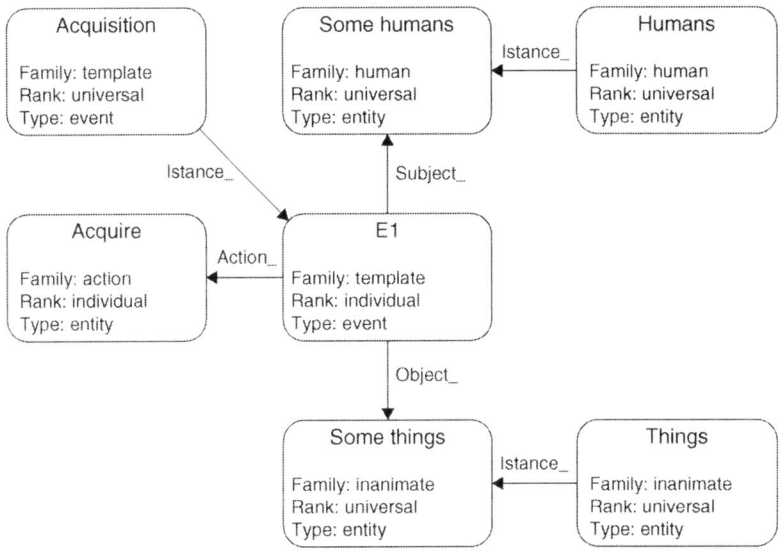

Figure 5.9: The acquisition prototype.

since the *acquisition* prototype should ensure that the appropriate acquisition event is correctly built for all semantic structures (see Figure 5.9).

Company target

The company target slot should be filled with the name of the company acquired by the company predator. The company target slot is filled in a similar way as the company predator. The company target is the object of the acquisition event (Figure 5.9) under the condition that it must necessarily be a company, since we only consider company takeovers. Therefore others kinds of takeovers are not considered. In the following sentence (from The Financial Times on CD-ROM) the takeover event is not relevant for the takeover template, since the object of the event is not a company:

Barder & Marsh, the Lloyd's agency, has reached agreement in principle with Wendover Underwriting Agency, to take over the management of five syndicates administered by Wendover, Richard Lapper writes.

The event is referring to as a management takeover rather than a company and is therefore not relevant.

Type of takeover

A takeover can be defined as hostile when the company target does not want to be acquired, friendly otherwise. Takeovers are generally friendly. In the set of 80 takeovers articles, only two occurrences of hostile takeovers were found. In both cases the takeover was hostile because the node hostile had been used as qualification of the takeover, for example:

Mr Vijay Mallya assaulted the UK drinks distribution market via the hostile takeover of Wiltshire Brewery, the UK quoted drinks company.

The rule for this slots is therefore as follows:

hostile is chosen if the main takeover event is related to the concept hostile. This analysis should be produced by the LOLITA core system when hostile is used as qualification of the takeover, for example in the sentence "*FIAT acquired Renault in a hostile takeover.*"
friendly is chosen in all other cases.

Value of the takeover
The takeover value slots should contain the monetary value that the company predator has paid for acquiring the company target. Three different semantic structures have been identified in the 80 source articles, from which three different rules have been defined.

Semantic structure 1: 43% of cases

```
Event 1:
   action:     acquire | purchase | buy | take-over
   subject:    company | person
   object:     company
   instrument: monetary value
```

In this case the monetary value is directly connected to the main takeover event. The value is the *instrument* of the takeover, thus the element that allows one company to acquire another company (free acquisitions are not considered here).

The slot rule for this semantic structure will therefore select any nodes which are linked as *instrument_* of the main takeover event and are monetary values. The following sentence from The Financial Times belongs to this semantic structure:

BF Goodrich, the Ohio-based specialty chemical and aerospace company, is to acquire Rosemount Aerospace from the Emerson Electric Company for 300 million dollars in cash, pending regulatory approval.

Semantic structure 2: 17% of cases

```
Event 1:
   action:  acquire | purchase | buy | take-over
   subject: company | person
   object:  company
```

```
Event 2:
  action:   relate_
  subject:  Event 1
  object:   monetary value
```

This semantic structure considers cases in which the monetary value is directly mentioned in the acquisition main event, but is given as qualification of the event. The following sentence (from The Financial Times on CD-ROM) shows an example of this semantic structure:

Cementos Mexicanos (Cemex), North America and Mexico's largest cement producer, is expected to launch a 1.7 billion dollars takeover for Spain's biggest producer, Valenciana de Cementos.

The slot rule for this semantic structure will look for any nodes which are related (action *relate_*) to the main takeover event and are monetary values.

Semantic structure 3: 36% of cases

```
Event 1:
  Action:   pay
  Subject:  company | person
  object:   monetary value
  goal:     company
```

In this case the acquisition main-event is the *goal_* of the event having as action *to pay*: the first company pays an amount of value with the goal of acquiring the second company. The rule for this case will therefore look for any events connected to the main acquisition event with the *goal_of* link. The events connected are checked and the objects of the events with action *pay* (or similar) and that are monetary values are chosen.

Semantic structure 4: 2% of cases

```
Event 1:
  action:   cost
  subject:  acquisition event
  object:   monetary value
```

In this case the monetary value is not directly linked to the main event but is stored into a separated event. The rule for this case will look for any event with action *cost* (or similar) which have as subject the acquisition main-event and, as object, a monetary value. The slot will be filled with the object.

Semantic structure 5: 2% of cases

```
Event 1:
  action:   is_a
  subject:  cost | price
  object:   monetary value
Event 2:
  action:   relate_
  subject:  subject of Event 1
  object:   acquisition event
```

In this case the slot will be filled with the object (which must be a monetary value) of an event with *is_a* action and subject cost, price (and similar) which is related (*relate_* action) to the main acquisition event.

An important note for this slot concerns with the correct **unification** of the events. The likelihood that the cost of the acquisition is not directly connected to the main event is, in fact, much higher than for other slots (13.21% in the sample population). If the system does not unify correctly the events, the template application will be unable to retrieve the appropriate information. In the following sentence (from The Financial Times on CD-ROM), for example, the information regarding the value of the takeover is stored in another event which should be unified by the system: "Samsung has acquired a former East German manufacturer of glass for colour TV picture tubes... Samsung is expected to pay dollars 30m for the acquisition."

Bank adviser predator
This slot should contain the name of the company or person which is advising the predator in the takeover operation. Only one occurrence of bank adviser has been found in the 80 articles of the sample population. This is probably due to the fact that the big companies are normally advised by the same company for all different kinds of operation and is therefore unlikely that the adviser is chosen in the specific occasion of a takeover.

The rule for this slot chooses any company which is an *adviser* (subjects of an event with action *is_a* and object *adviser*) and related to the *company predator* slot (*relate_* action).

Bank adviser target
The bank adviser of the target is, in the same way as the predator, the company or person who advises the target during the takeover. Similarly, the slot is defined in the same way as the *bank adviser predator*.

The slot is filled with any company which is an *adviser* (subject of an event with action *is_a* and object *adviser* and related to the company target slot (*relate_* action).

Expiry date

This slot should contain the reference to an eventual expiry date of the takeover. The date is usually stated when the takeover has not yet been performed and the company predator is offering a certain amount of money for a fixed amount of time. The company target can then accept or refuse such offer within the expiry date. The expiry date can only refer to the main-event, since for other slot it would not have any sense. Only an occurrence of expiry date in the 80 articles of the sample population has been found.

The rule for the expiry date slot fills the slot with the object linked with the *time_* link to an event with action *to expire* and subject the acquisition main-event.

Takeover attribution

This slot should contain the person, company, organisation who reported, announced or said something about the takeover event. The attribution information is extremely important for the financial operator. Knowing the source of the information, the operator can judge whether the facts are likely to be true, possible, or just rumours. For being included in the attribution slot, the person or company needs only to say, report or announce something about any of the slots. This is because if a person or company reports something about a particular slot which is related to the main event (e.g. value of the takeover), it is likely to be that it has also reported the main event.

Two different semantic structures have been identified in the 80 takeover articles of the sample population:

Semantic structure 1: 71.42% of cases

```
Event 1:
   action:   announce | say | report | inform
   subject:  company | person
   object:   acquisition event
```

In this case the person or company announces directly the takeover. The attribution event is therefore directly connected to the main event and its recognition is therefore straightforward. The attribution slot will be filled with the subject of any event with action *say, announce, report* and *inform* and object the acquisition main-event. The subject must be either a person or an organisation. The following sentence (from The Financial Times on CD-ROM) is an example of this semantic structure:

AJ Archer Holdings, one of two Lloyd's agency group listed on the Stock Exchange, yesterday announced that it would continue its expansion by acquiring a fellow agency, Kellett Holdings.

Semantic structure 2: 28.57% of cases

```
Event 1:
  action:   announce | say | report | inform
  subject:  company | person
  object:   any information in any of the other templates slots
```

In this case, the subject of the acquisition does not announce or report directly the main acquisition event, but other information, consisting in any of the other slots (apart from the slot denial). The template application will therefore infer that the attribution slot can be filled with such person. Since there is the possibility that the attribution event is wrong, the full event (sentence) is reported in the slot, rather than the only subject. In this way, the user has the possibility of verifying that the subject is relevant for the acquisition. The rule for the slot will look for any event with action *say, announce, report, inform*, subject organisation or person and object any node stored in any other slot.

Current stake predator
This slot should contain the amount or value of the shares already owned by the predator in the company target at the time of the takeover. The implementation of such rule, however, implies that the core system must be able to deal with time information in an extremely complete way. In fact, if the takeover occurred in the past, the system should understand that the ownership of part of the target occurred even in a farer past. Currently, however, the LOLITA core system is not able to deal with time in such a great detail. Therefore, the rule locates any event where the company predator is owner of part of the company target. In the 80 articles of the sample population only one occurrence of this slot appears which suggests that the information is not very common and, therefore, the fact that the temporal information is not checked is likely to be non-influent on the slot's fills.

Denial
The slot should contain the name of the person or company who denies any of the information in the template. Two occurrences of denial slots have been identified in the 80 takeover articles of the sample population and are both referring to some slots of the template. The following sentence (from The Financial Times on CD-ROM) is an example of denial of the *takeover value* slot.

Schroders, the City merchant bank, confirmed yesterday that it is considering taking full control of Wertheim, the Wall Street securities house in which it has held a 50 per cent stake since 1986, writes David Barchard. However, the bank denied that active negotiations for a cash sale had got under way.

The financial topic
A specific kind of text, for example financial articles, usually contains specific meanings of words and jargon and the probability that such meanings are used in that context is much higher than in other kinds of texts.

We can therefore define the topic of a specific kind of text as the *theme*, the subject of discourse or the probable reasoning of that article. If, for example, we are reading a The Financial Times article, we would expect that it will regard information about companies, economics, finance and business and, less likely, information about art, travel etc. If, in this context, we are reading about a takeover, we would expect the meanings of the words *buy* or *acquire* to be:

To buy: to take, to purchase, to acquire.
To acquire: to take, to purchase, to buy.

rather than:

To buy: to corrupt, to bribe, to pay.
To acquire: to produce, to grow, to get, to develop.

Choosing the topic of an article is basically making an assumption of what the article is more likely to contain and what has to be expected in the text. This helps to disambiguate the meaning of words, for example in cases like the one above.

The topic for the financial application includes the appropriate meanings of words and concepts one would expect in a financial context, for example *buy*, *takeover*, etc. The information stored in the *topic* influences the choice of the word meanings. The meanings preferred are those which are semantically closer to the context and the meanings in the topic. The semantic closeness is computed depending on the distance between the nodes in the semantic network. The choice of the appropriate meaning depends also on other factors, such as the system's knowledge of the concept and its frequency of use.

5.7 Performance

The evaluation of the results was carried out focusing on the performance of the IE module, which is essential for the system's success. This is because if any relevant information is missed or non-relevant information is mistakenly extracted, the investment suggestions produced by the expert system could be misleading.

The performance of the IE module was evaluated scoring the results of the information extracted for the user-defined takeover template shown in Figure 2.10 from an evaluation set of 55 financial articles (25 relevant takeover articles and 30 non-relevant financial articles). A complete discussion of the methodologies for evaluating IE systems is beyond the scope of this book. More information regarding this topic can be found in [114, 115]. Figure 5.10 shows a relevant takeover article from the evaluation set.

The scores have been computed using the MUC-6 scoring program which was released to the developers of the MUC-6 systems [114]. The template definition of the scoring program was changed to the user-defined takeover template in place of the original MUC-6 templates, while the evaluation measures and criteria of the

Cowie Group, the car leasing and motor trading company, yesterday announced a big
expansion of its bus operations with the 29.9 million pounds acquisition of Leaside Bus
Company, the subsidiary of London Regional Transport (LRT). The deal, involving a
25.5 million pounds cash payment and 4.4 million pounds to settle intra-group loans,
will enlarge Cowie's bus fleet from 128 vehicles to more than 600 and is expected to
lead to a fourfold sales increase.
"We paid slightly more than we wanted to, but it was worth it for the enormous growth
that it promises" said Mr Gordon Hodgson, chief executive. The acquisition follows
four months of talks between LRT and Cowie, which has been seeking a larger stake in
the London bus network for more than two years.
At present, the group's bus and coach operations are dominated by Grey-Green – acquired 14 years ago – which serves 13 bus routes in London and employs 450 drivers.
Leaside, by comparison, has a work force of about 1800 and operates 28 routes.
Mr Hodgson, who is meeting Leaside managers today, said he was determined to introduce private sector efficiency to the business, which last year made profits of just
607,000 pounds on turnover of 43 million pounds. In the same period, Grey-Green
made profits of 1.6 million pounds on sales of 14.4 million pounds. Cowie shares fell
3 1/2 p to 218 1/2p yesterday – a new low for the year.

Figure 5.10: A relevant article of the evaluation set.

```
Report for the standard takeover templates finalEval2:
```

SLOT	POS	ACT	COR	PAR	INC	MIS	SPU	NON	REC	PRE	UND	OVG	ERR	SUB
takeover	36	38	28	0	0	8	10	0	78	74	22	26	39	0
companytar	36	21	12	0	5	19	4	0	33	57	53	19	70	29
companypre	35	31	18	0	3	14	10	0	51	58	40	32	60	14
typetakeov	36	38	28	0	0	8	10	0	78	74	22	26	39	0
value	28	7	3	0	1	24	3	1	11	43	86	43	90	25
badviserpr	0	0	0	0	0	0	0	0	0	0	0	0	0	0
badviserta	0	0	0	0	0	0	0	0	0	0	0	0	0	0
expirydate	0	0	0	0	0	0	0	0	0	0	0	0	0	0
attrib	9	2	1	0	1	7	0	0	11	50	78	0	89	50
currentsta	0	0	0	0	0	0	0	0	0	0	0	0	0	0
denial	0	0	0	0	0	0	0	0	0	0	0	0	0	0
ALL OBJECTS	144	99	62	0	10	72	27	1	43	63	50	27	64	14

F-MEASURES		P&R	2P&R	P&2R
		51.03	57.41	45.93

Figure 5.11: The final score report for the user-defined takeover financial template.

scorer were not modified. The scoring program matched the templates produced
by the system for each article against the corresponding key templates producing a summary reporting the precision, recall and the combined F-measure (see
Sections 4.1 and 4.4.1).

Figure 5.11 shows the overall results for the 55 articles of the evaluation set.
The final results showed that the system's overall performance measures were:

F-measures 51.03

precision 63%

recall 43%

The overall figure is rather high, and the precision is significantly higher than the recall. The high performance of the IE module should allow the expert system to produce correct investment suggestions.

5.8 Integration with elementised news systems

Dow Jones Elementized News Feed is a new news system launched by Dow Jones in March 2007. Instead of providing the articles in text form, it offers them in structured Extended Markup Language (XML) format. The main information regarding all publicly traded US and Canada companies and largest UK companies is:

- corporate news,
- earnings,
- merger announcements,
- analyst upgrades and downgrades,
- executive changes,
- bankruptcy,
- stock splits,
- restatements,

and over 150 world's numeric economic indicators. Historical data from January 2004 for companies' earnings and economic indicators is also provided.

Since all companies' qualitative data are already in XML format they may be handled by computer programs without any extra interpretation, as if they were quantitative data. For example, from a merger announcement the takeover template of many NLP systems can be filled with a simple automatic filter which converts the XML structure to the template one. This format, therefore, skips entirely the analysis process of NLP systems and can directly be integrated with the LOLITA SemNet. The elementised knowledge can be inserted directly into the semantic network, skipping also the pragmatic analysis, since we may assume that information from Dow Jones system is carefully checked and fully compatible with standard knowledge, and the inference module, since every elementised concept is self-contained without any reference to other ones.

However, Dow Jones Elementized News Feed is still missing a lot of news and market rumours, especially for non-American companies. Those news must still be analysed with NLP systems, and the on-line enrichment of SemNet's content through the elementised news can improve the general knowledge of the system, especially when templates are filled with information coming from both sources. For example, the elementised news of a merger can contain the predator company's name, the target company's name, the price, but be missing the type of takeover (friendly or hostile). Once these information are acquired by SemNet, a news containing the same information may be better analysed and the takeover type may be deducted.

5.9 The IE-expert system

This section describes how LOLITA can be integrated to successfully make use of the qualitative information available to traders in order to suggest possible investment and hedging decisions and link the results to the quantitative real-time information.

The qualitative information available to equity traders can be grouped in two different categories: news articles from on-line news providers and in-house research material. IE-Expert is able to process these two categories of qualitative information and produce investment suggestions. In addition, it is able to provide a link between existing quantitative information and the investment decisions produced. The analysis is carried out in three main steps. The first step consists of the identification of relevant qualitative information from both real-time news and research material using the IE capabilities of IE-Expert. The second step consists of processing this information. Finally, the investment decision is shown to traders by linking it to existing quantitative information such as prices.

First of all, IE expert processes each of the incoming real-time news articles trying to identify any relevant information. The system processes all information using its IE capabilities. If no relevant information is found, the system skips the article and analyses the next incoming news. If any relevant information is found, a template is extracted according to the list of predefined templates shown in Figures 2.9 and 2.10. Figure 2.8 shows a financial news article and the corresponding template extracted by the system.

At this point IE-Expert retrieves from the database any information available regarding the two companies involved in the takeover and the market sector (according to the relevant region) which they belong to. For example, the system could retrieve the following information:

```
Company:        Tele-Communications Inc.
Negative:       Market under-performer

Company:        Bell Atlantic
Positive:       Buy

Market sector:  American Telecommunications
Positive:       Expanding rapidly.
```

Once the relevant qualitative information has been identified and processed from both sources, it is fed to the financial expert system, which processes it according to specific rules and suggests an investment decision. The expert system's knowledge consists of a set of investment decision rules which match the financial templates shown in Figures 2.9 and 2.10, which represent the most likely causes of share prices changes.

From the information shown above, the expert system would produce the following investment suggestions:

```
1) Bell Atlantic:

    Market Sector:   positive (expanding rapidly)
    Company:         positive (buy)
    Financial event: positive (takeover, company_predator)
    Investment decision suggested: share price likely to
    rise - buy

2) Tele-Communications Inc.

    Market Sector:   positive (expanding rapidly)
    Company:         negative (market under-performer)
    Financial event:  positive (takeover, company_target)
    Investment decision suggested: share price likely to
    rise - buy
```

The expert system suggested a likely positive impact of the takeover event for both companies and that, as a consequence, the share price of the two companies is likely to increase.

News can also refer to the market as a whole and, in this case, the investment decision suggested by the expert system will be linked to the relevant market index (e.g. the Standard & Poor's 500 index). This is because news regarding macro-economical data such as a reduction in the level of unemployment, generally affect the market globally.

The last step of the system is to display the investment decisions suggested by the expert system in real-time to traders. This is done using a specifically designed spreadsheet which reports the live quantitative information together with the information produced by the expert system. Figure 5.12 shows an example spreadsheet for part of the companies belonging to the S&P/MIB index.

The colour of a row changes whenever a relevant news is processed by IE-Expert and an investment decision is suggested. The colour becomes red for events with negative impact on the share price, green, for events with positive impact and blue for events with no impact on the share price. The trader is also able to click on the financial event and display the relevant article and market analysis which originated the event, to better understand its scope and impact on the share price.

IE-Expert therefore helps traders overcome their qualitative data-overload and link the quantitative and qualitative information together, which allows them to quicker define their current view of the market for the next investment and hedging decisions.

Name	Price	% Change	Min	Max	News Impact
Aem	2.625	0.42	2.5725	2.63	
Alitalia	0.7845	0.15	0.77	0.7865	Takeover–company target
Alleanza Ass	9.52	−0.68	9.45	9.58	
Atlantia	25.56	0.24	25.32	25.65	
Autogrill Spa	16.18	−1.05	16.1	16.39	
Banco Popolare	19.96	−0.94	19.72	20.29	
Bca Mps	4.98	−1.05	4.935	5.02	
Bca Pop Milano	11.35	0.06	11.07	11.38	Takeover–company predator
Bulgari	11.58	0.84	11.35	11.62	
Buzzi Unicem	25.23	−0.94	25.04	25.35	
Capitalia	7.225	−1.2	7.14	7.255	
Enel	7.885	0.28	7.825	7.89	
Eni	27.93	−0.82	27.79	28.28	
Fastweb	39.2	−0.61	38.8	39.41	
Fiat	23.48	0.64	22.98	23.76	Dividend forecast announcement
Finmeccanica	22.41	−1.32	22.25	22.69	New factory
Fondiaria-Sai	35.48	−1.66	35.33	35.95	

Figure 5.12: Merging real-time quantitative and qualitative information.

Although IE-Expert includes a set of pre-defined templates and expert system rules, it has been designed as a fully customisable system. This is because different traders and financial institutions might have different views and trading strategies.

The system is customisable at two different levels: the financial templates and the expert systems rules. New templates can be easily added to the system using a specific user-definable template interface. The user interface allows new users to define new templates using sentences in natural language using specific formal elements (e.g. the takeover template definition shown in Figure 2.10). The user can also customise the expert system providing the rules for processing the extracted templates and the research analysis available.

5.9.1 Implementation

IE-Expert is based on two main components. The first component is the **IE engine** which identifies and extracts the relevant information from the incoming real-time financial news. The second component is the **expert system**, which is used to process the templates extracted by the IE component and the market analysis to produce investment suggestions. In addition, a **PostgreSQL database** stores the market data associated to a specific company or sector and a spreadsheet is used to display the results. The architecture of the system is shown in Figure 5.13.

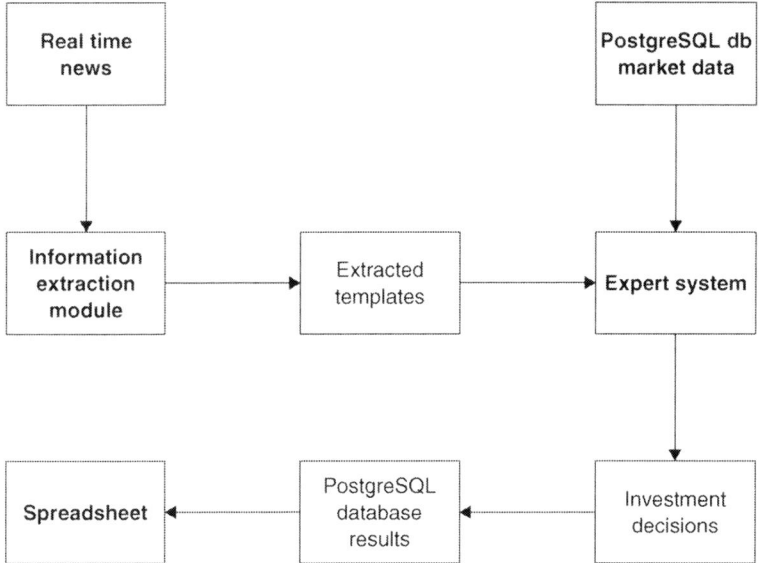

Figure 5.13: The architecture of IE-Expert.

5.9.2 The expert system component

Once the templates have been produced by LOLITA system, the system retrieves any associated market data information from the database which is currently based on a PostgreSQL server. The text of the template and the market data information are subsequently fed to the expert system.

The expert system currently employed is relatively straightforward. The templates definitions and the market data available are parsed and stored in memory. At this stage, the information is processed using a set of rules corresponding to each of the pre-defined templates available in the IE module. The rule corresponding to the template is matched against the new information and an investment decision is produced. The expert system rules are represented as a table of True/False conditions which are matched against the slots of the template produced and of the associated market data.

The basic rules of IE-Expert for the takeover template are displayed in Figure 5.14. While the system currently allows the user to enter new template definition using the user-definable template interface, the user is unable to enter new rules for the expert system, considerably limiting the global performance of the system. Further work is also being carried out to increase the number of standard templates directly available in the system and the corresponding expert system rules, the first one being the *merger* template, which has already been defined and it is shown in Section 5.4.5.

COMPANY_PREDATOR-investment suggestions		
Positive	**Neutral**	**Negative**
Company profile: positive Market sector: positive	Company profile: negative / negative Market sector: positive or Company profile: positive Market sector: neutral / negative	Company profile: negative / neutral Market sector: negative / neutral

COMPANY_TARGET-investment suggestions		
Positive	**Neutral**	**Negative**
Company profile: positive / neutral / negative Market sector: positive positive / neutral / negative		

Figure 5.14: The expert system rules for the takeover event.

The investment decision produced by the expert system, together with the associated template and market information is subsequently stored in a database. Finally, a spreadsheet is used to retrieve the information from the database and display the results.

The IE system is written in the functional language Haskell and C language. The expert system is written in C. A PostgreSQL database is used for storing the market data information and the investment decisions and templates produced by the system. The information is displayed using an Applix spreadsheet which accesses directly the PostgreSQL database. The system has been mainly written in C rather than in other languages for performance reasons. This choice, however, does not potentially prevent the system from being used within the Internet. The Applix spreadsheet, in fact, could be easily substituted with web pages interfaced directly to the core system and the interface to the core system could be written using Java.

6 Conclusions

Finance is a wide discipline, embracing many aspect of modern society, from business to banks, from accounting to global markets. In this book, we concentrated on the secondary financial markets, where stocks, bonds, derivatives and other securities and currencies are traded. All the systems presented here have mostly the stock exchange market in sight, since it is the largest and most common one, but any system may be without difficulty adapted to any other secondary market.

IE is a recent field of scientific research, developed together with the spreading of cheap computers. It consists of selecting the relevant text among thousands of documents but, as an extent to information retrieval, uses this text to report structured information to the user, answering some predetermined questions. Its utility in many disciplines is very large, and this is especially true when the mass of documents is huge and the user's time is precious, such as in securities' trading.

The systems presented in this book apply IE to financial documents and some of them go further giving some tools to present the retrieved information in an user-friendly way. Some systems do not deal directly with finance, however their algorithms are designed to collect information with a structure similar to many financial domains. Other systems do not extract information but summarise articles, which is also a very good tool for the financial investor.

The basis of this research are the first TREC conferences and especially the MUC conferences of the 90s, where the first really working systems have been presented and compared using a common training and testing set of documents and common templates. Since then, two families of systems have appeared: pattern matching systems and statistical systems. The former proved to be more successful, due to a strict adherence to language rules, while the latter proved to be much more portable and adaptable to error-prone documents such as e-mails. Therefore in the last years mixed systems have appeared, using statistical techniques to automatically or semi-automatically build pattern matching rules, thus improving portability. With the appearance of the WWW these algorithms have an even wider field of application, being the basis of search engines, automatic answering web services and, at the same time, being more and more necessary due to the exponential spreading of possible source of financial information.

Appendix A: Other MUC systems

This appendix contains a more detailed description of systems which participated in MUC-6 and MUC-7 competitions, described in Section 4.4.

A.1 Hasten

The MUC-6 system developed by SRA uses the combination of two sub-systems: **NameTag**, a commercial software for recognising proper names and other key phrases in the source text and **Hasten**, a text extraction system. The key part of the combined system is Hasten, which is built around the concept of **extraction examples**: the user provides source articles and annotates the text with what to extract and Hasten uses the information to analyse subsequent text [3]. The system, in fact, computes the similarity between the annotations provided by the user from the sample articles and the key phrases currently being analysed. The more examples the user enters, the more accurate should be Hasten's extraction from the real data. The system consists of four main modules depicted in Figure A.1: the analyser, the reference resolver, the collector and the generator.

The **analyser** extracts semantic information from the text using a set of pre-defined examples regarding the text by matching the new information against the similar one available in the examples. The module makes use of the **reference resolver** to link the references to their referents. The subsequent step is the **collector** which collects and merges the semantic information extracted by the analyser according to the concept specifications. Finally, the **generator** produces the output according to an arbitrary output format using an output script.

The system basically matches the new input against the collection of examples available in the system. This process is done taking into account specific parameters and produces a set of similarity values for each new sentence which are used to decide the relevance of the new input. If the similarity value overcomes a certain threshold value, the information is considered to be relevant and will be further processed. In Figure A.2 the matching process for each of the input sentences of a source article is shown.

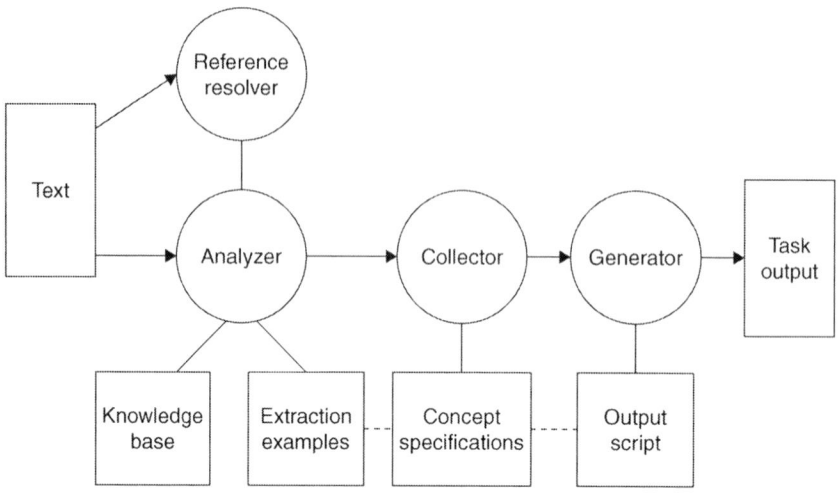

Figure A.1: The Hasten MUC-6 system (from Ref. [3]).

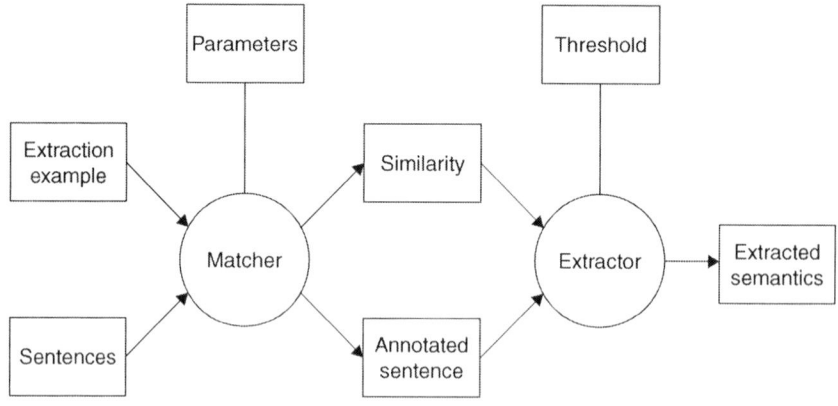

Figure A.2: The extraction by example in the Hasten system (from Ref. [3]).

The Hasten system shows some improvements with respect to other systems based on finite-state analysis techniques and, in particular, those used in MUC-5. The system, in fact, allows the developers to specify the patterns by inputting directly the examples, rather than having to input the patterns using specific notations. The system, however, is still based on pure finite-state analysis techniques and, therefore, the user must supply each of the possible patterns encountered in the specific domain. Moving the system towards new domains can therefore be expensive, since new examples have to be provided. For example, the scenario template task required a total of 132 egraphs (examples) which compares with only few semantic structures of the LOLITA MUC-6 scenario template.

A.2 Alembic

The Alembic system [4] never competed in the scenario template evaluation, but successfully participated in the template element. The system is based on an evolution of the Alembic system which competed in MUC-5 [133]. Not surprisingly, its evolution consisted in the introduction of simpler syntactic analysis modules, rather than performing deeper natural language understanding as its predecessor. The new system comprises three main modules (see Figure A.3): the tagger, the phraser and the inference. The **tagger** is implemented in C and is primarily responsible for part-of-speech tagging enriching the source text using SGML tags. The algorithm is based on an improvement of the work regarding rule sequences by Brill [134].

The central part of the system is the **phraser** which performs the syntactic analysis in the system. It is basically similar to many other systems based on finite-state analysis techniques with the difference of being driven by rule sequences. The rule sequences are applied against all the phrases of the current sentence. The phraser step is finished when all rules have been applied.

The third main module of the system is the **inference** which performs phrase interpretation, the so-called **equality reasoning**, and infers new facts from the source text using forward inference rules.

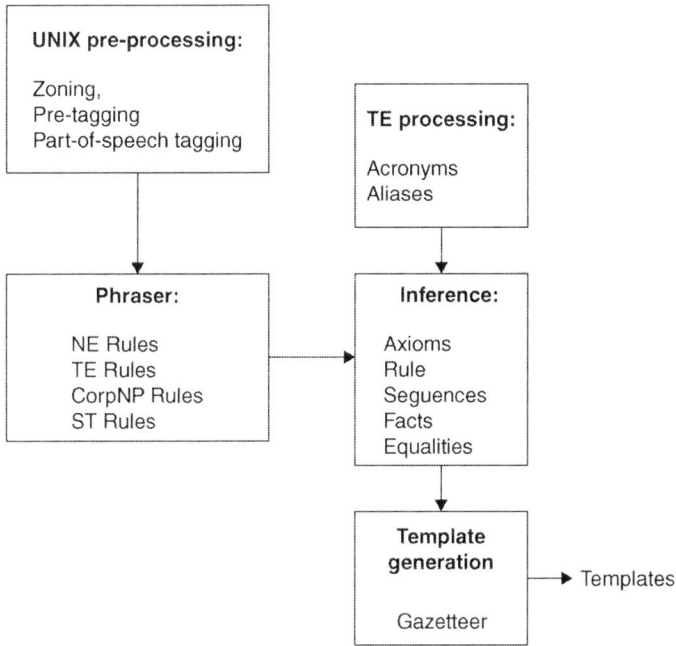

Figure A.3: The Alembic system (from Ref. [4]).

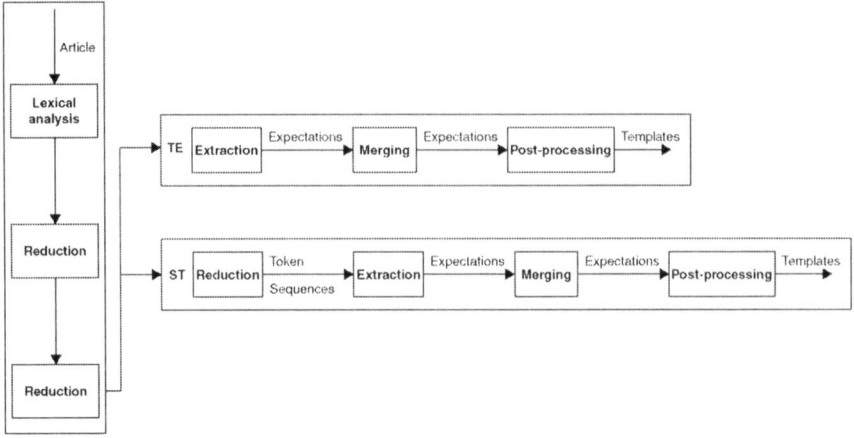

Figure A.4: The NLToolset system (from Ref. [5]).

Differently from its predecessor, the new Alembic system is more similar to other conventional systems based on finite-state analysis techniques. Therefore, the system does not perform semantic analysis of the source text nor analysis of words meanings.

A.3 NLToolset

The NLToolset system, developed by Sterling Software in collaboration with Lockheed-Martin, was originally designed for working in the counter-narcotics domain and was converted for the MUC-6 competition [5].

The system is based on finite-state analysis techniques and does not perform any semantic analysis of the input text. The core of the system is a pattern matcher which is repeatedly used in the processing of the source text. The pattern matcher is employed in the **reduction** modules. The text is repeatedly matched to each of the system's patterns obtaining the relevant information. The **extraction** module subsequently uses the results of the reduction modules to generate **expectations** which are used to fill the templates. Finally, a **merging** module is used to merge expectations which refer to the same type (person, organisation, etc.). The way in which template elements and scenario templates are generated by the system is slightly different (see Figure A.4) but is conceptually equivalent.

A.4 Oki

Oki submitted two systems to MUC-7: the English system for MUC-7 and the Japanese system for MET-2. In order to develop the systems in a short period, Oki utilised parsing module of the MT system for a sentence analyser. The systems are then developed using the different sentence analysers [6].

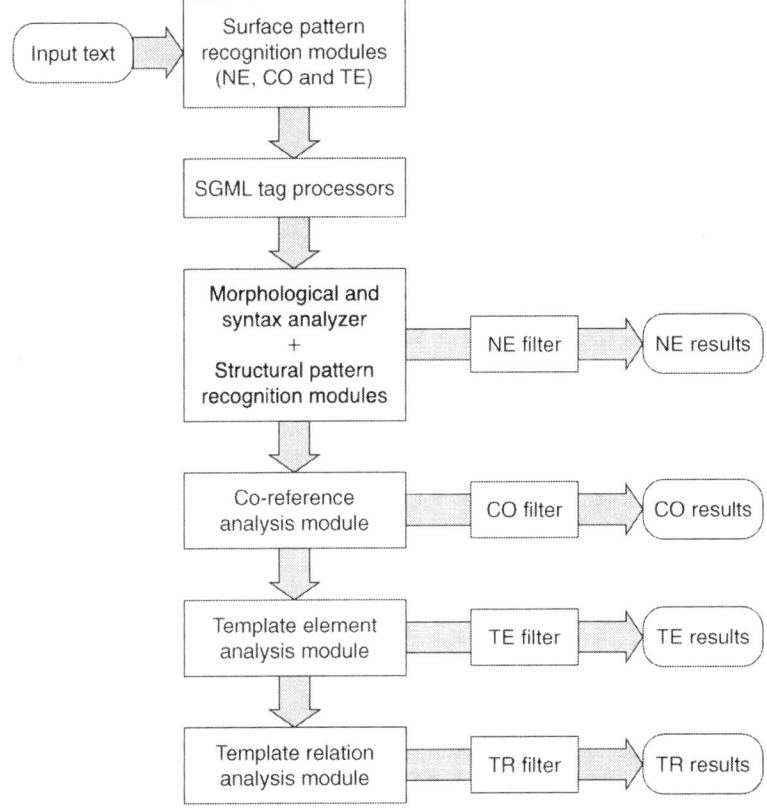

Figure A.5: Oki system architecture (from Ref. [6]).

The Oki IE system used for MUC-7 is composed of a surface pattern recognition module and a structural pattern recognition module. The **surface pattern recognition** module traces a text at surface linguistic level and detects named-entity's elements and co-referred elements without any language analysis system such as lexical analysis and syntax analysis. The **structural pattern recognition** module traces parse trees of a text, which is generated by parser of MT system. Moreover, there is a **filtering program** to convert internal expression of parser to surface expression, and two **tag processing modules**. Architecture of the system is shown in Figure A.5.

A.5 IE²

Information Extraction Engine (IE²) [135], developed by SRA, uses the standard modular architecture with five modules for the template element and template relationship tasks and six for the scenario template task.

The three core modules, namely NameTag, PhraseTag and EventTag, use SRA's multilingual IE engine called **TurboTag**.

The first two modules are a commercial **entity name recognition** software by **IsoQuest** and a **pattern matcher** which recognise and tag names of people, organisations and places, as well as time and numeric expressions. In addition to its name recognition capability, it provides subtypes and aliases of organisations, people and places (e.g., "U.S." for "United States" or "province" as a place subtype). The third module is a high-performance **noun phrase tagger** especially targeted to recognise noun phrases describing people, organisations and artifacts. Moreover, it is specially designed to work with relative clauses, reduced relatives, and prepositional phrases, and to add local links between phrases with high accuracy. Finally, a **rule-based phrase tagger** completes the parsing modules. The **discourse** module employs three different co-references resolution strategies: a rule-based one, a machine-learning one which uses a decision tree trained on previously submitted corpora, and an hybrid one which uses rules to reduce the decision tree's width. The last module generates the templates, interprets and normalises time expressions and performs event merging.

A.6 New York University: MUC-6 system

The system developed by the New York University [80] is a system based on finite-state analysis techniques. Differently from the systems developed at New York University for the previous MUC competitions [136], the MUC-6 system does not perform any semantic analysis of the input text. The system comprises seven main stages: tokenisation and dictionary look-up, four stages of pattern matching, reference resolution and output generation.

The **tokenisation** and **dictionary look-up** module is responsible for the identification of each word of the input text and makes use of various databases: a country database, a company dictionary, a government agency dictionary, a dictionary of common first names and a dictionary of scenario-specific terms specific for the MUC-6 competition. Once the words have been identified in the dictionary, a **post-tagger** is used to identify the most likely part-of-speech for each word. The output of the tokenisation module is later processed by the **pattern matching** module which recognises four different forms of patterns: names, nouns, verbs and semantic patterns. Semantic patterns are scenario-specific patterns, such as: *start-job(person,position)* or *add-job(person,position)*. The output of the pattern matching module is later analysed by the **reference resolution** module which unifies and integrates them in case they refer to the same object or event. Finally, the system generates the output according to the output required for the specific task.

The NYU system is therefore a pattern-matching system without any form of understanding of the input text. The system was the best system in the scenario template MUC-6 competition.

A.7 SIFT

For MUC-7 competition BBN developed a new system called SIFT [79], **Statistics for Information From Text**. It employs a unified statistical process to map from words to semantic structures: part-of-speech determination, name finding, parsing and relationship finding all happen as part of the same process. This allows each element to influence the others, and avoids the assembly-line trap of having to commit to a particular part-of-speech choice when only local information is available to inform the choice.

The SIFT sentence-level model was trained from a corpus of one million words from The Wall Street Journal text and from half million words of on-domain text annotated with named-entities, descriptors and semantic relations. For extraction in a new domain, the names and descriptors of relevant items are marked, as well as the target relationships between them that are signaled syntactically: the model can thus learn the structures that are typically used in English to convey the target relationships.

While the bulk of the task happens within the sentence-level decoder, some further processing is still required to produce answer templates. After the names, descriptors and local relationships have been extracted from the decoder output, a merging process is applied to link multiple occurrences of the same name or of alternative forms of the name from different sentences. A second, cross-sentence model is then invoked to identify non-local relationships that have been missed by the decoder, as when the two entities do not occur in the same sentence. Finally, type and country information is filled in using heuristic tests and a database, and output filters are applied to select which of the proposed internal structures will be included in the output.

A.8 TASC

TASC developed a technology for learning scenario template extraction grammars from examples provided by users with no special computational nor linguistic knowledge [81]. For straightforward scenario template problems, complete extraction systems can be learned from scratch. These learned systems are fast, robust and as accurate as carefully handcrafted systems. For more complex extraction problems the grammars can still be learned automatically with some computational-linguistic work for complex template merging and inference.

IsoQuest's commercial software is first used to mark up entities as a preprocessing step, recognising many categories such as dates, locations, people and organisations. Three different extractors, one for each task, are then applied with a common shared slot to let templates merge. The grammars TASC uses to perform scenario template extraction are highly tolerant of corrupted data, ungrammatical sentences and other types of noise. These grammars are learned from scratch through a combination of statistical and search algorithms. There is no base grammar from which the learning starts: the system begins with no grammatical knowledge at all because it was designed to be able to learn extraction grammars for any natural language, or for technical sub-languages that may contain unusual constructions. Once a grammar is learned, a corresponding extractor is generated automatically.

The process of learning these extraction grammars begins by defining the template through a simple graphical user interface. That interface allows the names of the slots to be entered, and the category of the corresponding filler to be chosen from a simple menu. For instance, the interface can be used to specify that there is a *payload owner* slot that should be filled by an organisation. Once the slots and fillers have been specified, an initial extractor is automatically constructed. The training program runs, and its graphical interface allows the user to interactively correct the wrongly filled slots. Examples can also be sorted by ambiguity.

A.9 New York University: MENE

New York University participated in the named entity task with another system called **Maximum Entropy Named Entity** (MENE) [7]. This system is rather innovative when compared to the other rule-based MUC-7 systems. It relies entirely on statistical training and probabilistic measures. As we have already seen, these techniques have the advantage to be ported to a new domain providing new annotated data and without any major technical intervention.

MENE system starts from the assumption that the task of finding named entities can be reduced to the task of assigning $4n + 1$ tags to each language token (usually words). There are four basic tags *start*, *continue*, *end* and *unique* for each of the n named entities, plus the tag *other* for tokens not belonging to any named entity. During the running of the system the tokens receive the tags which maximise the total probability found using a Viterbi search algorithm.

Probabilities assign is the hearth of the system. For each token a possible set of feature is decided. Features are properties of the token, expressed in a binary yes/no form, which may be **binary features** such as "the first letter is capital", **lexical features** such as "it is preceded by token *the*", **section features** such as "it is in the abstract", or **dictionary features** such as "it belongs to the list of company names". Once these features are decided, the frequency of appearance of every token-feature combination is automatically evaluated on the training set and the probability that this combination appears is calculated using probability combinatory rules. The bulk of the training set usually are the lexical features, which determine the probability due to the history of the sentence, since they look at previous words. The developer needs therefore only to concentrate on determining the lexical features for each domain, leaving to the training system the task of calculating probabilities. There are many binary, dictionary and lexical features that in MENE system may be taken into account but which will cause confusion to a standard rule-based system. For example, the feature that "a token following *to* is probably a destination" may not be inserted in a rule-based system because it is

Articles	425	350	250	150	100	80	40	20	10
MENE	92.9	92.2	91.3	90.6	89.2	87.9	84.1	81.0	76.4
MENE+Proteus	95.7	95.6	95.6	94.5	94.3	93.4	91.7		

Figure A.6: NYU MENE system's F-measures as a stand-alone system and together with NYU Proteus (from Ref. [7]).

false in many cases and creates a lot of errors, but in MENE system this feature has to compete with the feature that "a token following *to* is a verb" and other similar ones, all with their probability calculated on the training set.

MENE system may also be used in combination with other named entity systems, using the recognised named entity as another type of features, called **external systems features**, and running the system with the knowledge of another system without any further technical modification. MENE summarised results can be seen in Figure A.6 for different number of training articles as a stand-alone system and as a system after NYU's Proteus.

A.10 FACILE

FACILE is an IE tool [8] supporting four different languages: English, Italian, German and Spanish. The main aims of the FACILE project were to advance the state of the art in classification and IE techniques and to show that these techniques could successfully be applied to real applications in different industrial fields. The project was sponsored by the EU as a RTP project. A total of eight partners participated in the projects, including three research institutions, two industrial partners and three user organisations (Quinary SpA, ITC-Irst, Italrating SpA, FAI, Sema SAE, Caja de Segovia, Sis, UMIST-CCL).

The development of the project was performed working in parallel on two different tasks. The first one was to collect and analyse user requirements, through a strict interaction between the researches and end users organisations. At the same time, the architecture of the system was developed with the aim to define a core and kernel tools which would enable the quick development of several applications in the most effective way.

The most relevant application for the purpose of this book is the fourth application. The customer of this application was a major Italian financial agency (Radiocor), which was not among the participants to the project. FACILE was used to support automatic classification of news written in Italian. Classified news feed several pay-to-view services provided on the web and at selected customers' sites through Intranet deployment. The domain coverage is similar to that described for the Italian rating company, from which most of the domain specific knowledge has been derived.

FACILE is implemented as a collection of modules implementing several steps. A control module is used to activate all other modules when required. The main modules in the system are three largely application-independent modules (the

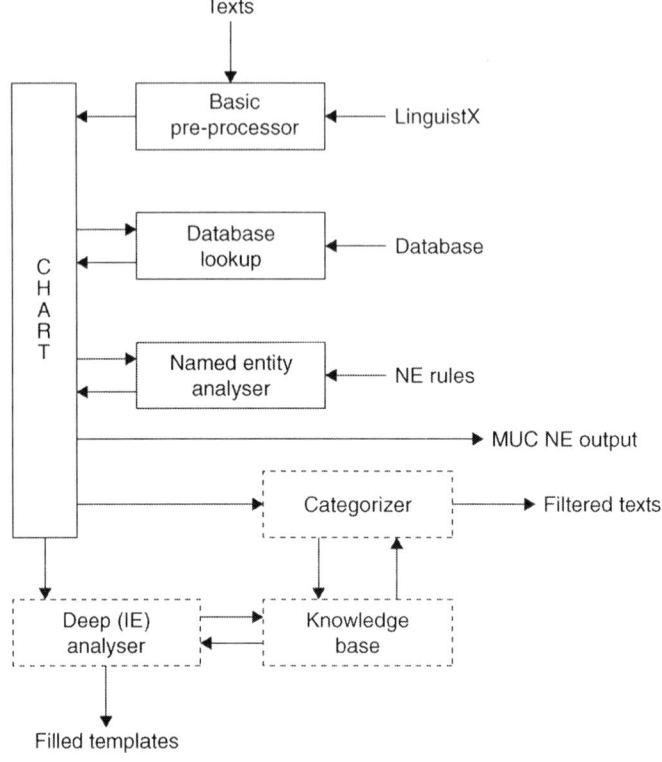

Figure A.7: FACILE architecture (from Ref. [8]).

pre-processor, the shallow analyser and the deep analyser) and some application-specific modules. Figure A.7 shows the main system architecture for the FACILE system.

The first module is the **pre-processor**, whose main task is to transform a input set of characters into analysed tokens. The main steps performed by the pre-processor are:

(a) tokenisation (splits the input text and assigns specific orthographic features);
(b) morphological analysis (stemming and assignment of morpho-syntactic information);
(c) part-of-speech tagging (disambiguation of multiple morpho-syntactic categories);
(d) database lookup (assignment of semantic features);
(e) named-entity analysis.

Then the **shallow classifier module** is the core pattern matching engine of the system. The first step performed by this model is recognition of domain relevant concepts in the source text and categories assignments. This step is performed by the **shallow analyser**. This includes both domain objects (e.g. share, bond, warrant, etc.) and domain events (e.g. takeover, merger etc.). The pattern matching techniques are integrated within the knowledge representation system. The output of the shallow analyser is a set of text portions matched with concepts with associated scores which represent confidence factors. The next step is identification of the text's main topic using application-specific heuristics (based on both concept matches and context) and domain knowledge. This step is performed by the **rule-based categoriser**. This modularisation should allow the system to be ported to new languages and domains.

The next module is the **deep analyser module**, whose main goal is to perform IE to achieve the desired level of classification in the form of output templates. This is achieved starting from the pre-processed and classified text supplied by the shallow classifier module. Texts are classified according to their content, allowing the user to run natural language queries such as *Send me any texts concerning bonds issued by European-based financial institutions whose amount exceeds 1 million Euro*. The task performed by the deep analyser module are somehow similar to the scenario template task of the MUC competition [25]. However, the templates generated by this module tend to be much flatter.

The main technique employed is a cascade of **finite-state transducers**. Each transducer operates on a string of tokens. Tokens are abstract representations of lexical elements that have three types of realisations accessible at any time during analysis: lexical (strings, named-entities, etc.), syntactic (parse trees, typed feature structures) and semantic (quasi logical forms).

The first module applied is the **parser**. The parser assumes that there is only one single possible parse tree in the source text. It then attempts to produce the best approximation of such a parse tree.

Default reasoning is applied to the generated parse tree. In this way, additional information is included which was not originally present in the source text, but it is needed for template filling. **Discourse processing** is subsequently performed.

Finally, the templates are filled applying an additional **default reasoning** step. Some merging and recovery actions are taken to cope with missing information.

One of the key goals of the FACILE project, as we mentioned above, was to show that NLP and IE techniques can be successfully applied to real industrial applications. In order to make this possible the design of the system had to allow for it to be integrated into the user environment. As a consequence, the system has been split into two main blocks:

- the **classification kernel**, composed by the four modules described above. This is deployed as a stand alone UNIX module;
- the **application layer**, this module can be customised and modified so that the system can be integrated within the existing user's systems.

Appendix B: Recent systems

In this appendix we present more recent systems, developed after the MUC competition series, but which are still based on the basic ideas of the previous systems: pattern matching or statistical analysis.

One of the new key issues is **portability**, i.e. building a system which can be moved to a different domain. While for statistical systems this simply means having a new training corpus, for pattern-matching system a major challenge in IE is developing rules which can be adapted to new domains with the minimum of human intervention. Early systems were based on knowledge engineering approaches but suffered from a knowledge acquisition bottleneck. One approach to this problem is to use machine learning to automatically learn the domain-specific information required to port a system. Weakly supervised algorithms, which bootstrap from a small number of examples, have the advantage of requiring only small amounts of annotated data, which are often difficult and time consuming to produce. However, this also means that there are fewer examples of the patterns to be learned, making the learning task more challenging. Providing the learning algorithm with access to additional knowledge can compensate for the limited number of annotated examples.

Another new issue is the **technological platform**, which now is required to run on the WWW, to process several documents in different languages, formats (text, HTML, XML, PDF, etc.) and in different alphabets or character encodings. Moreover, the birth of many IE systems which use alternative approaches requires a common evaluation tool, both as open source technological infrastructure and as common data set, to compare the systems. MUC-6 data are still used by many authors as common evaluation data set, while the GATE system developed at University of Sheffield is the leading common IE framework.

B.1 University of Utah system

Most IE systems use rules or patterns to extract words based on the context, since many patterns are very specifically related to an event. The common technique of these approaches is to simultaneously decide whether a context is relevant and at the same time whether a pattern is to be extracted or not. Therefore, they consider features related to the words and to the context, and pattern matchers must take into consideration also the surrounding words, up to a large extent.

The system developed at University of Utah [9] proposes an approach which splits the task of finding relevant regions of text from that of extracting the words themselves: it first detects the regions of the document that contain relevant information, and then applies the extraction patterns only to those parts. This approach presents several advantages:

- it avoids false positives, for examples metaphors;
- it avoids omissions when relevant information is not specifically linked to an event. For example, if a weapon is cited in a sentence, it may or may not be used in a crime depending on whether the sentence is crime relevant or not;
- it may apply more general patterns, aggressively searching for extractions without using too many surrounding words, since it supposes that all the considered areas do not contain non-relevant information.

B.1.1 Architecture

The first part of the system is the **self-trained classifier**, a program which discriminates between relevant and non-relevant sentences. The program is self-trained, which means that from an example of few seed patterns, it is able to run through the training set and to automatically learn the new relevant patterns. The training set consists of a **non-relevant sentences pool**, a set of documents containing only non-relevant sentences, and an **unlabelled sentences pool**, a set of documents containing a mix of relevant and non-relevant sentences. A **support vector machine classifier** [137, 138] is trained with three iterations using relevant sentences and an equal number of sentences drawn from the non-relevant pool (see Figure B.1).

The second part of the system consists of learning new extraction patterns, to use in the sentence classifier, which are semantically affine. Therefore, a specific metric called **semantic affinity** has been introduced to automatically assign roles to event patterns . This metric measured the tendency for a pattern to extract nouns or verbs that belong to a specific category (see Ref. [139]). To determine the semantic category of nouns the **Sundance parser** [140] or **WordNet** [141] may be used. To calculate the semantic affinity between pattern p and event role r, the program

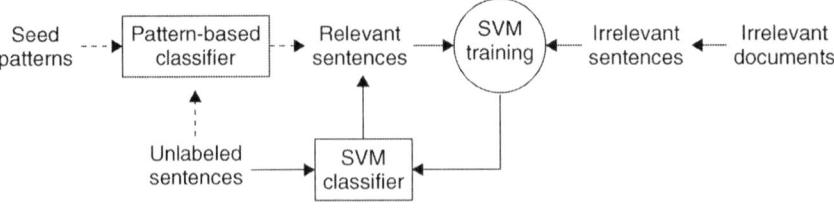

Figure B.1: University of Utah's self-training system (from Ref. [9]).

computes the frequency fr(p, r) of p's extraction that have a noun belonging to r and then uses the formula

$$\text{affinity}(p, r) = \frac{\text{fr}(p, r) \log_2 \text{fr}(p, r)}{\sum_{\forall r} \text{fr}(p, r)}.$$

Finally, **AutoSlog extraction pattern generator** (see Ref. [142]) is applied exhaustively to the whole training corpus to extract patterns which are then ordered by semantic affinity for the considered role. It is very interesting to note that as training corpus the WWW may also be used, as described in Ref. [143], where through specific Google's queries, searching only for English documents on the CNN's website, and through an appropriate HTML parser, more than 5000 suitable documents on terrorism were extracted in 2005.

Patterns are then divided into **primary patterns** and **secondary patterns**. The former are patterns which show a high correlation with relevant documents and are therefore assumed to be reliable patterns: if they are found in a sentence marked as non-relevant, it is assumed that the sentence classifier is wrong. The latter are patterns with a not so high correlation with relevant documents, which will be used for searching only inside relevant documents. Moreover, patterns with a too low correlation with relevant documents are excluded from the search since they usually match with too generic sentences (for example, patterns such as *<subject>saw* or *<subject>did*) which will cause a loss in precision.

B.1.2 Evaluation and results

The system was evaluated using MUC-4 terrorism corpus and ProMed disease corpus; we concentrate here our attention on the former evaluation.

This MUC-4 testset consists of 1300 development texts, 200 for tuning and 200 as testset. Even though MUC-4 has answer key templates, this system is currently not able to fill templates and therefore it is only evaluated on the extraction themselves. Even though this is a good test anyway, it must be taken into account that it is an easier task than a full template generation test, since it does not have to handle co-reference and to deal with the problem of discriminating multiple events in the same document.

Concerning the sentence classifier, after three iterations it produced a precision of 0.92 and a recall of 0.85 on irrelevant sentences and a precision of 0.46 with a recall of 0.63 on relevant sentences. The final results of IE on five different categories show an F-measure ranging from 0.43 to 0.50 with precision from 0.39 to 0.58 and recall from 0.36 to 0.56, depending on the category.

B.2 University of Sheffield pattern extraction

The university of Sheffield proposes a variant for pattern extraction, called **linked chains** [144], where extracted patterns are pair of chains which share the same verb but no direct descendants. This pattern representation encodes most of the information in the sentence with the advantage of being able to link together event participants which neither of the SVO nor chain model can. On the other hand, it generates a polynomial number of patterns while the sub-tree model is exponential. There is a clear tradeoff between the complexity of pattern representations and the computing power necessary to handle them. Some pattern representations can represent better the language and cover more situations, since they use a large amount of information from the dependency tree, than others and are probably able to produce more accurate extraction patterns. However, they add extra computational complexity since they generate a large number of patterns. This complexity, both in the number of patterns to be handled and in the computational effort required to actually produce them, limits the algorithms that can be applied to learn useful extraction patterns, thus preventing the analysis of more available training documents. The ideal model is therefore the one with sufficient language-expressive power and at the same time does not include extra information which would make its use impossible or very hard. Experiments on MUC-6 executive management succession comparing SVO, chains, linked chains and sub-trees models on the pattern coverage showed that there is a big gap between the first two models (15.1 and 41.1% coverage respectively) and linked chains (94.8%), while it is not so large between linked chains and sub-trees model (99.7%).

The same authors from University of Sheffield propose another variant [145] based on another scoring function. Instead of using a document-centric scoring function, they propose a semantic scoring function. The approach is inspired by the vector space model which is commonly used in information retrieval: each pattern can be represented as a set of pattern element-filler pairs. For example, the pattern *COMPANY fired ceo* consists of three pairs: subject *COMPANY*, verb *fired* and object *ceo*. Once an appropriate set of pairs has been established, a pattern is represented as a binary vector in which an element with value 1 denotes that the pattern contains a particular pair and 0 that it does not. The similarity of two **pattern vectors** is compared using the measure:

$$\text{score}(a, b) = \frac{a \times Wb}{\|a\| \, \|b\|},$$

where a and b are pattern vectors and W the **semantic similarity matrix** that lists the similarity between each of the possible pattern element-filler pairs. It contains information about the similarity of each pattern element-filler pair stored as non-negative real numbers. Appropriate values for the elements of W are built using the **WordNet** (see Section 2.2.1) **hierarchy**. Tokens not included in WordNet are manually mapped onto the most appropriate node in the WordNet hierarchy. For further details, see Ref. [145].

This similarity measure can be used to create a weakly supervised pattern acquisition algorithm, where each candidate pattern is compared against the set of currently accepted patterns using this measure. The best technique for ranking candidates turned out to be comparing the score of each pattern candidate against the centroid vector of the set of currently accepted patterns and taking the four highest scoring patterns whose score is within 0.95 of the best pattern. Evaluation of this measure applied to sentence filtering on MUC-6 data produced a significant (Wilcoxon signed rank test is significant with $p < 0.001$) improvement in precision and recall (up to 0.30 for precision and 0.20 for recall) with respect to a traditional document-centric approach.

B.3 GATE framework

General Architecture for Text Engineering (GATE) has been in development at the University of Sheffield since 1995 [11, 146, 147] and has been used in a wide variety of research and development projects [148]. Its first version dates back to 1996, and since then GATE was licensed by several hundred organisations and used in many language-analysis contexts including IE in English, Greek, Spanish, Swedish, German, Italian and French. Version 4 of the system, a complete re-implementation extension of the original 1996 version, is from July 2007 freely available from http://gate.ac.uk/download.

GATE is a generic infrastructure for developing and deploying software components that process human language. GATE is able to help researchers in three ways:

- specifying a standard architecture and organisational structure for language-processing software;
- providing a framework, or class library, which implements the specified architecture and that can be used to embed language-processing capabilities in diverse applications without developing a natural language software from scratch;
- providing a development environment built on top of the framework made up of convenient graphical tools for developing components;
- providing a standard environment to perform tests, substituting one of GATE's component with the researcher's own module and thus testing different interchangeable modules within the same framework.

The architecture uses component-based, object-oriented, mobile code. The framework and the development environment are written in Java and are available as open-source free software under the GNU library licence (http://www.gnu.org/licenses). GATE uses Unicode character encoding and therefore can be used with several different languages which uses non-ASCII alphabets. From a scientific point of view, GATE's main contribution is in the quantitative measurement of accuracy and repeatability of results for verification purposes.

GATE includes a family of processing resources for language analysis, which are:

- ANNIE, **A Nearly-New Information Extraction system**, which uses finite-state techniques to perform various tasks such as semantic tagging, tokenisation and verb phrase chunking;

- JAPE, **Java Annotation Patterns Engine**, provides rules for annotation based on regular expressions. JAPE is a version of CPSL Common Pattern Specification Language (for details, see Ref. [149]);
- the **annotation diff tool** in the development environment calculates performance metrics such as precision, recall and F-measure for comparing different annotations. Typically the researcher marks manually some documents and then uses these along with the diff tool to automatically measure the performance of the tested components.
- GUK, **GATE Unicode Kit**, solves some technical problems with the Java Development Kit's support for Unicode.

B.3.1 ANNIE

ANNIE is an IE system originally derived from LaSIE (see Section 4.5.2), designed to be a portable IE system and useable in many different applications, on many different kinds of text and for many different purposes. Portability has a number of positive implications:

- it is able to handle at the same time documents in many different formats, from HTML pages to documents retrieved via optical character recognition, from very well-structured XML documents to unformatted e-mail messages with minor orthographic mistakes;
- it is very hardware-scalable. It can process large data volumes at high speed, scaling from small computers running personal desktop operating systems to very large parallel supercomputers;
- developers may adapt it to new circumstances with a minimum of effort;
- even its users may adapt the system up to the most possible extent;
- different languages can be processed, including editing and display of diverse character standards and conversion of diverse encodings into Unicode.

These issues are addressed by ANNIE in a variety of ways:

- it provides a development environment for technicians and programmes to adapt the core system. The advantages are that the core system can be designed for robustness and portability, computational complexity in extracting data is not limited by a learning algorithm, the engineering aspects of the process are taken in charge by the infrastructure (e.g. data visualisation, WWW component loading, performance evaluation). The disadvantage of this choice is that the adaptation process is labour intensive and it is difficult for end-users to acquire the necessary skills;
- the system learns part or all of the extraction knowledge from annotated training data. The advantage is a reduction in the need for human staff to port the system. The disadvantages are that extracted data must be either simple data or complex data from simple texts, such as seminar announcements, and that large volumes of training data are usually required;

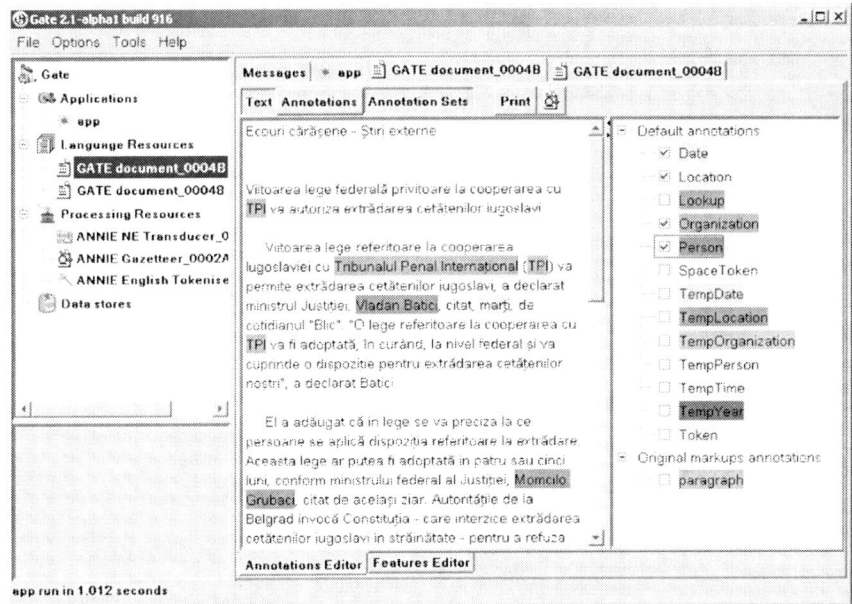

Figure B.2: GATE and ANNIE annotating a Romanian text (from Ref. [10]).

- the system enables end-users to customise it through a simplified access to the rules languages, the domain models and the gazetteers;
- the system embeds an error learning procedure within the end-user tools and in this way users may correct extraction's suggestions (see Figure B.2);
- ANNIE is written in Java and has cross-platform test suites to ensure portability from desktop to mainframe computers;
- Java's Unicode support has been extended to many different languages.

B.3.2 Architecture

ANNIE components are displayed in Figure B.3. Three components are taken directly from LaSIE system used in MUC-6, the **Lemmatiser**, the **Buchart parser** and the discourse interpreter **DisInt**, and are not described here.

The first component is the **tokeniser**, which splits the text into very simple tokens such as numbers, punctuation and words of different types, for example distinguishing between words in uppercase and lowercase and between certain types of punctuation marks. The aim is to limit the work of the tokeniser and therefore to maximise efficiency and enable more flexibility placing the burden on the grammar rules, which are more adaptable. A rule has a left-hand side and a right-hand side. The left-hand side is a regular expression, which can use the operators *or* and *and* and some typical regular expression quantity's operators (such as *one or more*) and

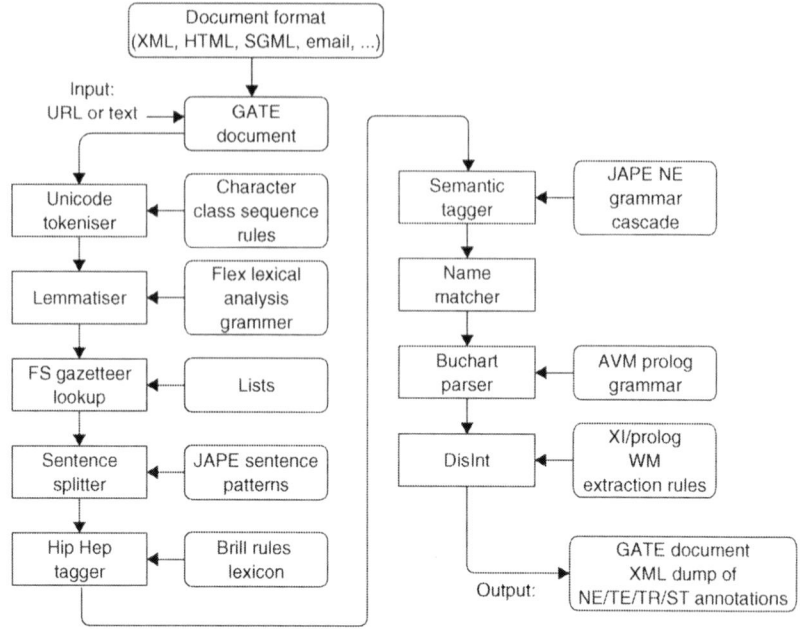

Figure B.3: ANNIE system architecture (from Ref. [11]).

which has to be matched on the input; the right-hand side describes the annotations to be added to the **annotation set**. In the default set of rules, the following kinds of tokens are possible:

Word: any set of contiguous capital or small letters, including a hyphen. No form of punctuation may be included. A word also has the attribute *orth*, which can take four possible values: *upper initial* (the initial letter is capital and the other ones are small, such as a personal name or the beginning of a sentence), *all caps* (all letters are capital, such as acronyms), *lower case* (all letters are small), *mixed caps* (a mixture of capital and small letters, such as in some acronyms);

Number: any combination of consecutive digits;

Symbol: *currency symbol* (e.g. $) and *symbol* (e.g. &). These are represented, respectively, by any number of consecutive currency or other symbols;

Punctuation: *start punctuation* (e.g. the left parenthesis), *end punctuation* (e.g. the right parenthesis) and *other punctuation* (e.g. the colon). Each punctuation symbol is a separate token, even when this breaks ellipses;

Space token: space characters and control characters. Any contiguous and homogenous set of space or control characters is defined as a single space token.

The above description applies to the default tokeniser, while, as for every module of GATE framework, alternative tokenisers with different rules can be created if necessary. The **English tokeniser** is a processing resource that comprises a normal tokeniser and a JAPE transducer. The transducer's task is to adapt the generic output of the tokeniser to the requirements of the English part-of-speech tagger. One such adaptation is the joining together in one token of constructs like years abbreviations (*'70s*), common spoken language abbreviations (*'cause*), Saxon genitive (*'s*), contractions (*'ll, 're, 've*), etc. Another task of the JAPE transducer is to convert negative contraction constructs like *can't* into two tokens *can* and *not*.

The **gazetteer** is a collection of lists containing a set of names, such as personal names, names of nations, companies, days of the week, etc. An index file is used to access these lists; for each list, a major type and an optional minor type are specified. These lists are compiled into finite-state machines. Any text tokens that are matched by these machines will be annotated with features specifying the major type and, when present, the minor type. Grammar rules then specify the types to be identified in particular circumstances. So, for example, if a specific day needs to be identified, the minor type *day* should be specified in the grammar, in order to match only information about specific days; if any kind of date needs to be identified, the major type *date* should be specified, to enable tokens annotated with any information about dates to be identified. In addition, the gazetteer allows other values to be associated with particular entries in a single list. ANNIE does not use this capability, but enables it for other system's gazetteers.

The **sentence splitter** is a sequence of finite-state transducers which segment the text into sentences, using mostly information from the punctuation. This module is required for the tagger. The splitter uses a gazetteer list of abbreviations to help distinguish the punctuation symbol indicating a full stop from the one indicating an abbreviation. Each sentence is annotated with the type sentence. Each sentence break, such as a full stop, is also given a *split* annotation. The sentence splitter is a domain-independent and application-independent module.

The **tagger** (see Ref. [150]) is a modified version of the **Brill tagger**, which produces a part-of-speech tag as an annotation on each word or symbol. The tagger uses a default lexicon and rule set which comes from training on a very large corpus taken from The Wall Street Journal. Both these modules can be modified manually if necessary.

ANNIE's **semantic tagger** is based on the Java Annotation Patterns Engine (JAPE), which allows the recognition of regular expressions in annotations on documents through a finite-state transduction over annotations based on regular expressions (JAPE is a version of CPSL Common Pattern Specification Language. For details, see Ref. [149]). It contains rules which, through regular expressions, modify annotations assigned in earlier modules.

The **OrthoMatcher** module adds identity relations between named-entities found by the semantic tagger, in order to enable later co-reference. It does not find any new named-entities, but it assigns a type to an unclassified proper name, using the type of a matching name. The matching rules are only invoked if the names being compared are both of the same type, i.e. both already tagged as organisations, or if one of them is classified as *unknown*. This prevents a previously classified name from being re-categorised.

B.3.3 Processing resource modules

The **pronominal co-reference** module is in charge of resolving anaphora using the JAPE grammar formalism. Anaphora are references to previously appeared words, while reference to implicit words (exophora) or to forward words (cataphora) are not taken care of.

This module is not automatically loaded with the other ANNIE modules, but can be loaded separately as a processing resource. The main module consists of three submodules: quoted text module, pleonastic *it* module and pronominal resolution module. The first two modules are helper submodules for the pronominal one, because they do not perform anything related to co-reference resolution except the location of quoted fragments and pleonastic *it* occurrences in text. They generate temporary annotations which are used by the pronominal submodule. For each pronoun the co-reference module generates an annotation of type *co-reference* containing two features: *antecedent offset*, a pointer to the starting node for the annotation which is proposed as the antecedent and *matches*, a list of pointer to annotations that comprise the co-reference chain comprising this anaphor/antecedent pair.

The **quoted speech submodule** identifies quoted fragments in the analysed text, using mostly quotation symbols. The identified chunks are used by the pronominal co-reference submodule for the proper resolution of pronouns referring to the first singular person which appears in quoted speech fragments. The module produces *quoted text annotations*. The submodule itself is a JAPE transducer which loads a JAPE grammar and builds a finite-state machine over it, which matches the quoted fragments and generates appropriate annotations that are used later by the pronominal module. The JAPE grammar consists of only four rules, which create temporary annotations for all punctuation marks that may enclose quoted speech, such as quotations, dashes, etc. Finally all temporary annotations generated during the processing, except the ones of type *quoted text*, are removed.

The **pleonastic *it* submodule** matches occurrences of words *it*, *its* and *itself*. It is a JAPE transducer similar to the quoted speech submodule, which operates with a grammar containing patterns that match the most commonly observed pleonastic it constructs.

The main functionality of the co-reference resolution module is in the **pronominal resolution submodule**. This uses the results from the execution of the quoted speech and pleonastic *it* submodules and works according to the following algorithm: first it preprocesses the current document, locating the annotations that the submodule need and prepares the appropriate data structures for them. Then, for each pronoun, it inspects the context and all the suitable antecedent candidates for this kind of pronoun and chooses the best one, if any. Finally, it creates the co-reference chains from the couple anaphora antecedent to the co-reference information supplied by the OrthoMatcher (this step is performed from the main co-reference module).

B.4 Ontotext Lab: KIM

Among the IE systems based on GATE infrastructure (see Section B.3), it is note-worthy mentioning **Knowledge and Information Management** (KIM) platform developed by Ontotext Lab [12, 151]. This platform provides semantic annotation, indexing, retrieval services and an infrastructure. The most important difference between KIM and other systems and approaches is that it performs semantic anno-tation and provides services based on the results. To do this in a consistent way, it uses as a basis for its data an ontology and a massive **knowledge base** (KB). The automatic semantic annotation is a classical named-entity recognition together with an annotation process. The traditional flat named-entity sets is composed of several general types. The semantic annotation provides specifically more precise type information, because the named-entity type is specified by reference to an ontology. Further, and more important, the semantic annotation requires a precise identification of the entity. While in a classical named-entity recognition guessing the type is the only goal of the task, a semantic annotation needs to recognise the entity and create a direct reference to it in a KB.

The KIM platform consists of **KIM Ontology** (KIMO), knowledge base, KIM Server with its API and the front-ends. The KIM API provides the program inter-face for semantic annotation, indexing and retrieval services. KIM ontologies and knowledge bases are kept in semantic repositories based on standard Semantic Web technology, including **RDF repositories** such as **SESAME9** [152]. In gen-eral, KIM provides a mature infrastructure based on GATE system for scalable and customisable IE as well as annotation and document management. The **Lucene information retrieval engine**, a high performance full text search engine available on http://jakarta.apache.org/lucene, is used and has been adapted to index docu-ments by entity types and measure relevance according to entities, along with tokens and stems. It is important to mention that KIM, as a software platform, is domain and task independent as are GATE, SESAME and Lucene.

B.4.1 Ontology and knowledge base

The KIM ontology KIMO consists of 250 general entity types and 100 entity rela-tions. The top classes are *entity, entity source* and *lexical resource*. The entity class is further subdivided into *object, abstract* and *happening*. The lexical resource branch is dedicated to encoding various data aiding the IE process, such as company suf-fixes, person first names, etc. An important sub-class of this branch is *alias*, which represents the alternative names for entities. The *has alias* relation is used to link an entity to its alternative names, while the official name of an entity is referred by the *has main alias* property. The instances of the entity source class are used to separate the trusted (pre-populated) information in the KB from those which will be automatically extracted later.

The KIM KB represents a projection of the world, according to the domain on which the system has to work. Each entity has information about its specific type, aliases, attributes and relations. For every new domain, independently from the IE engine, the system needs a starting KB to represent the basic entities that are considered important in the new domain. Moreover, KIM KB has been pre-populated with entities of general importance, that allow enough clues for the IE process to perform well on inter-domain web content. It consists of about 80,000 entities with more than 120,000 aliases from the WWW in the form of online encyclopedias, public servers, directories and gazetteers, including 50,000 locations and 8400 organisations.

The IE involved in KIM is concentrated mostly on the named-entity recognition task, which is considered to be the first step for further attribute, relation, event and scenario extraction. In order to identify the references of entity relations in the content, we should first identify the entities. Usually the entity references are associated with a NE type, such as *location, date*, etc. Then entities are organised in a deep hierarchical structure of NE types, to have a very fine grained specification and identification of world concepts. For example, it would be natural for an IE application performing company intelligence to keep more specialised sub-classes of *organisation* (e.g. such as *public company*).

The KIM IE process uses light-weight ontology KIMO defining the entity types. In addition to the hierarchical ordering, each class is coupled with its appropriate attributes. The relation types are also defined with their domain and range restrictions. Given the ontology, the entities in the text could be linked to their type. However the system goes further, and identifies not only the type of the NE but also keep its semantic description and extends it with the IE process. Thus the NE references in the text are linked to an entity individual in the KB. The accessibility of the semantic descriptions of entities in the KB would allow the IE process to later base on attributes and relations as clues for recognition and disambiguation. For example, if a person appears along with a town in the content, and there are two town that have the same name (alias), there is an ambiguity. KIM checks whether the person has some previously defined relations with one of the towns, and if so, the related town will be chosen as a better candidate and associated with the NE reference in the content.

B.4.2 Architecture

KIM IE is based on the GATE framework, which has proved its maturity, extensibility and task independency for many natural language applications. Ontotext has reused much of GATE's document management functionality, namely generic NLP components as the tokeniser, the tagger, and the sentence splitter. These processing layers are provided by the GATE platform, together with their pattern-matching grammars, NE co-reference and others, as standardised modules for a further construction of sophisticated IE applications. Ontotext has changed the grammar components to handle entity class information and match rules according to it. Moreover, the grammar rules are based on the ontology classes, rather than on a flat set of NE types as in GATE. This allows much more flexibility in the creation of

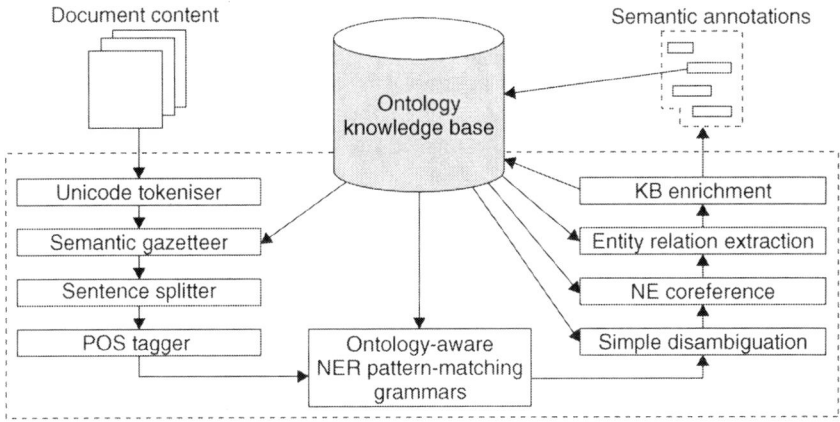

Figure B.4: KIM information extraction architecture (from Ref. [12]).

recognition rules at the most appropriate level of generality, giving the opportunity to handle more specific NE types.

The KIM architecture can be seen in detail in Figure B.4. Here we describe only the modules which change from standard GATE architecture.

In the **semantic gazetteer** the lists of a traditional text-lookup component are changed with a knowledge base that keeps the entities with their aliases and descriptions, as well as the lexical resources (such as possible male person first names). These are used to initialise the semantic gazetteer component, which keeps the various aliases and their type and instance references as Uniform Resource Identifiers (URI), a compact string of characters used to identify or name a resource, with a syntax is defined through schemes (the most famous example of URI are addresses of web pages). When a known lexical resource or entity alias is found in the text, the semantic gazetteer generates an annotation with a link to a class in the ontology. Since many entities share aliases (e.g. *New York* is both a *state* and a *city*) it often happens that one NE reference in the text may be associated with different possible types and instances. At this phase, the system associates all the equivalent possibilities as annotations. Later, simple disambiguation techniques are applied to filter out some of the alternative annotations. This phase is the entry-point for association of annotations in the text with a class in the ontology and with an instance in the KB.

A **grammar processor** called JAPE is a part of the GATE platform, and allows the specification of rules that deal with patterns of annotations. Ontotext has modified the JAPE processor to handle class information and, according to this information, match patterns of annotations. The NE grammars are based on the ones used in ANNIE within the GATE project. In the modified grammars, the definition of a rule goes through specification of the class restrictions for the entities in the pattern. The matching process takes information from the ontology to decide whether the possible annotation has the same class as (or a sub-class of) the class in the considered pattern. Thus it can be specified a pattern referring to a more general class (e.g. organisation), allowing all of its sub-classes (e.g. commercial, educational, non-profit and other organisations) to be compatible with the grammar rule. At this point the suggested candidates for entities are evaluated. Some of them are taken into account and are transformed to final NE annotations. These inherit the type and instance information from the lookup annotations generated by the gazetteer. Other NE annotations are constructed by the grammar processor according to the patterns in the text. These annotations have an entity type, but lack the instance information since they have not yet been associated with an existing KB entry. Later, template relations extraction takes place, identifying some relations that the entities show in the text.

The next module is the **orthographic NE co-reference** component, that generates lists of matching entity annotations within the same type, according to their text representation. It re-uses GATE's co-reference module, extending it to also include the instance information of the recognised entities, thus enabling different representations of an entity to be matched if they are aliases of the same KB individual. The result of the co-reference component is that groups of matching entities are created. Then, these groups are used to determine the instance information and the aliases of new entities.

Theoretically there are many different entity aliases in the KB that are equivalent to a NE reference in the text. For such references the semantic gazetteer generates different annotations. Thus, an over-generation of semantic annotations is produced due to the richness of the KB and the human habit of naming different things with same names. During the gazetteer lookup phase it is impossible to disambiguate because of the lack of clues since the gazetteer layer uses only its raw content and does not have access to information from other components. Therefore, **simple disambiguation** techniques take place in the pattern-matching grammars phase.

The last phase is not part of the standard IE systems. The newly recognised entity annotations lack instance information and are still not linked to the KB. However these entity annotations can represent entities that are in the already recognised part of the KB. At first, the system matches the entity annotations by their class information and string representation against the set of recognised entities. If it finds a matching entity individual, the annotation gets its instance identifier. Otherwise it builds a new entity individual and adds it to the KB together with its aliases derived from the list of matching entities. At this point the system has linked all generated named-entity annotations to the ontology (through their type information) and to the KB (through their specific instance). The relation annotations generated by the template relation extraction grammars are used to generate the corresponding entity relations in the KB.

B.4.3 Evaluation and results

To measure the named-entity recognition performance of KIM a modified version of **GATE Corpus Benchmark Tool** was used. Two sequential versions of the KIM platform were compared against a human annotated corpus, thus counting the changes of the performance from version to version. The evaluation corpus contains 100 documents of news articles from UK media sources (The Financial Times, The Independent and Guardian). We have to note that this evaluation does not take into account the fact that KIM provides much more information than a simple named-entity recogniser, since is semantic annotation is much more specific and linked to the KB. The final result of KIM is a precision of 0.86 and a recall of 0.84. Further details can be found in Refs. [12, 151].

B.5 LoLo

Local Grammar for Learning Terminology (LoLo) system is developed by University of Surrey [153] and has three distinguishing features:

- it is built for English and Arabian languages,
- it extracts pattern for the pattern matcher using N-grams without introducing any keyword, thus being adaptable to any new domain;
- for the financial domain, it focuses its evaluation on **sentiment analysis**, which means that it considers the impact of news on market movements. Therefore it extracts mostly templates which deal with rise and fall rumours, especially how and when they appear and disappear from the news.

The objective of this system is to use methods and techniques of IE in the automatic analysis of specialist news that streams in such a way that information extracted at an earlier period of time may be contradicted or reinforced by information extracted at a later time. As we pointed out in Chapter 1, the impact of news on financial and stock markets is extremely important and its analysis takes the name of sentiment analysis. The prefix *sentiment* is used to distinguish this kind of analysis from fundamental analysis and technical analysis. Engle's statistical analysis suggests that the bad news has longer lasting effect than good news (see Refs. [154, 155]). Usually, sentiment analysis is performed using news proxies which include news' dates and times and the names of agencies releasing the news.

B.5.1 Architecture

LoLo is developed using the Microsoft.NET platform and contains four components: the **corpus analyser**, the rules editor, the information extractor and the information visualiser. The first module starts with denoting numbers as <no> and then it automatically extracts patterns from a corpus of domain-specific texts without prescribing the metaphorical keywords and organisation names. This is achieved looking at the **lexical signature** of a specialist domain and extracting typical patterns of the individual items of the lexical signature. The lexical signature includes key vocabulary items of the domain (for the financial domain, typical verbs such as "*buy*") and names of people, places and things typical of the domain. Given a specialist corpus, keywords are identified and **collocates**, words which appear near each other in a text more frequently than it would be expected by chance, of the keywords are extracted. The keyword may appear close to words that have frequencies higher than the keyword itself – and in this case they are usually grammatical words – or close to words that have lesser frequency – and in this case they are usually lexical words such as nouns, adjectives and are therefore good candidates for compound words. Sentences containing these keyword's collocates are then used to construct a sub-corpus, which is then analysed and **word tri-grams**, ordered triplet of words such as "it is not", above a frequency threshold in the sub-corpus are extracted; the position of the tri-grams in each of the sentences is also noted. The sub-corpus is searched again for contiguous tri-grams and these couples of tri-grams are used to build the pattern for the pattern matching. For example, if a tri-gram is noted for its frequency as a sentence initial position and appears with another frequent tri-gram at the next position, then the two tri-grams are used to form a pattern. This process is continued until all the tri-grams in the sentence are matched with the significant tri-grams. These domain-specific patterns are then used to extract similar patterns and information from a test corpus to validate the patterns found in the training corpus.

The **rules editor** exports the extraction patterns as regular expressions, which are then used by the IE for pattern matching. The **visualiser** displays a time-series that shows how the extracted events emerge, repeat and fade over time in relation to other events or in relation with a previously defined time series of financial events. This is very useful for analysing any relations between different events or understanding the trends in the appearing of information.

B.5.2 Evaluation and results

For each of the two languages, English and Arabian, a corpus of 1.72 million tokens was created. Each corpus was then divided into two equally sized training corpus and testing corpus, which was further divided into two testing corpora. The system was tested on the first and on the second corpus.

The evaluation is, as for every system focused on pattern creation, without a template filling system. However, in this case the system task is not necessarily easier, since it produces also a very useful time sequence information. Unfortunately the system's evaluation was very concentrated on time variations and therefore only the results of the first four typical market variations patterns (share goes up, share goes down, index goes up, percentage variation) were considering, instead of considering complete precision and recall measures on the whole set of events to extract, yielding a precision in English from 0.88 to 1.

B.6 University of Wisconsin's systems

University of Wisconsin's system [156] uses **Hidden Markov Models** (HMMs) [157] to extract couples of relevant words from biomedical scientific articles. Even though the subject is not the same, the task has some strong similarities with the extraction of data from financial articles, since both aim at extracting the name of an

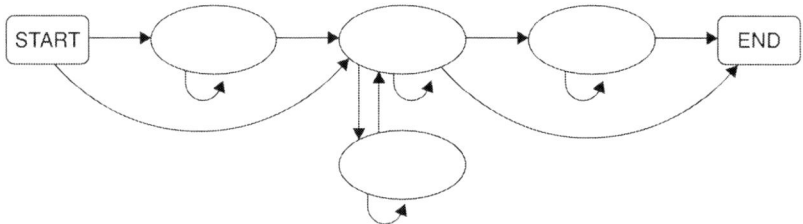

Figure B.5: An example of HMMs.

actor (the protein in this case or the company in our case) and its effect or its relation with other entities (for example, a disorder in this case and a predator company in our case). Therefore this system does not aim at extracting single words, but the relation between couples of words.

HMMs are the components of a statistical process, called Markov process, composed of a set of states (see Figure B.5) and a set of transitions between states. Each state may emit tokens with a certain probability distribution and each transition has a probability distribution to lead the process into another state. The University of Wisconsin's approach starts from a syntactic parsing of the sentences using **Sundance system**, developed by University of Utah (see http://www.cs.utah.edu/nlp), producing a sequence of sentence segments, each consisting of the words and of their grammatical type. Moreover, if a word is found in the relevant sentences which belongs to a template's keywords set, it is annotated with the corresponding template's label. The state of HMMs represent these annotated segments and each state can emit only segments with the same grammatical type.

Once HMMs are built on relevant and non-relevant sentences, they are trained using Baum–Welch algorithm and modified forward, backward and Viterbi algorithms (further information on the algorithm used by this system can be found in [156] and on HMMs training algorithms in [157, 158]). Using this modified algorithms the system then determines the most likely path through the states and it fills a template extracting a couple (or, more generic, a N-uple) when the probability of emission of the sentence by the model trained on relevant document is larger than the probability of emission by the model trained on non-relevant documents and when the two template's slots (or, more generic, the N slots) are filled. When the sentence contains more than one template to be filled, they are filled in the order in which they occur (which probably is fine in the biomedical sector but may cause severe misinterpretations for complex financial news sentences) and in case less slots, than the template required number, of a type are filled, the last slots of that type is used several times (i.e., if the sentence contains A1 B A2 A3, the extracted couples are (A1, B), (A2, B), (A3, B)), which again may cause severe misunderstanding in financial information extraction (IE).

The system was tested with two templates on 1 437 relevant sentences (containing 1 544 couples) and over 18,000 non-relevant sentences against similar models which do not use HMMs or use a simplified version. According to the template results vary, in the best case an increase of precision by 0.30 with a constant recall.

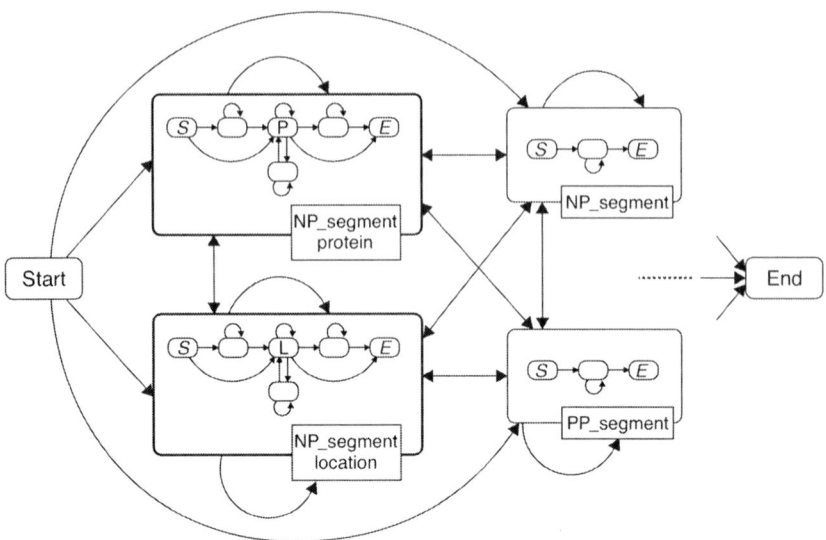

Figure B.6: HHMMs used by University of Wisconsin (from Ref. [13]).

A suggested variant [13] uses **Hierarchical Hidden Markov Models** (HHMMs), which are HMMs at different grammatical level, i.e. a model for the words inside sentences and a model for the sentences inside a document. HHMMs were first introduced by [159] and are now adopted by many sectors of computational linguistics, especially automatic speech recognition. Experiments on the same two templates' extraction tasks shows a further improvement of precision and recall (Figure B.6).

B.7 Elie

Elie system [160, 161] is developed at University College Dublin and applies relatively standard machine learning algorithms to extract the start and the end positions of every pattern which is going to fill a template. Its innovative contribution is to apply a parser with a high precision but low recall, and then to retrieve the missed positions using a high recall parser. The first module, called **L1**, is a **tag-matcher** which is trained on a large quantity of non-relevant sentences and few relevant sentences. Its task is to find start and end positions of tokens and, due to its peculiar training, its precision is very high, so this module can be seen as very reliable. Each position is annotated with its token, its part-of-speech, orthographic information and information taken from a gazetteer containing names of people, countries and cities, titles. Moreover, to each couple of start-end positions a probability is assigned based on the length of the matching. However, due to a low recall, L1 misses a lot of positions. Whenever a start position is identified but not its respective end position, or viceversa, the **L2** module is applied. This module is focused on a high recall performance, and quite often manages to find the missing position.

This system was tested on three data sets: the seminar announcements set from Carnegie Mellon University [162], the job position data set [163] and the Reuters corporate acquisition data set [162]. Each set was split in two parts used for training and testing. Experimental results show significative improvements with respect to other systems. In particular, the last data set consists of 600 articles from which seven template slots were extracted. The results were not so good as for the other two sets (precision from 0.28 to 0.63 and recall from 0.09 to 0.62), however the application of L2 module managed to increase recall from L1 by more than 50% with a precision loss below 30% and a general significative increase in the F-measure.

Appendix C: Other systems

This appendix presents systems that perform different tasks which may not strictly be qualified neither as IE nor information retrieval. However, these tools can produce interesting results such as surfing automatically the WWW and writing summaries of the most relevant articles, like Newsblaster in Section C.3, or message filtering like Assentor. Moreover, the ideas and techniques underlying these systems can be adapted in information extraction systems, such as the domain-specific terminology extraction algorithm of TermExtractor in Section C.4.

C.1 Assentor

C.1.1 Introduction and scope

Financial institutions, investment banks, and some companies that strongly rely on confidential research projects are heavily regulated entities where employees are subject to important restrictions such as policies and physical arrangements designed to manage confidential information and prevent the inadvertent spread and misuse of inside information, limitations in the way they can interact with their customers, etc. In addition, there are various financial regulations regarding important problems such as money laundering, insider trading, etc. With the advent of electronic methods of fast communications, such as e-mail and, more recently, instant messaging (e.g. in financial applications Bloomberg instant messaging or Reuters 3000 XTra instant messaging), companies are even more exposed and responsible for what their employees communicate to the outside area. Monitoring such activities is extremely difficult without the use of automatic tools, and doing it manually may also be forbidden by national privacy laws.

Therefore, filtering these messages has become an area where information extraction tools applied to finance are being progressively introduced. While these tools are not used directly for taking or helping to take investment decisions, they are extremely important for the financial institutions because of the importance of aspects such as compliance for their success.

One of the key tools in this area is Assentor. Assentor was originally developed by SRA. The rights to the Assentor products were subsequently bought by

Ilumin and by CA, which expanded the Assentor range to comprise several different tools:

Assentor archive: The archiving solution that is the foundation of all Assentor product line.

Assentor mailbox manager: A personal and end-user access to Assentor archive.

Assentor compliance: A content inspection and quarantining tool in support of a wide-range of regulatory (Securities and Exchange Commission, National Association of Securities Dealers and New York Stock Exchange) and corporate requirements.

Assentor list examiner: A tool that monitors and provides language specific analysis on national, international and customer proprietary lists of restricted entities (Office of Foreign Assets Control, Federal Bureau of Investigation, World Bank, etc.).

Assentor discovery: A searching and retrieval tool.

The most interesting tool for IE is the Assentor compliance module because it uses pattern matching techniques and has a direct application to the financial area. Assentor compliance uses intelligent natural language patterns to identify and flag a wide range of regulatory, industry specific and corporate policy violations. One of its main uses is **intelligent message surveillance**. Through the use of IE techniques, it is able to quarantine suspect messages that could potentially violate federal, industry and corporate regulations. If it finds unacceptable or suspect communications in the message content, it stops the message from leaving (or entering) the company e-mail stream and routes it to an authorised compliance officer for review. In detail, Assentor compliance performs the following tasks:

- It reviews incoming and outgoing messages and attachments, retains a permanent record of the results, and tracks all associated events.
- It scans e-mail and attachments for non-compliant language and breaches in corporate policy.
- It fulfills SEC rules number 17a-3 and 17a-4 archiving requirements, NASD rule number 3010(d) and NYSE rule number 342.
- It has customisable message surveillance capabilities.
- It provides centralised management of content policies.
- It is transparent to the user and requires no change in existing e-mail usage to deploy.

Assentor compliance is therefore able to identify cases such as firm preservation patterns, jokes or profanity and confidential information. And, more in particular, is able to stop illegal financial activities such as stock manipulation, insider activity, unauthorised rumours, inside knowledge, money laundering, high-pressure tactics, stock hype and restricted issues.

C.1.2 Architecture and performance

Being a commercial package currently being offered to high-profile financial institutions, it is very difficult for us to access technical information. However, we do know that the system was originally developed by SRA and that this would have profited from SRA's strong experience in the field of pattern matching based IE. Therefore, the technologies employed are most likely related to the other products which have been developed by SRA, in particular their IE systems which competed in the MUC competitions, such as the Hasten system described in Section A.1.

As far as the performance of the system is concerned, we again do not have access to any specific statistics regarding this. Ilumin, however, stressed the fact that the system was licensed to over 250,000 users and it was being used by over 100 of the top financial firms.

C.2 NewsInEssence

C.2.1 Introduction and scope

NewsInEssence (NIE) is a summarisation system in development by the University of Michigan since March 2001 [14]; a full working version can be accessed on the web (in December 2007) at http://lada.si.umich.edu:8080/clair/nie1/nie.cgi. NIE retrieves news from on-line versions of British, Canadian, South African and Australian newspapers, as well as English language versions of on-line newspapers from India, Singapore and China. Then NIE performs a clustering of articles, a topic tracking and multi-document summarisation.

The main feature of NIE compared to other systems is that it focuses on the summarisation and grouping of news which are available online on the Internet. The number and quality of news available on the WWW has been growing very quickly over the past few years. Many newspaper or news agency make available to their customers electronic versions of their articles either free or on subscription. As a result users have access to a huge amount of information which provides many benefits over traditional printed news in terms of quantity and quality, but together with these benefits come challenges. On the WWW, there are hundreds of on-line reliable news sources (e.g. *Reuters, The Financial Times*, etc.) and they usually publish several articles each day, sometimes more than in their paper version. As a result users are overwhelmed with the sheer volume of news. For a reader interested in a given topic, this overload threatens to negate the benefits of on-line news because finding and reading all related articles becomes impractical.

The goal of NewsInEssence (http://www.newsinessence.com) is to help alleviate these problems by acting as the user's secretary and gather and produce a concise summer of the related online news articles. As soon as the user specifies a topic (which may be indicated through an example article or, more traditionally, through keywords), NIE searches across tens of news sites to build a **cluster** of related stories. It then generates a summary of the entire cluster, highlighting its most important content.

C.2.2 Architecture of the system

To build a news summarisation service, it is important to consider the way journalists write news. Traditionally, they are trained to use the so-called **inverse pyramid**

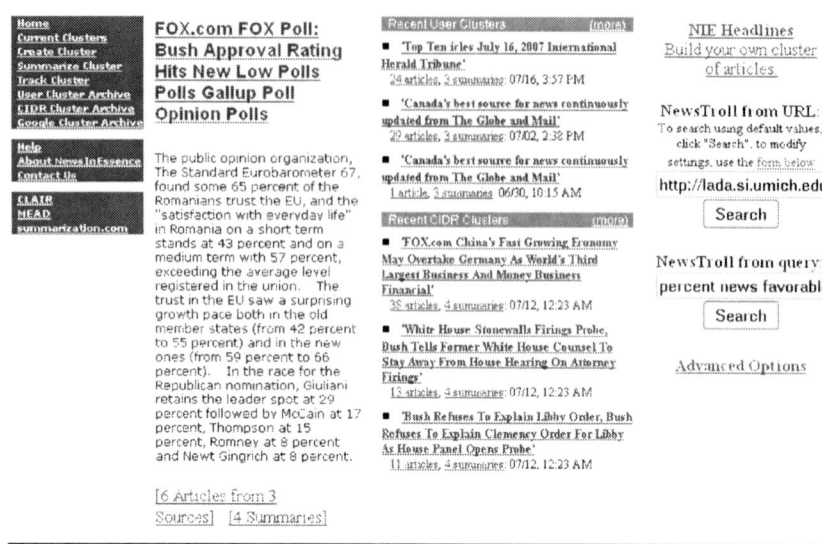

Figure C.1: NewsInEssence application example.

structure technique [164]. The article usually begins with a broad overview of the situation of event, to give the human reader an immediate grasp of the content, followed by finer details.

Many summarises, including NIE, create a summary by extracting important sentences from the input documents. The challenging aspect of this extractive summarisation technique is that content and writing style vary significantly according to the source (on-line version of paper newspaper, news agency short articles, advertisement, etc.), to the writer and to the topic (financial information, sport news, political events, etc.). These stylistic differences make it difficult to detect that there is a relationship between two articles. This is particularly true on the Internet, where NIE finds related articles published by news organisations in different countries, or intended for different audiences.

The central object in NewsInEssence is the cluster. A cluster consists of typically 2–30 topically related news articles. For each document in the cluster, NIE displays the article's title, source, publication date and original URL. Figure C.1 shows how the end application displays the cluster information.

C.2.3 Implementation

NewsInEssence's topic-focused search is implemented by a web-crawling agent called **NewsTroll** [165]. Beginning with a given news story's URL or with keywords, NewsTroll attempts to gather a cluster of related stories from the Internet in real time.

The agent runs in two phases. In the first phase, it looks for related articles by traversing links from the page containing the seed article. Using the seed article and any related articles it finds in this way, the program then decides on a set of keywords, using a modified **TF-IDF technique** to pick out words used often in this cluster but rarely in general. The TF–IDF weight (term frequency and inverse document frequency) is a weight used in information retrieval to evaluate how important a word is to a document in a collection. The importance increases proportionally to the number of times a word appears in the document but is offset by the frequency of the word in the corpus. For other examples of this scoring technique, see Section 4.5.1.

Once settled on a set of keywords to use, it enters the second search phase. In this phase, it attempts to add articles to the cluster using the search engines of six news websites and using the keywords that have been found in the first phase as search terms.

In both phases, NewsTroll selectively follows hyperlinks from its start page, i.e. the seed URL in the first phase and the news site search pages in the second phase. In selecting which links to follow, NewsTroll aims to reach pages which contain related stories or further hyperlinks to such pages. The program uses several levels of rule-based filtering in order to reduce the number of non-relevant harvested pages. Only when NewsTroll determines that a URL is interesting according to these rules, it goes to the Internet and fetches the linked page. That page's hyperlinks are then extracted for review. A more stringent set of (mostly site-specific) rules are applied to determine whether the URL is likely to be a news story itself. In this case, the similarity of its text to that of the original seed page is taken into account. This similarity is measured as the cosine distance between IDF-weighted n-dimensional vector representations of the two documents. Cosine similarity is a measure of similarity between two vectors of n-dimensions by finding the angle between them. Their vectors are built using keywords (for detailed information see Refs. [166, 167]). If the measured similarity is above a given threshold, the page is considered to contain a related news article and is added to the cluster.

By using the logic of its rules and employing successively rigours layers of filtering as described above, NewsTroll is able to filter out large numbers of web pages.

The NewsTroll algorithm is briefly described in a programming language format in Figure C.2.

Standardisation of input HTML documents is achieved translating all the documents into Extensible Markup Language (XML), with source, URL, headline, description, title, keywords, date and text. Then a XSL-based translation is performed, taking as input the XML documents and producing a single XML index

```
Input : SeedUrl, SitesToSearch, ExitConditions
Output: Cluster

Cluster-<SeedUrl
WeightedKeywords<-get_common_keywords(SeedUrl, SeedUrl)
LinkedUrls-<get_links(SeedUrl)

//first search
while UrlToTest<- next(LinkedUrls) && PrimaryExitCondition ! = true
  if follows_useful_rules(UrlToTest)
    LinkedUrls<- LinkedUrls + get_links(UrlToTest)
  if follows_article_rules(UrlToTest) && (similarity(SeedUrl,
  UrlToTest) > threshold)
    Cluster<- Cluster + UrlToTest
    WeightedKeyWords<- WeightedKeyWords + get_common_keywords(SeedUrl,
    UrlToTest)

SecSearchKeyWords<- max_n(WeightedKeyWords)

//second search
while SearchSite<-next(SiteToSearch) && SecondaryExitCondition != true
  SearchPage<- generate_search(SearchSite, SecSearchKeyWords)
  LinkedUrls<- get_links(SearchPage)
  while UrlToTestc<- next(LinkedUrls) && SecondaryExitCondition != true
    if follows_useful_rules (UrlToTest)
      LinkedUrls<- LinkedUrls + get_links(UrlToTest)
    if follows_article_rules(UrlToTest) && (similarity(SeedUrl,
    UrlToTest) > threshold)
      Cluster<- Cluster + UrlToTest

Return Cluster
```

Figure C.2: NewsTroll algorithm (from Ref. [14]).

file which contains index data for each of the articles in the cluster. Once the stories found by the NewsTroll agent are translated into XML and an index file generated, the user can use the system's graphical interface to visualise the cluster. The interface uses the document metadata extracted in the conversion process to represent each article.

C.3 Newsblaster

C.3.1 Introduction and scope

Newsblaster, a project developed by the Columbia Natural Language Processing Group [168], represents the next level of evolution for news on the web. The service monitors 17 major web news services (*CNN, Reuters, Fox News*, etc.), and groups related stories together for easy access, reading the news, using natural language and AI techniques, and then actually writes short summaries of each major news event based on what it has understood.

As the underlying technology improves and is extended, it is easy to see how this sort of approach can be used to develop customised web crawlers that users tailor to understand their own interests and send out on autonomous search missions [169]. If such a system were combined with a URL monitoring service and a set of subjects interesting for the user, it can effectively be a web advisory service, automatically creating directories of relevant websites annotated with high-level summaries that would spare time of manual searching.

The Newsblaster system is already under attention of the press and public. A recent analysis indicates that Newsblaster receives tens of thousands of hits a day, and news agencies that have written articles about Newsblaster include *The New York Times, USA Today* and *Le Monde*. From 2007 Newsblaster is no more open to general public use, but is still running for educational and research purposes (Figure C.3).

Even trough Newsblaster does not perform any information extraction, its clustering and the information retrieval techniques it uses to produce summaries can be adapted to information extraction tasks in finance.

C.3.2 Centrifuser

Newsblaster system uses the summarisation engine Centrifuser, developed by Columbia University [15, 170, 171], a domain- and genre-specific multi-document summarisation system. It builds both extract-based summaries as well as indicative document cluster summaries. The extract summary gives a wide overview of the

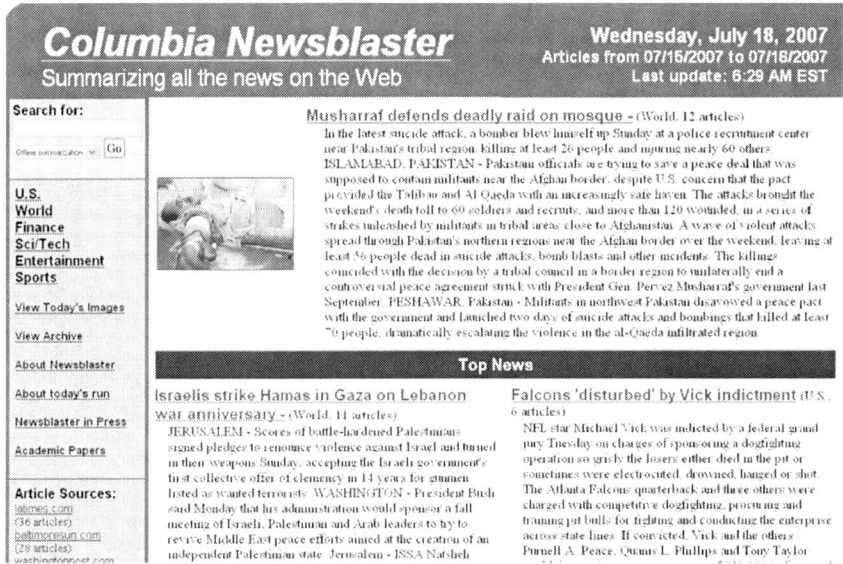

Figure C.3: Newsblaster application example (from Natural Language Processing Group website at Columbia University).

query topic suitable for browsers. The latter summaries differentiate the documents from each other as much as possible to route lead to particular documents that can meet their information needs. Even though Centrifuser focuses on patient health care documents, its techniques can be adapted to the financial domain.

The query results also include details, such as relative length that differ among types of documents taking correctly into consideration the average length of each article type. The results also detail whether or not a document in the set has certain specified sections, or which documents contain figures and tables. In order to compare results, the system sets up a topic tree for every query term by comparing all the sub-heads in the documents.

Each document is viewed as a tree of topics (Figure C.4) and these trees are intersected to find similarities and differences. In the heartburn domain, the *definition, symptoms* and *causes* of most problems are nearly always signaled by distinct section headings within documents. Each of these branches can have five sub-branches. Once a search engine knows that the document is relevant to the search query, the system matches the query to a particular node of each document, which may be the root node of the tree, as in the case of *heartburn treatments*, or in another position, as in the case of *facts about heartburn*.

The system sets up a composite tree by comparing all the documents to get an idea of what an average document is like. For example even if the heartburn documents do not have *prognosis* as a topic, the system can infer the typical structure of patient information documents by looking at related documents that have the same structure. The software sorts references and sub-heads, focusing on those that occur more often in the query documents. When a section is not featured in another document and is too far down from the main branches, it might be discarded as non-relevant. Centrifuser then generates natural language summaries of text based on the types of information that are really useful, extracting sentences or list items that occur across documents and checking morphological and subject–verb agreements. The software also extracts descriptors such as the author's name, media format and categorisation keywords if they are available as metadata in the documents.

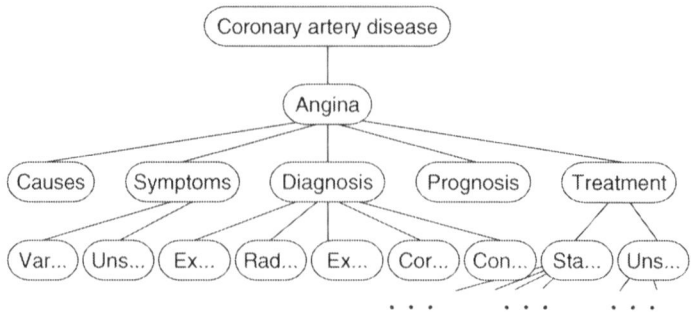

Figure C.4: Centrifuser's tree structure (from Ref. [15]).

C.3.3 System description

In Centrifuser, each document is represented by a tree, which breaks the document's topic into sub-topics. They are built automatically for structured documents using a simple approach that takes into account section headers. Other methods such as layout identification and text segmentation are used as a basis to build such trees in structured and unstructured documents. The **composite topic tree** contains also normative values calculated for each document feature to properly compute differences between documents. Figure C.5 shows a partial view of such a tree constructed for consumer healthcare articles. The composite topic tree carries topic information for all articles of a particular domain and genre combination. It encodes each topic's relative typicality, its prototypical position within an article, as well as variant lexical forms that it may be expressed as. For instance, in the composite topic tree in Figure C.5, the topic *Symptoms* is very typical, may be expressed as the variant *Signs* and usually comes after other its sibling topics (*Definition* and *Cause*). The system aligns multiple document topic trees using similarity metrics, and then merges the similar topics, resulting in a composite topic tree.

Centrifuser works in three steps to generate the summary: **content calculation**, planning and realisation. In the first, potential summary content is evaluated determining which input topics are present in the document set. For each topic, the system determines its relevance to the query and its similarity to the prototype, given knowledge about the topics covered in the domain. In detail, each document is converted to a tree of topics and each of the topics is assigned a topic type according to its relationship to the query. In the **planning** phase, the content planner uses a text plan to select information to be included in the summary. The system

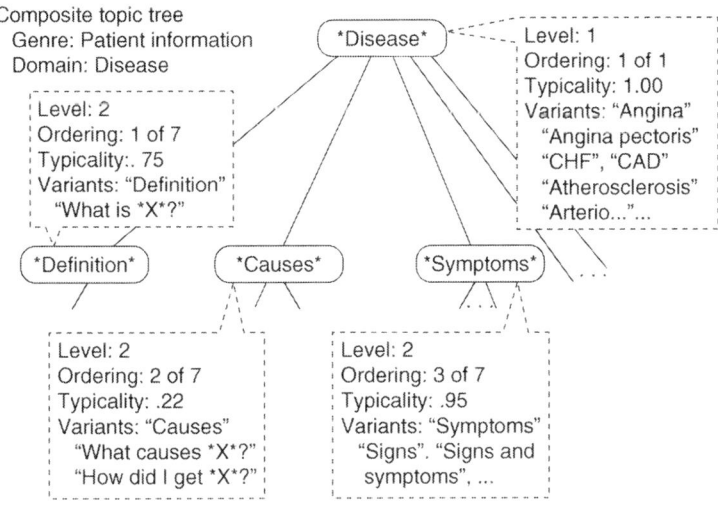

Figure C.5: Centrifuser's composite topic tree structure (from Ref. [15]).

determines that of seven document types each document belongs to, based on the relevance of its topics to the query and their similarity to the prototype. The plan generates a separate description for the documents in each document type. In the final **realisation** step, the resulting description is put in a lexical form to produce the summary.

C.4 TermExtractor

TermExtractor, developed by University of Rome La Sapienza [172, 173], is a terminology extractor. Terminology extraction is a sub-task of information extraction, whose goal is to automatically extract relevant terms from a given corpus.

In the last years, an ever growing number of communities and networked enterprises started to access and interoperate through the Internet. Modelling these communities and their information needs is important for several web applications, like web crawlers or web services. One of the first steps to model the knowledge domain of a virtual community is to collect a vocabulary of domain-relevant terms, thus building the linguistic surface manifestation of domain concepts. Typically, approaches to automatic term extraction use linguistic processors (part of speech tagging) to extract terminological candidates, i.e. syntactically plausible terminological noun phrases (e.g. *"credit card"*, *"board of directors"*). These word entries are then filtered from the candidate list using statistical and machine learning methods. Once filtered, since they show a low ambiguity and high specificity, these terms are particularly useful to define a knowledge domain or to support the creation of a domain ontology. Moreover, terminology extraction is a very useful starting point for semantic similarity, knowledge management, and information extraction.

TermExtractor extracts terminology in a specific application domain. The software takes as input a corpus of domain documents, parses them and extracts a list of syntactically plausible terms (compounds, adjective-nouns, etc.). Documents parsing assigns a greater importance to terms with text layouts (title, abstract, bold, italic, underlined, etc.). Two entropy-based measures, called domain relevance and domain consensus are then used. **Domain consensus** is used to select only the terms that are consensually referred throughout the corpus documents. **Domain relevance** is instead used to select only the terms which are relevant to the domain of interest and it is computed with reference to a set of contrastive terminologies from different domains. Finally, extracted terms are further filtered using **lexical cohesion** that measures the degree of association of the words in a terminological string.

In 2007, TermExtractor has been submitted for large-scale evaluation in the domain of enterprise interoperability by the members of a network of excellence, the INTEROP NoEc. Given the good performance of the tool, a public web application has been developed, and is currently available at http://lcl2.uniroma1.it/termextractor.

Bibliography

[1] Yangarber, R., Grishman, R. & NYU, Description of the proteus/PET system as used for MUC-7 st. *Proceeding of the Seventh Messages Understanding Conference (MUC-7)*, DARPA, 1998.

[2] TPS Group & BBN, Description of the plum system as used for MUC-6. *Proceeding of the Sixth Messages Understanding Conference (MUC-6)*, DARPA, Morgan Kaufmann Publishers, 1995.

[3] Krupka, G.R. & SRA, Description of the SRA system as used for MUC-6. *Proceeding of the Sixth Messages Understanding Conference (MUC-6)*, DARPA, Morgan Kaufmann Publishers, 1995.

[4] Aberdeen, J., Burger, J., Day, D., Hirschman, L., Robinson, P., Vilain, M. & MITRA, Description of the alembic system used for MUC-6. *Proceeding of the Sixth Messages Understanding Conference (MUC-6)*, DARPA, Morgan Kaufmann Publishers, 1995.

[5] Lee, R. & Sterling Software, A nltoolset-based system for MUC-6. *Proceeding of the Sixth Messages Understanding Conference (MUC-6)*, DARPA, Morgan Kaufmann Publishers, 1995.

[6] Fukumoto, J., Masui, F., Shimohata, M., Sasaki, M. & Oki Electric Industry, Description of the Oki system as used for MUC-7. *Proceeding of the Seventh Messages Understanding Conference (MUC-7)*, DARPA, 1998.

[7] Borthwick, A., Sterling, J., Agichtein, E., Grishman, R. & NYU, Description of the mene named entity system as used in MUC-7. *Proceeding of the Seventh Messages Understanding Conference (MUC-7)*, DARPA, 1998.

[8] Black, W.J., Rinaldi, F., Mowatt, D. & Facile, Description of the NE system used for MUC-7. *Proceeding of the Seventh Messages Understanding Conference (MUC-7)*, DARPA, 1998.

[9] Patwardhan, S. & Riloff, E., Effective information extraction with semantic affinity patterns and relevant regions. *Proceedings of the 2007 Joint Conference on Empirical Methods in Natural Language Processing and Computational Natural Language Learning (EMNLP-CoNLL)*, Prague, Czech Republic, June 28–30, 2007.

[10] Bontcheva, K., Maynard, D., Tablan, V., Cunningham, H. & GATE: A unicode-based infrastructure supporting multilingual information extraction. *Proceedings of the Workshop on Information Extraction for Slavonic and other Central and Eastern European Languages*, Borovets, Bulgaria, 8–9 September, 2003.

[11] Cunningham, H., Maynard, D., Bontcheva, K., Tablan, V. & Ursu, C., The Gate User Guide, University of Sheffield, 2007. Available at http://gate.ac.uk/sale/tao/index.html or http://gate.ac.uk/sale/tao/tao.pdf.

[12] Popov, B., Kiryakov, A., Manov, D., Kirilov, A., Ognyanoff, D. & Goranov, M., Towards semantic web information extraction. *Proceedings of the Second International Semantic Web Conference (ISWC-03)*, Sanibel Island, FL, October 20–23, 2003.

[13] Skounakis, M., Craven, M. & Ray, S., Hierarchical hidden Markov models for information extraction. *Proceedings of the 18th International Joint Conference on Artificial Intelligence (IJCAI-03)*, Acapulco, Mexico, 11 August, 2003.

[14] Radev, D., Otterbacher, J., Winkel, A., Blair-Goldensohn, S., & NewsInEssence, Summarizing online news topics. *Communications of the Association for Computing Machinery (ACM)* Vol. 10, University of Michigan, 2005.

[15] Kan, M., McKeown, K.R. & Klavans, J.L., Applying natural language generation to indicative summarization. *Proceedings of 8th European Workshop on Natural Language Generation at the ACL/EACL*, Toulouse, France, 6–7 July, 2001.

[16] Costantino, M., Collingham, R.J. & Morgan, R.G., Natural language processing in finance. *The Magazine of Artificial Intelligence in Finance*, 2, pp. 42–47, 1996.

[17] Harman, D.K. (ed.), *Proceedings of the Second Text Retrieval Conference (TREC-2)*, NIST and DARPA, 1994.

[18] Harman, D.K. (ed.), *Proceedings of the Third Text Retrieval Conference (TREC-3)*, NIST and DARPA, 1994.

[19] Harman, D.K. (ed.), *Proceedings of the Fourth Text Retrieval Conference (TREC-4)*, NIST and DARPA, 1995.

[20] Harman, D.K. (ed.), *Proceedings of the Fifth Text Retrieval Conference (TREC-5)*, NIST and DARPA, 1996.

[21] DARPA, *Proceeding of the Third Message Understanding Conference (MUC-3)*, Morgan Kaufmann Publishers, 1991.

[22] DARPA, *Proceeding of the Fourth Message Understanding Conference (MUC-4)*, Morgan Kaufmann Publishers, 1992.

[23] DARPA, *Proceedings of Fifth Message Understanding Conference (MUC-5)*, Morgan Kaufmann Publishers, 1993.

[24] DARPA, *Proceedings of the Sixth Message Understanding Conference (MUC-6)*, Morgan Kaufmann Publishers, 1995.

[25] DARPA, *Proceeding of the Seventh Messages Understanding Conference (MUC-7)*, 1998.

[26] Morgan, R., Garigliano, R., Callaghan, P., Poria, S., Smith, M., Urbanowicz, A., Collingham, R., Costantino, M., Cooper, C. & The LOLITA Group, University of Durham, Description of the LOLITA system as used in MUC-6. *Proceeding of the Sixth Messages Understanding Conference (MUC-6)*, DARPA, Morgan Kaufmann Publishers, 1995.

[27] Garigliano, R., Urbanowicz, A., Nettleton, D.J. & University of Durham, Description of the LOLITA system as used in MUC-7. *Proceeding of the Seventh Messages Understanding Conference (MUC-7)*, DARPA, 1998.

[28] Costantino, M., *Financial Information Extraction using Pre-Defined and User-Definable Templates in the LOLITA System*. Ph.D. Thesis, Department of Computer Science, University of Durham, 1997.

[29] Costantino, M. & IE-Expert, Integrating natural language processing and expert system techniques for real-time equity derivatives trading. *The Journal of Computational Intelligence in Finance*, 7, pp. 34–52, 1999.

[30] Costantino, M., Natural language processing and expert system techniques for equity derivatives trading: The IE-Expert system. *Proceedings of the International Conference on Information Technology Interfaces*, 1999.

[31] Edwards, R.D., Magee, J. & Bassetti, W.H.C. (eds.) *Technical Analysis of Stock Trends*, Amacom Books: New York, NY, 2001.

[32] Appel, G., *The Moving Average Convergence-Divergence Trading Method*, Traders Press: Greenville, SC, 1985.

[33] Hatamian, T., Price forecasting Linear prediction. *The Magazine of Artificial Intelligence in Finance*, **2**, pp. 48–54, 1995.

[34] Soofi, A.S. & Cao, L., A modelling and forecasting financial data: Techniques of non-linear dynamics. *Studies in Computational Finance*, Springer: New York, NY, 2002.

[35] Ruey, T., *Analysis of Financial Time Series*, Wiley: Hoboken, NJ, 2005.

[36] Walczak, S., Selecting between AI Technologies. *The Magazine of Artificial Intelligence in Finance*, **2**, pp. 48–54, 1995.

[37] Beinhocker, E.D., *The Origin of Wealth: Evolution, Complexity, and the Radical Remaking of Economics*, Harvard Business School Press: Boston, MA, 2006.

[38] Colander, D. (ed.), *The Complexity Vision and the Teaching of Economics*, Edward Elgar Publications: Northampton, UK, 2000.

[39] McCarthy, J., Minsky, M. & Rochester, N., A proposal for the Dartmouth summer research project on artificial intelligence, University of Stanford, 1955. Available at: http://www-formal.stanford.edu/jmc/history/dartmouth/dartmouth.html or http://www-formal.stanford.edu/jmc/history/dartmouth.pdf

[40] McCarthy, J. & Hayes, P.J., Some philosophical problems from the standpoint of artificial intelligence. *Machine Intelligence*, **4**, pp. 463–502, 1969.

[41] Russell, S.J. & Norvig, P., *Artificial Intelligence: A Modern Approach*, Prentice Hall, 2003.

[42] Newquist, H.P., Why is AI still in finance? *The Magazine of Artificial Intelligence in Finance*, **2**, 1995.

[43] Sowa, J.F., *Principles of Semantic Networks: Explorations in the Representation of Knowledge*, Morgan Kaufmann Publishers: San Francisco, CA, 1991.

[44] Sowa, J.F., *Knowledge Representation: Logical, Philosophical, and Computational Foundations*, Course Technology: Boston, MA, 1999.

[45] Sowa, J.F., Semantic Networks, Available on: http://www.jfsowa.com/pubs/semnet.htm, 2006.

[46] Fellbaum, C. & WordNet, *An Electronic Lexical Database*, MIT Press: Cambridge, MA, 1998.

[47] Refenes, A.P. (ed.) *Neural Networks in the Capital Markets*, Wilcy: Hoboken, NJ, 1996.

[48] Zahedi, F., *Intelligent Systems for Business: Expert Systems with Neural Networks*, Course Technology Press: Boston, MA, 1993.

[49] Shadbolt, J. & Talor, J.G., *Neural Networks and the Financial Markets: Predicting, Combining and Portfolio Optimisation*, Springer: Gateshead, UK, 2006.

[50] Lisboa, P.J.G., Edisbury, B. & Vellido, A. (eds.) *Business Applications of Neural Networks: The State-Of-The-Art of Real-World Applications*, World Scientific Publishing Company: Singapore, 2000.

[51] Kirkpatrick, S., Gelatt, C.D. & Vecchi, M.P., Optimization by simulated annealing, *Science*, **220(4598)**, pp. 671–680, 1983.

[52] Dempster, A., Laird, N. & Rubin, D., Maximum likelihood from incomplete data via the EM algorithm. *Journal of the Royal Statistical Society*, **39**, pp. 1–38, 1977.

[53] Ackley, D.H., Hinton, G.E. & Sejnowski, T.J., A learning algorithm for Boltzmann machines. *Cognitive Science*, **9**, pp. 147–169, 1985.

[54] Azoff, E.M., *Neural Network Time Series Forecasting of Financial Markets*, Wiley: Hoboken, NJ, 1994.

[55] Refenes, A.P., Zapranis, A.D. & Francis, G., Modelling stock returns in the framework of APT: A comparative study with regression models. *Neural Networks in the Capital Markets*, ed. A.P. Refenes, Wiley, pp. 101–125, 1994.

[56] Peterson, D.D., Mesa 8. *Technical Analysis of Stocks and Commodities*, **24(7)**, pp. 68–71, 2006.

[57] Jacobs, L., Tradingsolutions. *Traders World*, **39**, p. 29, 2005.

[58] Steurer, E., Nonlinear modelling of the DEM/USD exchange rate. *Neural Networks in the Capital Markets*, ed. A.P. Refenes, Wiley: Hoboken, NJ, pp. 199–211, 1994.

[59] Levitt, M.E., Machine learning for foreign exchange trading. *Neural Networks in the Capital Markets*, ed. A.P. Refenes, Wiley: Hoboken, NJ, pp. 233–243, 1994.

[60] Kingdon, J., Criteria for performance in gilt futures pricing. *Neural Networks in the Capital Markets*, ed. A.P. Refenes, Wiley: Hoboken, NJ, pp. 261–276, 1994.

[61] Sen, T.K. & Oliver, R., Predicting corporate mergers. *Neural Networks in the Capital Markets*, ed. A.P. Refenes, Wiley: Hoboken, NJ, pp. 325–340, 1994.

[62] Egeli, B., Meltem, O. & Badur, B., Stock market prediction using artificial neural networks. *Hawaii International Conference on Business*, 2003.

[63] Schmitt, L.M., *Theoretical Computer Science*, Vol. **259**, Chapter: Theory of Genetic Algorithms, Elsevier Science Publishers, pp. 1–61, 2001.

[64] Eiben, A.E. & Smith, J.E. (eds.) *Introduction to Evolutionary Computing. Natural Computing*, Springer: New York, NY, 2003.

[65] Chen, S.H. (ed.) *Genetic Algorithms and Genetic Programming in Computational Finance*, Springer, 2002.

[66] Mahfoud, S. & Mani, G., Financial forecasting using genetic algorithms. *Journal of Applied Artificial Intelligence*, **10**, pp. 543–565, 1996.

[67] Costantino, M., Collingham, R.J. & Morgan, R.G., Qualitative information in finance: Natural language processing and information extraction. *NeuroVest Journal*, **4(6)**, pp. 14–19, 1996.

[68] Sell, S., *Expert Systems*, MacMillan: London, UK, 1986.

[69] Luconi, F.L., Malone, T.W. & Morton, M.S.S., Expert systems: The next challenge for managers. *Decision Support Systems: Putting Theory into Practice*, eds. R.H. Sprague & H.J. Watson, Prentice-Hall: Upper Saddle River, NJ, pp. 365–379, 1994.

[70] Cowell, R.G., Lauritzen, S.L. & Spiegelhater, D.J., *Probabilistic Networks and Expert Systems. Information Science and Statistics*, Springer: New York, NY, 2005.

[71] Watkins, P.R. & Eliot, L.B. (eds.) *Expert Systems in Business and Finance: Issues and Applications*, Wiley: Hoboken, NJ, 1993.

[72] O'Keefe, R.M., O'Leary, D.E., Rebne, D. & Chung, Q.B., The impact of expert systems in accounting: System characteristics, productivity and work unit effects. *International Journal of Intelligent Systems in Accounting Finance and Management*, **2**, pp. 177–189, 1993.

[73] McCarthy, W., Denna, E., Gal, G. & Rockwell, S., Expert systems and AI-based decision support in auditing: Progress and perspectives. *International Journal of Intelligent Systems in Accounting Finance and Management*, **1**, pp. 53–63, 1992.

[74] Wright, G. & Rowe, G., Expert systems in the UK life insurance industry: Current status and future trends. *International Journal of Intelligent Systems in Accounting Finance and Management*, **2**, pp. 113–127, 1993.

[75] Gilbert, J., Artificial intelligence on wall street: An overview and critique of applications in the finance industry. Technical Report, Department of Computer Science, Brandeis University, 1995.

[76] Riloff, E. & Lehnert, W., Information extraction as a basis for high-precision text classification. *ACM Transactions on Information Systems*, **12**, pp. 296–333, 1994.

[77] Jacobs, P.S., Krupka, G., Rau, L., Mauldin, M.L., Mitamura, T., Kitani, T., Sider, I. & Childs, L., GE-CMU: Description of the shogun system used for MUC-5. *Proceeding of the Fifth Messages Understanding Conference (MUC-5)*, Morgan Kaufmann Publishers, 1993.

[78] The PLUM System Group, BBN: Description of the plum system as used for MUC-5. *Proceeding of the Fifth Messages Understanding Conference (MUC-5)*, Morgan Kaufmann Publishers, 1993.

[79] Miller, S., Crystal, M., Fox, H., Ramshaw, L., Schwartz, R., Stone, R., Weischedel, R., the Annotation Group, & BBN: Description of the sift system as used for MUC-7. *Proceeding of the Seventh Messages Understanding Conference (MUC-7)*, DARPA, 1998.

[80] Grishman, R., The NYU system for MUC-6 or where's the syntax? *Proceeding of the Sixth Messages Understanding Conference (MUC-6)*, DARPA, Morgan Kaufmann Publishers, 1995.

[81] Patten, T., Hoffman, B., Thurn, M. TASC, Description of the TASC system used for MUC-7. *Proceeding of the Seventh Messages Understanding Conference (MUC-7)*, DARPA, 1998.

[82] Garigliano, R., Morgan, R.G. & Smith, M.H., The LOLITA system as a contents scanning tool. *Proceedings of the 13th International Conference on Artificial Intelligence, Expert Systems and Natural Language Processing*, Avignon, France, 1993.

[83] Boguraev, B., Garigliano, R. & Tait J., Editorial. *Journal of Natural Language Engineering*, **1(1)**, pp. 1–7, 1995 [Cambridge University Press].

[84] Smith, M.H., Garigliano, R. & Morgan, R.G., Generation in the LOLITA system: An engineering approach. *Seventh International Workshop on Natural Language Generation*, Kennebunkport, ME, 1994.

[85] Reuters, *Reuters 3000 Xtra: Getting Started. Reuters*, 2001.

[86] Sabbagh, D., Computers that digest the news to change trading. *The Times*, 2006.

[87] Voorhees, E. & Buckland, L., *The Fifteenth Text Retrieval Conference Proceedings (TREC-2006)*. NIST, DARPA and ARPA, 2006.

[88] Lewis, D.D. & Jones, K.S., Natural language processing for information retrieval. *Communications of the Association for Computing Machinery (ACM)*, **39**, pp. 92–100, 1996.

[89] Rijsbergen, C.J.V., *Information Retrieval*, 2nd edn, Butterworths: London, UK, 1979.

[90] Langville, A.N. & Meyer, G.D., *Google's PageRank and Beyond: The Science of Search Engine Rankings*, Princeton University Press: Princeton, NJ, 2006.

[91] Grossman, D.A. & Frieder, O., *Information Retrieval: Algorithms and Heuristics*, Springer: New York, NY, 2006.

[92] Strzalkowski, T., Document representation in natural language text retrieval. *ARPA Workshop on Human Language Technology*, Morgan Kaufmann Publishers: Plainsboro, NJ, pp. 328–334, March 8–11, 1994.

[93] Meadow, C.T., Boyce, B.R., Kraft, D.H. & Barry, C.L., *Text Information Retrieval Systems*, Academic Press: Oxford, UK, 2007.

[94] Belkin, N.J. & Croft, W.B., Information filtering and information retrieval: Two sides of the same coin? *Communications of the Association for Computing Machinery (ACM)*, **35**, pp. 29–38, 1992.

[95] Salton, G., Another look at automatic text-retrieval systems. *Communications of the Association for Computing Machinery (ACM)*, **29**, pp. 548–556, 1986.

[96] Croft, W.B. & Turtle, H.R., Text retrieval and inference. *Text-Based Intelligent Systems: Current Research and Practice in Information Extraction and Retrieval*, Lawrence Erlbaum Associates: Mahwah, NJ, 1992.

[97] Jones, K.S., Assumptions and issues in text-based retrieval. *Text-Based Intelligent Systems: Current Research and Practice in Information Extraction and Retrieval*, Lawrence Erlbaum Associates: Mahwah, NJ, 1992.

[98] Stanfill, C. & Waltz, D.L., Statistical methods, artificial intelligence, and information retrieval. *Text-Based Intelligent Systems: Current Research and Practice in Information Extraction and Retrieval*, Lawrence Erlbaum Associates: Mahwah, NJ, 1992.

[99] Voorhees, E.M. (Conference Manager), *Proceedings of the Fourteenth Text Retrieval Conference (TREC-2005)*, NIST, DARPA and ARPA, Gaithersburg, MD, November 15–18, 2005. Available on: http://trec.nist.gov/pubs/trec14/t14_proceedings.html.

[100] Voorhees, E.M., Overview of Trec-2005. *Proceedings of the Fourteenth Text Retrieval Conference (TREC-2005)*, NIST, DARPA and ARPA, 2005.

[101] Buckley, C., Trec Evaluation Package, 2006. See http://trec.nist.gov/trec_eval/ for reference.

[102] Hobbs, J. & Israel, D., Principles of template design. *ARPA Workshop on Human Language Technology*, Morgan Kaufmann Publishers, pp. 172–176, 1994.

[103] Onyshkevych, B., Template design for information extraction system. *Proceeding of the Fifth Messages Understanding Conference (MUC-5)*, Morgan Kaufmann Publishers, 1993.

[104] Tait, J.I., *Automatic Summarising of English Texts*. Ph.D. Thesis, University of Cambridge, 1982.

[105] Moens, M.F., *Information Extraction: Algorithms and Prospects in a Retrieval Context*, Springer: New York, NY, 2006.

[106] Schank, R.C. & Riesbeck, C.K., *Inside Computer Understanding*, Lawrence Erlbaum Associated: Mahwah, NJ, 1981.

[107] DeJong, G.F., An overview of the frump system. *Strategies for Natural Language Processing*, Elbaum: Hillsdale, NJ, pp. 149–176, 1982.

[108] Hederman, L., Natural language processing and information extraction from texts. Technical Report, University of Dublin, 1992.

[109] Lytinen, S.L. & Gershman, A., Atrans: Automatic processing of money transfer messages. *Ninth International Joint Concerence on Artificial Intelligence*, M.K. Publishers, pp. 821–825, 1986.

[110] Grishman, R. & Sterling, J., Preference semantics for message understanding. *Speech and Natural Language Workshop*, M.K. Publishers, pp. 71–74, 1989.

[111] Chinchor, N., MUC-4 evaluation metrics. *Proceeding of the Fourth Messages Understanding Conference (MUC-4)*, DARPA, Morgan Kaufmann Publishers, pp. 22–29, 1992.

[112] Chinchor, N., MUC-5 evaluation metrics. *Proceeding of the Fifth Messages Understanding Conference (MUC-5)*, Morgan Kaufmann Publishers, 1993.

[113] Sundheim, B.M., TIPSTER/MUC-5 information extraction system evaluation. *Proceeding of the Fifth Messages Understanding Conference (MUC-5)*, Morgan Kaufmann Publishers, 1993.

[114] Chinchor, N. & Dungca, G., The scoring method for MUC-6. *Proceeding of the Sixth Messages Understanding Conference (MUC-6)*, Morgan Kaufmann Publishers, 1995.

[115] Callaghan, P.C., *An Evaluation of LOLITA and Related Natural Language Processing Systems*. Ph.D. Thesis, Department of Computer Science, University of Durham, 1998.

[116] Hobbs, J., The generic information extraction system. *Proceeding of the Fifth Messages Understanding Conference (MUC-5)*, Morgan Kaufmann Publishers, 1993.

[117] Sudo, K., Sekine, S. & Grishman, R., Automatic pattern acquisition for Japanese information extraction. *Proceedings of the First International Conference on Human Language Technology Research*, 2001.

[118] Matsumoto, Y., Kurohashi, S., Yamaji, O., Taeki, Y. & Nagao, M., Japanese morphological analyzing system: Juman. Technical Report, Kyoto University and Nara Institute of Science and Technology, 1997.

[119] Sekine, S., Grishman, R. & Shinnou, H., A decision tree method for finding and classifying names in Japanese texts. *Proceedings of the Sixth Workshop on Very Large Corpora*, 1998.

[120] Murata, M., Uchimoto, K., Ozaku, H. & Ma, Q., Information retrieval based on stochastic models in IREX. *Proceedings of the IREX Workshop*, 1994.

[121] Sudo, K., Sekine, S. & Grishman, R., An improved extraction pattern representation model for automatic IE pattern acquisition. *Proceedings of the 41st Annual Meeting of the Association for Computational Linguistics (ACL-03)*, 2003.

[122] Gaizauskas, R., Wakao, T., Humphreys, K., Cunningham, H. & Wilks, Y., University of sheffield: Description of the LASIE system as used for MUC-6. *Proceeding of the Sixth Messages Understanding Conference (MUC-6)*, Morgan Kaufmann Publishers, 1995.

[123] Humphreys, K., Gaizauskas, R., Azzam, S., Huyck, C., Mitchell, B., Cunningham, H. & Wilks, Y., Description of the LASIE system as used for MUC-7. *Proceeding of the Seventh Messages Understanding Conference (MUC-7)*, DARPA, 1998.

[124] Grishman, R., TIPSTER phase II architecture design document (tinman architecture), 1995. http://www.itl.nist.gov/iaui/894.02/related_projects/tipster/.

[125] Ogden, W., Cowie, J. & Rauls, V., Tabula rasa meta-tool text extraction tool builder. Technical Report MCCS-94-264, Computing Research Laboratory, New Mexico State University, 1994.

[126] Parker, B., *Spell Checking in LOLITA*. Master's Thesis, Department of Computer Science, University of Durham, 1994.

[127] Tomita, M., *Efficient Parsing of Natural Language: A Fast Algorithm for Practical Systems*. Kluwer Academic Publishers: New York, NY, 1986.

[128] Bokma, A.F. & Garigliano, R., Uncertainty management through source control: A heuristic approach. *International Conference on Information Processing and Management of Uncertainty in Knowledge-Based Systems*, 1992.

[129] Long, D. & Garigliano, R., *Reasoning by Analogy and Causality, a model and application*. Ellis Horwood: Westgate, UK, 1994.

[130] Smith, M.H., *Natural Language Generation in the LOLITA System: An Engineering Approach*. Ph.D. Thesis, Department of Computer Science, University of Durham, 1996.

[131] Costantino, M., Collingham, R.J. & Morgan, R.G., Financial information extraction at the university of Durham. *Proceedings of the Second Meeting of Artificial Intelligence in Accounting, Finance and Tax*, University of Huelva, 1996.

[132] Costantino, M., Collingham, R.J. & Morgan, R.G., Information extraction in the LOLITA system using templates from financial news articles. *Proceedings of the 18th International on Information Technology Interfaces '96*, June 18–21, 1996.

[133] Aberdeen, J., Burger, J., Roberts, S. & Vilain, M., MITRA-bedford: Description of the alembic system as used for MUC-5. *Proceeding of the Fifth Messages Understanding Conference (MUC-5)*, Morgan Kaufmann Publishers, 1993.

[134] Brill, E., Some advances in transformation-based part of speech tagging. *National Conference on Artificial Intelligence*, 1994.

[135] Aone, C., Halverson, L., Hampton, T., Ramos-Santacruz, M., & SRA, Description of the IE2 system used for MUC-7. *Proceeding of the Seventh Messages Understanding Conference (MUC-7)*, DARPA, 1998.

[136] Grishman, R., Sterling, J. & NYU, Description of the proteus system as used for MUC-5. *Proceeding of the Fifth Messages Understanding Conference (MUC-5)*, DARPA, Morgan Kaufmann Publishers, 1993.

[137] Vapnik, V., *The Nature of Statistical Learning Theory*, Springer: Berlin, Germany, 1995.

[138] Joachims, T., Text categorization with support vector machines: Learning with many relevant features. *Proceedings of the Tenth European Conference on Machine Learning*, Chemnitz, Germany, pp. 137–142, April 21–24, 1998.

[139] Patwardhan, S. & Riloff, E., Learning domain-specific information extraction patterns from the web. *Proceedings of the Workshop on Information Extraction Beyond The Document*, Sidney, Australia, p. 66–73, 22nd July, 2006.

[140] Riloff, E. & Phillips, W., An introduction to the sundance and autoslog systems. Technical Report UUCS-04-015, School of Computing, University of Utah, 2004.

[141] Fellbaum, C. (ed.) *WordNet: An Electronic Lexical Database*. MIT Press: Cambridge, MA, 1998.

[142] Riloff, E., Automatically constructing a dictionary for information extraction tasks. *Proceedings of the Eleventh National Conference on Artificial Intelligence*, Seattle, WA, pp. 811–816, August 1–4, 1993.

[143] Patwardhan, S. & Riloff, E., Learning domain-specific information extraction patterns from the web. *Proceedings of the Workshop on Information Extraction Beyond The Document*, Sidney, Australia, pp. 66–73, 22nd July, 2006.

[144] Stevenson, M. & Greenwood, M.A., Comparing information extraction pattern models. *Proceedings of the Workshop on Information Extraction Beyond The Document*, pp. 12–19, Sidney, Australia, 22nd July, 2006.

[145] Stevenson, M. & Greenwood, M.A., A semantic approach to IE pattern induction. *Proceedings of the 43rd Annual Meeting of the Association for Computational Linguistics (ACL 05)*, University of Michigan, Ann Arbor, MI, 25–30 June, 2005.

[146] Cunningham, H., Wilks, Y. & Gaizauskas, R., GATE a general architecture for text engineering. *Computers and the Humanities*, **36**, pp. 223–254, 2002.

[147] Cunningham, H., Maynard, D., Bontcheva, K. & Tablan, V., GATE: A framework and graphical development environment for robust NLP tools and applications. *Proceedings of the 40th Annual Meeting of the Association for Computational Linguistics (ACL 02)*, Philadelphia, PA, July 6–12, 2002.

[148] Maynard, D., Cunningham, H., Bontcheva, K., Catizone, R., Demetriou, G., Gaizauskas, R., Hamza, O., Hepple, M. & Herring, P., A survey of uses of GATE. Technical Report CS-00-06, Department of Computer Science, University of Sheffield, 2000.

[149] Cunningham, H., Maynard, D. & Tablan, V., Jape: A java annotation patterns engine. Technical Report CS-00-10, Institute for Language, Speech and Hearing, University of Sheffield, 2000.

[150] Hepple, M., Independence and commitment: Assumptions for rapid training and execution of rule-based POS taggers. *Proceedings of the 38th Annual Meeting of the Association for Computational Linguistics (ACL-2000)*, Hong Kong, 1–8 October, 2000.

[151] Kiryakov, A., Popov, B., Manov, D., Ognyanoff, D., Kiutchukov, I. & Terziev, I., Automatic semantic annotation with kim. *Proceedings of the Second European Semantic Web Conference (ESWC-2005)*, Crete, Greece, May 29–June 1, 2005.

[152] Broekstra, J., Kampman, A. & van Harmelen, F., Sesame: An architecture for storing and querying RDF data and schema information, *Semantics for the WWW*, MIT Press: Cambridge, MA, 2001.

[153] Almas, Y. & Ahmad, K., Lolo: A system based on terminology for multilingual extraction. *Proceedings of the Workshop on Information Extraction Beyond The Document*, Sidney, Australia, pp. 56–65, 22nd July, 2006.

[154] Engle, R. & Ng, V.K., Measuring and testing the impact of news on volatility. *Journal of Finance*, **48(5)**, pp. 1749–1777, 1993.

[155] Andersen, T., Bollerslev, T., Diebold, F. & Vega, C., Micro effects of macro announcements: Real time price discovery in foreign exchange. Working Paper 8959, National Bureau of Economic Research, 2002.

[156] Ray, S. & Craven, M., Representing sentence structure in hidden Markov models for information extraction. *Proceedings of the 17th International Joint Conference on Artificial Intelligence (IJCAI-01)*, Seattle, WA, August 4th–10th, 2001.

[157] Rabiner, L.R., A tutorial on hidden Markov models and selected applications in speech recognition. *Proceedings of the IEEE*, **77**, pp. 257–286, 1989.

[158] Baum, L.E., An equality and associated maximization technique in statistical estimation for probabilistic functions of Markov processes. *The Annals of Mathematical Statistics*, **41**, pp. 164–171, 1970.

[159] Fine, S., Singer, Y. & Tishby, N., The hierarchical hidden Markov model: Analysis and applications. *Machine Learning*, **32**, pp. 41–62, 1998.

[160] Finn, A. & Kushmerick, N., Multi-level boundary classification for information extraction. *Proceedings of the European Conference on Machine Learning*, 2004.

[161] Finn, A. & Kushmerick, N., Information extraction by convergent boundary classification. *Proceedings of the Workshop on Adaptive Text Extraction and Mining (AAAI-04)*, San Jose, CA, July 26, 2004.

[162] Freitag, D., *Machine Learning for Information Extraction in Informal Domains*. Ph.D. Thesis, Carnegie Mellon University, 1998.

[163] Califf, M.E. & Mooney, R.J., Relational learning of pattern-match rules for information extraction. *Proceedings of the 16th National Conference on Artificial Intelligence*, Orlando, FL, July 18–22, 1999.

[164] Mitchel, C. & West, M., *The News Formula: A Concise Guide to News Writing and Reporting*, Saint Martin's Press: New York, NY, 1996.

[165] Radev, D.R., Blair-Goldensohn, S., Zhang, Z. & Raghavan, R.S., Newsinessence: A system for domain-independent, real-time news clustering and multi-document summarization. *Proceedings of the First International Conference on Human Language Technology Research*, San Diego, CA, 2001.

[166] Salton, G., Wong, A. & Yang, C.S., A vector space model for automatic indexing. *Communications of the Association for Computing Machinery*, **18(11)**, pp. 613–620, 1975.

[167] Tan, P., Steinbach, M. & Kumar, V., *Introduction to Data Mining*, Addison Wesley: Upper Saddle River, NJ, 2005.

[168] McKeown, K.R., Barzilay, R., Evans, D., Hatzivassiloglou, V., Klavans, J.L., Nenkova, A., Sable, C., Schiffman, B. & Sigelman, S., Tracking and summarizing news on a daily basis with columbia's newsblaster. *Proceedings of the Human Language Technology Conference*, San Diego, CA, March 24–27, 2002.

[169] McKeown, K., Barzilay, R., Chen, J., Elson, D., Evans, D., Klavans, J., Nenkova, A., Schiffman, B. & Sigelman, S., Columbia's newsblaster: New features and future directions. *Proceedings of The Annual Conference of the North American Chapter of the Association for Computational Linguistics (NAACL)*, Edmonton, Canada, May 27–June 1, 2003.

[170] McKeown, K.R., Hatzivassiloglou, V., Barzilay, R., Schiffman, B., Evans, D. & Teufel, S., Columbia multi document summarization: Approach and evaluation. *Proceedings of the Document Understanding Workshop (DUC)*, New Orleans, LA, September 13–14, 2001.

[171] Kan, M., McKeown, K.R. & Klavans, J.L., Domain-specific informative and indicative summarization for information retrieval. *Proceedings of the Document Understanding Workshop (DUC)*, New Orleans, LA, September 13–14, 2001.

[172] Navigli, R. & Velardi, P., Learning domain ontologies from document warehouses and dedicated websites. *Computational Linguistics*, **30(2)**, p. 8, 2004.

[173] Sclano, F. & Velardi, P., Termextractor: A web application to learn the shared terminology of emergent web communities. *Proceedings of the third International Conference on Interoperability for Enterprise Software and Applications (I-ESA)*, Funchal-Madeira Island, Portugal, March 28th–30th, 2007.

Index

 **WIT**PRESS   *...for scientists by scientists*

Data Mining IX

Data, Text and Web Mining and their Business Applications

Edited by: C.A. BREBBIA, Wessex Institute of Technology, UK, N.F.F. EBECKEN, COPPE/UFRJ, Brazil, A. ZANASI, TEMIS Italia, Italy and D. ALMORZA GOMA, University of Cadiz, Spain

This book is a compilation of papers presented at the Ninth International Conference on Data Mining and Information Engineering. Data mining, including text mining and business applications, is a field of active current research and development that can yield substantial knowledge from data gathered from a wide range of applications. Many institutions have derived considerable benefits from these applications, and are now applying the methodology to increasing effect. Information engineering systems can be applied in many areas, including environmental conservation, economic planning, resource integration, cartography, urban planning, risk assessment, pollution control and transport management.

The conference reflected ways in which this technology plays an active role in linking economic development and environmental conservation planning. Of interest to researchers from academia and industry, as well as application developers from many areas, the papers in these proceedings are arranged into the following topics: Data Preparation; Clustering Technologies; Customer Relationship Management; Text Mining; Web Mining; Categorization Methods; Applications in Science and Engineering; Information Systems Strategies and Methodologies; Applications in Business, Industry and Government; Security Applications; Applications in Medicine and Genetics; Economic Intelligence.

WIT Transactions on Information and Communication Technologies, Vol 40
ISBN: 978-1-84564-110-8   2008   320pp £105.00/US$210.00/€157.50

WIT*Press*
Ashurst Lodge, Ashurst,
Southampton,
SO40 7AA, UK.
Tel: 44 (0) 238 029 3223
Fax: 44 (0) 238 029 2853
E-Mail: witpress@witpress.com

 **WIT**PRESS   *...for scientists by scientists*

Mobile Agents

Principles of Operation and Applications

Edited by: **A. GENCO**, *University of Palermo, Italy*

Mobile agents are intelligent agents with advanced mobility capabilities. A mobile agent must be provided with so-called strong mobility, a feature which allows it to carry its status with it and accomplish its mission by migrating from site to site on the Internet. A mobile agent can complete in one site what it started on another site.

Starting from the mobile agent concept, this book provides the reader with a suitably detailed discussion on mobile agent principles of operation, as for instance, migration, communication, co-ordination, interoperability, fault tolerance and security. As an example to application fields for mobile agents, this book discusses how they can be effective in implementing data mining and information retrieval systems.

Series: Advances in Management Information, Vol 6
ISBN: 978-1-84564-060-6   2008   304pp   £95.00/US$190.00/€142.50

Computational Finance and its Applications III

Edited by: **C.A. BREBBIA**, *Wessex Institute of Technology, UK*, **M. COSTANTINO**, *Royal Bank of Scotland Financial Markets, UK and* **M. LARRAN**, *University of Cadiz, Spain*

Many interesting applications in computational finance are closely related to the simulation work carried out by engineers and physical scientists. This makes computational finance a particularly attractive area for transdisciplinary research, a fact that is reflected by the range of topics included in this book. Originally presented at the Third International Conference on Computational Finance and its Applications, the papers in this volume cover the following subject areas: Modern Financial Services Technologies; Derivatives Pricing; Forecasting, Advanced Computing and Simulation; Portfolio Management and Asset Allocation; Risk Management; Time Series Analysis and Forecasting; Intelligent Trading Agents; Advanced Computing and Simulation.

This state-of-the-art book should be of interest to academics involved with financial modelling, markets, and computational finance, as well as members of the banking community and financial institutions.

WIT Transactions on Information and Communication Technologies, Vol 41
ISBN: 978-1-84564-111-5   2008   256pp   £95.00/US$190.00/€142.50